ENGAGING BOYS IN ACT1

Too many boys do not like to read, are choosing not to read, and are suffering academically as a result. All concerned adults need to redouble their efforts to ensure that boys who bring the greatest challenges to our classrooms and schools receive responsive literacy texts and practices to increase their chances for academic, personal, and occupational success. This book is more than a compendium of techniques; it also provides an analysis of the research literature on central issues and related aspects of literacy and learning for boys. The author identifies issues that impinge on boys' literacy development and explores what the research literature has to say about these issues. The descriptions of how teachers have used engaging texts and practices to help boys overcome low literacy engagement and skill in order to stay on course as readers and writers are highly informative and practical as models of best practice.

WILLIAM G. BROZO is Professor of Literacy in the Graduate School of Education at George Mason University, USA. On the Learning Metrics Task Force, he helped establish global learning and assessment standards and he contributes to iLit, a digital program for struggling adolescent readers.

ENGAGING BOYS IN ACTIVE LITERACY

Evidence and Practice

WILLIAM G. BROZO
George Mason University

CAMBRIDGE
UNIVERSITY PRESS

University Printing House, Cambridge CB2 8BS, United Kingdom

One Liberty Plaza, 20th Floor, New York, NY 10006, USA

477 Williamstown Road, Port Melbourne, VIC 3207, Australia

314–321, 3rd Floor, Plot 3, Splendor Forum, Jasola District Centre,
New Delhi – 110025, India

79 Anson Road, #06–04/06, Singapore 079906

Cambridge University Press is part of the University of Cambridge.

It furthers the University's mission by disseminating knowledge in the pursuit of education, learning, and research at the highest international levels of excellence.

www.cambridge.org
Information on this title: www.cambridge.org/9781108498630
DOI: 10.1017/9781108654111

© Cambridge University Press 2019

This publication is in copyright. Subject to statutory exception and to the provisions of relevant collective licensing agreements no reproduction of any part may take place without the written permission of Cambridge University Press.

First published 2019

Printed and bound in Great Britain by Clays Ltd, Elcograf S.p.A.

A catalogue record for this publication is available from the British Library.

ISBN 978-1-108-49863-0 Hardback
ISBN 978-1-108-72427-2 Paperback

Cambridge University Press has no responsibility for the persistence or accuracy of URLs for external or third-party internet websites referred to in this publication and does not guarantee that any content on such websites is, or will remain, accurate or appropriate.

Contents

List of Figures	*page* vii
Acknowledgements	viii

	Introduction	1
1	Boys' Reading and Learning: Identifying the Issues	7
	Boy Crisis: Nuancing the Issue	15
	What Does It Mean to Be a Reader in a Global Literacy Context?	18
	Boys' Reading and Learning: A Coda	21
2	Boys and Literacy: A Closer Look	24
	Boys and Socioeconomic Factors	25
	Immigrant Boys	28
	Boys as Additional Language Learners	30
	Identity Factors and Boys	33
	Boys and Reading Engagement	36
	Boys and New Technologies/Literacies	39
	Boys' Literacy Needs from Childhood to Adolescents	40
	A Closer Look at Boys and Literacy: A Coda	44
3	Boys' Masculinities and Identities: Evidence and Practice	45
	A Closer Look at Masculinities, Identities, and Boys' Literacy Achievement	45
	Promising Programs and Practices	53
	Boys' Masculinities and Identities: A Coda	88
4	Socioeconomics and Boys: Evidence and Practice	89
	The Poverty Penalty for Boys	93
	Family, Community, and School Buffers for Boys	97
	Promising Programs and Practices	99
	Socioeconomics and Boys: A Coda	109
5	Immigrant and New Language Learner Boys: Evidence and Practice	110
	Immigrant Youth: Evidence from PISA and PIRLS	111

Gender Differences in Academic Achievement for Immigrant Youth	113
Gender Differences in New Language Learning	115
Promising Programs and Practices	118
Immigrant and New Language Learning Boys: A Coda	138

6 Literacy Engagement and Boys: Evidence and Practice — 140
- Factors Influencing Boys' Reading Motivation — 144
- Promising Programs and Practices — 150
- Literacy Engagement and Boys: A Coda — 155

7 Boys and New Literacies: Evidence and Practice — 157
- Boys and Electronic Reading: Evidence from PISA and PIRLS — 158
- A Multiple Literacies Perspective on Boys — 160
- Guidelines for Using New Literacies with Boys — 164
- Promising Programs and Practices — 169
- New Literacies and Boys: A Coda — 178

8 Boys and Writing: Evidence and Practice — 179
- Writing in the Twenty-First Century — 180
- Writing and Reading — 184
- Enhancing Reading through Writing — 186
- Guidelines for Writing Instruction — 189
- Promising Programs and Practices — 192
- Boys and Writing: A Coda — 206

References — 207
Index — 249

Figures

3.1	Sample Pre-Unit Responses from "To Be a Man" Survey	page 59
3.2	Web of Class Brainstorm of a Television Man	61
3.3	Web of Class Brainstorm of a Real Man	62
3.4	Anticipation Guide for Chapter 6 of Scorpions	68
3.5	Sample Post-Unit Responses from "To Be a Man" Survey	86
8.1	Differences in Features of Persuasive Essay across Content Areas	191
8.2	11 Elements of Effective Writing Instruction	193

Acknowledgements

I want to recognize all the teachers and students who welcomed me into their classrooms and the parents and sons who invited me into their lives as I researched this book. Each one breathed life into this project and made it entirely worthwhile.

I want to extend a special thanks to the Cambridge University Press, particularly my editors Dave Repetto and Emily Watton for their commitment to this project, and to Ursula Acton, Allan Alphonse, Varun Kumar Marimuthu, and Jim Diggins for their assistance in making this book a more readable and useful resource. Two others, Jennifer Lindenauer and Kelly Usher, deserve a word of appreciation for their indispensable research skills.

Ultimately, I owe the most gratitude to my wife, Ursula, who kept me inspired throughout the many long months of writing and editing.

Introduction

It has now been over 40 years since the start of my career as an educator. I began my first job teaching English at an all-black high school in rural South Carolina, USA. In that single-level building with the leaky roof, undersized gymnasium, and no air conditioning system, I came face to face with boys who, in the words of Sven Birkerts (2006), "had never bathed in the energies of a book" (p. 84). These were boys who could not read at a level necessary to understand and enjoy the stories and plays from the required literature anthology. William, a 6'7" 17-year-old star basketball player, was in one of my 11th-grade sections. As I handed out textbooks on the first day of class, he leaned close to my ear and whispered, "I don't know how to read." I quickly came to the realization that to engage William and his classmates as readers, I would need to use every bit of my creative energy. Although it ran counter to my sensibilities as an English teacher, I made a fateful decision in those first weeks to dispense with my beloved Silas Marner and Julius Caesar, and the vaunted poets, playwrights, and novelists of the past and experiment with young adult literature.

I was looking for something that the students would find more accessible and meaningful. I found it in Alice Childress's (1973) *A Hero Ain't Nothin' But a Sandwich*. This story of a young adolescent boy's drug addiction and alienation while growing up in Harlem transformed my class. Attendance and behavior problems decreased noticeably. Students were eager to read, or at least try to read. When we finished the book, they clamored for more of the same. Even William made modest progress that first year, although he dropped out the next. I would often spot his looming frame hanging out on the only street of commerce in our small, poor town. Unfortunately, he was eventually arrested and found guilty of dealing narcotics. It was the last I ever heard of him.

Of course my own literate history is very different from that of African American teens growing up in hot, dusty tobacco country, whose ancestors were slaves and sharecroppers. Nonetheless, when it comes to literacy, we all have something in common – where we begin our literate journeys may have little resemblance to where the journey takes us and, certainly, where the journey ends.

Since those days as an inchoate literacy teacher, I have spent untold hours in general and remedial classrooms in numerous schools around the United States and across the globe, observing and learning from other teachers, conducting demonstration lessons, and gathering research data. The overwhelming impression I have been left with is that more must be done to reach the growing numbers of listless, detached, and struggling male readers. I have also found a clear and recurring pattern of concern among teachers: Too many boys do not like to read, are choosing not to read, and are suffering academically as a result.

I wrote this book based on an ongoing desire to share my experiences and ideas with the many teachers, parents, researchers, and others who are equally concerned about boys' literate futures. The guiding premise for this book, as for all my speaking and writing about boys, is *engaging boys in literacy should be the highest priority when developing reading curricula and seeking to foster independent reading habits.* To achieve engaged reading, I propose the use of a great variety of texts along with a range of practices that are likely to improve boys' thinking about what they read and increase their motivation to read.

My Perspective in *Engaging Boys in Active Literacy*

Although this book is filled with many descriptions of promising literacy-focused programs and practices for boys, I strived to do more than write a compendium of techniques text. Since opinions abound about boys' academic and social development, it is essential to establish and analyze the research literature on central issues and related aspects of this topic. Thus, in the first two chapters, I identify the big issues surrounding literacy and learning for boys, accompanied by salient research findings. Each of these issues is further developed in subsequent chapters where additional evidence from the research literature is brought to bear. Moreover, I draw principally upon the evidence base from North America and from across Europe. In doing so, I expand what is known about boys literacy development to inform instructional practices and programs. Readers of this book, then, will appreciate the balanced approach I establish, combining accessible descriptions and analysis of relevant research with instructional and programmatic approaches to increasing boys' reading and writing motivation and expanding their literacy and learning.

Why a Book Just about the Literacy Needs of Boys?

Boys need special attention with respect to their literacy development and attitudes. I make clear in the opening chapters that overwhelming evidence from North America and Europe (Chudowsky & Chudowsky, 2010; Mullis, Martin, Foy, & Drucker, 2012; OECD, 2016a) shows that boys have the lowest scores on standardized measures of reading and verbal ability. Furthermore, boys dominate the rolls of remedial reading classes and those who have difficulty learning to read (Lietz, 2006; Wheldall & Limbrick, 2010). They also make up the largest group of dropouts and delinquents (Child Trends Data Bank, 2015). These, however, are only school-related phenomena. When one considers that males (a) commit all but a small percentage of homicides, (b) are far more likely to be victims of violent crime than women, (c) take their own lives at alarming rates, and (d) make up most drug addicts and people who are homeless (Callanan & Davis, 2011; National Alliance to End Homelessness, 2016; National Institutes of Health, n.d.; Noguera, 2008), addressing boys' needs becomes all the more urgent.

It is well known that boys who drop out of school are likely to have weak or poorly developed literacy skills (Hernandez, 2012; Whitmire, 2010). These dropouts become vulnerable to a life of underemployment and unemployment and, far worse, are at a higher risk of becoming criminal offenders (Sum et al., 2009). It is also known, however, that engaged readers have a much greater chance of staying in school, expanding career and life options, and maturing into self-actualized adults (Hofstetter, Sticht, & Hofstetter, 1999).

This book, then, is devoted to identifying issues that impinge on boys' literacy development, exploring what the research literature has to say about these issues, and describing how teachers have used engaging texts and practices to help boys overcome low literacy engagement and skill and stay the course as readers and writers. Once boys develop a sense of self through active literacy, they increase their chances for an expansive intellectual journey throughout school and beyond. This is critical because it has been shown that possession of highly developed literacy abilities can ultimately lead to better lives for themselves and those around them (Hill, 2014). I have found that boys become more engaged readers and learners when motivated by exposure to texts and practices that capture their imaginations. These include the young adult novel that served as a central text in the "Real Men" unit described in Chapter 3, to the graphic novels employed by secondary teachers in science and math explained in Chapter 7, to a boys' book club that link soccer and reading as described in Chapter 6. These texts and approaches, as well as the many others presented in this book, serve as examples of how to build capacity and enjoyment in reading for male youth.

Organization and Content

Each chapter begins with a short advance organizer highlighting the big ideas and main chapter topics. Each chapter also contains a special feature called "Boys in the Real World." The goal of this feature is to capture the attitudes and practices of actual boys who struggle with reading and writing or are unmotivated by typical, school-based texts and literacy schemes. Within this feature are prompts designed to stimulate reflection on the scenario and creative ideas for increasing the boy's level of engagement with literacy and depth of understanding of text. In the final section of Chapters 3 through 8, "Promising Programs and Practices," I describe a variety of literacy practices from within classrooms and schools as well as those situated in homes and communities that have heightening boys' engagement and achievement.

Chapter 1 introduces the primary issues of the book and raises concerns about boys' literacy behavior. I present evidence that supports the need to help boys discover or become reacquainted with the pleasure and value of reading. I also discuss the connection between reading ability and academic success. While taking an advocacy position on behalf of boys, I also nuance notions of a "boy crisis" by drawing attention to those male youth at the greatest risk of failing to develop engaged and effective literacy abilities. Finally, I assert that reading engagement and skill will position boys for the competition and opportunities in the twenty-first century.

Chapter 2 digs deeper into the critical issues surrounding boys' literacy development. Keeping in focus those boys who, according to research, are the most needful of effective and responsive literacy practices and programs, I foreground factors of socioeconomics, immigrant status, language learning, technology/new literacies, engagement, and literate identity. Also explored in this chapter is the developmental nature of gender-based reading differences between boys and girls.

Chapter 3 trains a lens on masculinities and identities and their relationship to boys' literacy achievement and attitudes. One of the important goals of this chapter is to challenge and caution against hegemonic masculinity responses to boys' literacy needs. This chapter initiates a section entitled "Promising Programs and Practices" that appears in all subsequent chapters. In it, I provide a full description of a unit I participated in with lower-secondary level students. Named the "Real Men" unit, the goal was to expand literacy skills of struggling youth from a school in the barrio of Texas, USA, while helping them develop critical literacy practices for challenging stereotypic masculinity.

Chapter 4 presents additional ideas and research evidence related to socioeconomic factors and their impact on boys' literacy development and achievement. I take up related issues in this chapter, such as the rise of a skills-based global economy and the need for boys to possess sophisticated and flexible literacy abilities to compete in such a world. In the "Promising Programs and Practices" section, I describe and exemplify specific school- and home-based approaches that have been employed with male youth to expand reading and writing skills and heighten engagement in literacy.

Chapter 5 is devoted to the relationship between boys' immigrant status and new language learning on their literacy learning. In addition to bringing additional research evidence to bear on these factors, I also share examples of practices and programs, such as book clubs and the "my bag" strategy, that have had positive impact on linguistically and culturally different male youth.

Chapter 6 focuses on the importance of engagement in boys' literacy development. I demonstrate the universal significance of engagement for reading achievement and consider theoretical guidelines for crafting engaging literacy curriculum for boys. In the "Promising Programs and Practices" section of the chapter, I describe, among other approaches, a particularly outstanding program in Germany called "Kicking and Reading" that combines soccer training with reading training for upper-primary level boys.

Chapter 7 acknowledges the active role boys play in our digital world. As the evidence supports, boys are more engaged in literate activity when they are able to take advantage of new media and ICT tools. Moreover, boys have shown higher reading achievement on electronically mediated assessments. Because of the mounting evidence for this pattern, I describe, in the "Promising Programs and Practices" section of the chapter, instructional approaches that link school-based literacy learning with male youths' outside-of-school texts, such as graphic novels, and electronic media.

In Chapter 8, the last chapter of the book, I foreground what is known from the research literature about boys' writing development and achievement. As is the case with reading, boys often struggle with writing, though this area of literacy development for boys does not receive as much attention as it deserves. Several examples of teachers engaging boys in reading and learning through writing – from poetry to mathematics – are woven into this chapter and featured in the final chapter section.

CHAPTER I
Boys' Reading and Learning: Identifying the Issues

In this chapter, I

- Explore the "crisis" discourse around boys' literacy and learning and share counter narratives to this discourse
- Describe the authentic literacy, learning, and life challenges males experience in and out of school
- Explain why boys need to possess sophisticated literacy competencies in order to be successful in a global literacy context

---

A perusal of titles of popular press books, reports, and news articles will quickly leave one with the impression that boys are in serious trouble. Consider these attention grabbers:

"The Trouble with Boys"
"Boys Adrift"
"The War against Boys"
"Why Boys Fail: Saving Our Sons from an Educational
System That's Leaving Them Behind"
"Taking the Boy Crisis in Education Seriously"
"Boys are at the Back of the Class"
"Schools are Failing Our Boys"
"Affirmative Action for Boys"
"Boys Aren't Learning to Read and It's a Global Problem"
"The Boy Crisis: At Every Level of Education, They're
Falling Behind. What to Do?"

With media's sensationalizing of the issue, and publishers and authors grasping for headlines, it is not surprising to find large percentages of the public in both North America and Europe worried about the future of boys (EURYDICE, 2010; Whitmire, 2011). This widespread concern for boys being left behind in America has led to schools around the country going so

7

far as to implement approaches to gender-specific teaching advocated by David Gurian and his eponymous institute, such as boys learning in classrooms set at cooler temperatures and with bright lights where boy-friendly lessons are interspersed with energetic physical activity. In the European context, the EU High Level Group of Experts on Literacy (2012) report identified the gender gap in reading, in favor of girls, as one of the four gaps that needed to be closed. And the UK's National Literacy Trust established a Boys' Reading Commission, which published its report in 2012 outlining why boys are falling behind in reading and what can be done at the policy, school, and community levels to address the issue. In the United States and Canada, numerous reports have appeared over the past two decades drawing attention to the disparities between the reading achievement of boys and girls and warning of the consequences of boys' continued underachievement in reading. As recently as 2015, the *Brown Center Report on American Education* devoted the entire first part to boys, girls, and reading (Loveless, 2015), concluding with a rather dire speculation that the death of the novel may come when girls and women stop reading.

Morris (2011) has suggested that the charged "crisis" rhetoric surrounding issues of boys' academic achievement and the over-simplistic correctives being proffered have caused a backlash among scholars and feminists who take odds with the essential assertion of an educational crisis for boys. Nevertheless, behind the hype about a so-called boy crisis there remain some concerning trends that require our attention and analysis. This is needed in order to separate fact from fiction around the issues and to nuance the often jarring headlines that might otherwise lead one to believe boys and men are doomed.

Much is known about boys' challenges in school and in society. What follows is a summary of the evidence and what it actually tells us about male youth.

- **_Boys underperform relative to girls on most measures of verbal ability._** In the United States, on every state reading and writing high-stakes tests at both the primary and secondary levels, boys' scores are significantly below the achievement scores of girls (Chudowsky & Chudowsky, 2010). This same pattern holds true for 9-, 13-, and 17-year-old boys' and girls' performance on the National Assessment of Educational Progress (NAEP) test of reading, writing, and numeracy in the United States (Loveless, 2015). Global comparisons of gender performance in reading reveal a consistent trend. On PIRLS 2011

(Progress in International Reading Literacy Study), 9-year-old boys on average were 16 score points lower than their female counterparts (Mullis, Martin, Foy, & Drucker, 2012; Thompson et al., 2013). This gap at the primary level tends to widen for 15-year-olds on PISA (Program for International Student Assessment). On the 2015 PISA, the OECD average was 27 score points in favor of girls, with girls outperforming boys in all 71 participating countries and economies (OECD, 2016a). The United States, for instance, saw a 10-point difference on PIRLS 2011 and a 31-point difference on PISA 2012. Similarly, German 9-year-old boys scored 8 points lower than girls on PIRLS 2011, but 44 points lower on PISA 2012.

- ***Boys comprise a much greater percentage of weak readers on PIRLS (Progress in Reading Literacy Study) and PISA (Program for International Student Assessment) as compared with girls.*** On PISA 2012, across more than 30 OECD countries, 14 percent of boys as compared with 9 percent of girls did not meet level 2, considered the baseline-level of proficiency in the reading literacy domain (OECD, 2013a).

- ***Boys have significantly lower levels of reading engagement than girls.*** A close examination of PISA data reveals that when it comes to enjoyment of reading, time spent reading for pleasure, and diversity of texts read (such as newspapers, magazines, fiction, and nonfiction) girls had significantly higher indices than boys on all three dimensions of reading engagement among virtually all participating countries (Brozo et al., 2014). In addition to findings on international assessments, numerous studies report boys are less engaged and motivated to read as compared with girls (Guthrie & McRae, 2011; Kessels, Heyder, Latsch, & Hannover, 2014; Logan & Johnston, 2009; Marinak & Gambrell, 2010). The variable of engagement is critical to any discussion of success for boys as evidence points to the role engagement plays in producing higher levels of academic and reading achievement for struggling boys (Matthews et al., 2010) and boys of color, especially those who have experienced multiple risk factors in their lives (e.g., low parental education, single-care-giver households, economic poverty, maltreatment; Fantuzzo, LeBoeuf, Rouse, & Chen, 2012).

- ***Boys are overrepresented in remedial reading and learning disabilities classes.*** It has long been known that boys dominate the rolls of students in reading and learning disabilities classrooms (Shaywitz et al., 1990). Analysis of studies employing objective criteria for identifying students with reading disabilities demonstrates clearly that boys are more likely than girls to receive a learning disabilities diagnosis and placement (Liederman, Kantrowitz, & Flannery, 2005). This finding has been corroborated by researchers in both the North American and European contexts (Hawke et al., 2007, 2009; Wheldall & Limbrick, 2010). Among the 67 percent of boys who comprise the overall group of special education students, the largest share by far are black and Hispanic males at nearly 80 percent, making them more likely than any other groups to be placed in special education classes (Moore & Henfield, 2008; Pitre, Lewis, & Hillton-Pitre, 2007; Schott Foundation Report, 2015).

- ***Boys are far more likely to be retained at grade level than girls.*** Studies show that retained students are more likely to be male, minority, and of lower socioeconomic status (SES; Xia & Kirby, 2009). Specifically, boys were found to be much more likely to be retained than girls (Hong & Yu, 2007; Jacob & Lefgren, 2007). Furthermore, grade retention appears to be associated with depressed reading achievement (Silberglitt, 2006), poor overall academic performance (Jimerson & Ferguson, 2007), and an increased risk of boys dropping out of school (Guevremont, Roos, & Brownell, 2007), an issue I will discuss in more detail. Grade retention, along with school suspensions, has also been identified as one of the contributors to the school-to-prison pipeline (Aud, Fox, & KewalRamani, 2010; Redfield & Nance, 2016).

- ***Fewer boys than girls complete secondary education, attend, or graduate from postsecondary institutions.*** Males age 16 to 24 make up 55 percent of US high school dropouts (Child Trends Data Bank, 2015). The graduation rate for African American males is only 59 percent (Schott Foundation, 2015). Early leaving for boys has been associated with poverty, poor physical and mental health, and crime (Burrus & Roberts, 2012). At the same time, college participation rates for US 18–24-year-olds show a full 6 percent difference in favor of females (43 percent versus 37 percent; NCES, 2016). From another perspective, ninth-grader male students who completed secondary school were enrolled in postsecondary institutions at a rate 9 percent lower than their female cohorts (70 percent versus 79 percent) (NCES, 2016). Studies like Conger and Long's (2010) examination of male disadvantage in grade point average, credits earned, and persistence in college have revealed that males arrive at college with lower secondary school grades, earn lower marks and accumulate fewer credits in their first semester as compared with their female counterparts. As males progress through college they continue to fall further behind female students. According to Conger and Long, these widening gender disparities in academic performance contribute to males leaving postsecondary schools early and their lower overall graduation rates.

- ***Boys of color and immigrant boys have very low reading achievement.*** The gender gap favoring girls is most pronounced among minority and low-income populations. Sizeable gaps in reading achievement have been documented between white male youth and African American (Brunn & Kao, 2008; Husband, 2012) and Hispanic American male youth (Gandara & Contreras, 2009; Zickafoose, 2009). In the United States, the lowest performers on PISA, PIRLS, and NAEP are African American boys from low SES backgrounds, followed by Hispanic American males from equally low SES levels (Brozo & Crain, 2015; Brozo et al., 2014). For example, the 2013 NAEP results show that only 17 percent of black students were adequate readers by eighth grade, in stark contrast to the 46 percent of white eighth graders who were proficient in reading. Mead (2006) stresses that in spite of achievement gains made by both girls and boys, "There's no doubt that some groups of boys – particularly Hispanic and black boys and boys from low-income homes – are in real trouble" (p. 3).
- ***Boys from low-income households have very low reading achievement.*** In general, there is a persistent correlation, as evidenced by standardized intelligence tests, between poverty and lower cognitive achievement (Robinson & Lubienski, 2011). Low-SES students often earn below-average scores in reading and possess poor writing skills (Jensen, 2009; Reardon, Robinson-Cimpian, & Weathers, 2015). In some low-economy states, such as Mississippi, only 3 percent of African American students are proficient in English, reading, science, and math (Carnoy & Garcia, 2017). Boys at the highest risk of struggling as readers and learners are those from the lowest rungs of the socioeconomic scale (Entwisle, Alexander, & Olson, 2007). In the United States, this is especially true for black and Hispanic boys who come from poverty (Tatum, 2008; Martin et al., 2007). Carnoy and Garcia's (2017) analysis of trends in math and reading achievement reveals that students' poverty status was closely linked to their achievement in these areas. The researchers found the largest achievement gaps in reading, in the range of one standard deviation lower, between white students from economic privilege and black and Hispanic English language learner students who were eligible for free and reduced-price lunch, a proxy for

poverty status in the United States. Further evidence for the income-achievement connection comes from Hill's (2014) path analysis of 117 African American males who participated in PISA 2009. His findings revealed that reading scores of these students were linked directly to the financial well-being and occupational status of their fathers.

- *Male youth of color are over-represented among the ranks of school dropouts (early leavers).* As many as 1.2 million American youth drop out of high school every year (US Census Bureau, n.d.), which equates to over 3,200 students for each day of the year – a staggering figure by any measure. But just as disturbing is the number of Latino and black students who fail to graduate from high school (Brown & Rodriguez, 2009; Meade et al., 2009; Soza, Yzaguirre, & Perilla, 2007). Of the entire school population in 2015, Hispanic students dropped out at a rate of 9.2 percent and black students 6.5 percent. These figures compare with a 4.6 percent dropout rate for white students (NCES, 2017). To put these percentages into further perspective, data from that same year, 2015, reveal the graduation rate from four-year public high schools for black males was 59 percent while at 65 percent for Latino males. This means that 41 percent of African American boys and 35 percent of Hispanic boys are leaving school before completion. Although these rates reflect an improvement over the past two decades, they still pale in comparison to the 80 percent graduate rate of white males (Schott Foundation, 2015).

- *Boys of color disproportionately represent incarcerated youth who also have very low literacy skills.* There is an undeniable relationship between lack of literacy and the probability of being imprisoned in the United States. Cohen (2010) has shown that more than 60 percent of America's inmates are illiterate, and 85 percent of all juvenile offenders have reading problems. Hernandez (2012) determined a boy who can't read on grade level by third grade is four times less likely to graduate from secondary school by age 19 than one who does read proficiently at that time. If the boy who can't read on grade level also lives in poverty, then that same student is 13 times less likely to graduate on time. Many of these dropouts find themselves among the ranks of the United States' large prison population. Sum and his colleagues (2009) found that about 1 in every 10 young male school dropouts is in jail or juvenile detention center as compared to 1 in 35 young male high school graduates. The picture is even bleaker for African Americans, with nearly 1 in 4 young black male dropouts incarcerated or otherwise institutionalized on an average day. According to Sum et al. (2009), that equates to a shocking 22 percent daily jailing rate for young black men who drop out of high school.

The literacy and academic challenges I have outlined make a compelling case, I believe, for giving special attention to boys to ensure they develop the reading, writing, and learning skills needed for success in school and life. Equally compelling are these sobering facts about males in our society, both in North America and Europe:

- ***Males commit most suicides.*** Across North America (Wyllie et al., 2012) and around the globe (Bertolote & Fleischmann, 2002), the vast majority of suicide victims are boys and men. Overall, males commit suicide about four times as often as women (Callanan & Davis, 2011).
- ***Males perpetrate most homicides.*** Overwhelmingly, males commit and are victims of homicide (United Nations Office on Drugs and Crime, 2015). Black males as a subgroup are the most prone and susceptible to murder, whereas white females are the least. Furthermore, males between the ages of 15–30 are the highest offenders, making up 10 percent of the population, but commit 63 percent of the homicides in the United States (Shulman, Stienberg, & Piquero, 2013).
- ***Males commit most acts of family violence.*** Spouses, partners, and children are victims of numerous forms of physical abuse at the hands of men, while the percentage of female perpetrators of intimate partner abuse is negligible (Caldwell, Swan, & Woodbrown, 2012; Houry et al., 2008).
- ***Males comprise most of the homeless.*** In North America and in Europe, males outnumber females in the ranks of the homeless by a 75 to 25 percent margin. Furthermore, men are up to nine times more likely to die homeless than women (National Alliance to End Homelessness, 2016).
- ***Males comprise most drug addicts.*** Males use and abuse illegal substances in far greater numbers than females, and males are more prone than females to addiction (National Institutes of Health, n.d.).
- ***Males comprise most AIDS carriers.*** Of the 1.1 million people living with HIV infection in the United States, men account for 76 percent and comprise 80 percent of all new cases. Black men have the highest rates of new HIV infections among all men. Overall, 1 in 51 men will receive a diagnosis of HIV infection at some point in their lifetime; the figure is 1 in 16 for black males.

Taken together, there are unique academic and sociological challenges many boys and men pose for teachers, researchers, policy makers, parents, and all other concerned adults. Clearly, we vest our futures in all children, not just the boys. And most certainly all children need adults to imbue them with hope, imagination, and competencies that make it possible for them to achieve what they desire and become who they want to be. This book, however, focuses on stressing the importance of engaging and keeping teen and preteen boys as readers to improve their chances of successful academic futures and, consequently, richer and more meaningful lives. The mounting evidence I have presented suggests that the time has come to begin paying special attention to the literacy needs of male youth.

Boys in the Real World

"Kwame"

Kwame is a sixth grade African American boy. He is a high academic achiever and describes himself as good student and a good reader; however, he does not like to read nor does he choose to read in his free time. He explained that one of the few topics he will read is sports, and is currently reading a teacher-recommended book, *The Crossover* (Alexander, 2014), about twin brothers who are stars on their junior high basketball team. The words of the book are formatted to read like rap lyrics. Outside school, Kwame likes to play sports and video games.

One book Kwame read for a school project and he found that he enjoyed was entitled *Buddha Boy* (Koja, 2003). He said he liked it because the main character, who was Buddhist and bullied in school, was befriended by another student who helped him and became his friend. Their friendship and the way the situation was handled by both boys seemed compelling to Kwame. Kwame describes himself as a strong reader, but says he only reads when he has to and does not choose to read for pleasure. Like many adolescent boys, Kwame views "real" reading as novel reading and not the articles about sports, humorous pieces, or the Instagram and emails he reads for pleasure on his phone. He said required reading for school and reading long books was a "headache." Nevertheless, he wishes he enjoyed it more because he acknowledges the importance of reading.

Kwame described himself as a good writer who produces well-written compositions for school assignments. He said it is not as much of a "headache" to write because "I can make it my own. With a book, I have to read what is on the page." He said he likes when teachers ask him to write about his life and experiences and recounted a school project that required him to write about an experience that was very memorable. He described writing about a Halloween memory when he bit into a piece of candy with peanuts and had his first allergic reaction. He explained that up until that point he did not know he was allergic to peanuts. He recounted this writing assignment with enthusiasm.

Discussion and Activities

- What recommendations can you offer to teachers working with Kwame to help him develop the reading habit and continue to nurture his enthusiasm in writing?
- How can Kwame's interests in sports be exploited for further literacy development?
- In what ways can teachers take advantage of the kinds of topics Kwame enjoys to further his reading and writing abilities?

Boy Crisis: Nuancing the Issue

Despite the case I have presented to undergird my contention that boys – particularly struggling and disengaged boys, certain boys of color, boys in poverty, and immigrant boys – demand extra supports to meet their learning and life needs, many continue to question the validity of such a perspective (Kuhl & Martino, 2017; Weaver-Hightower & Skelton, 2013). I am ever mindful of the importance of understanding the counter-narrative to the advocacy position I have taken on behalf of boys' literacy development, because challenging myself about my interpretation of the evidence and my own beliefs is essential to establishing the credibility of my scholarship and the substance of my message.

One intriguing challenge to generalizations about boys' underachievement in reading relative to girls comes from critiques on technical grounds of international assessments of reading literacy, such as PISA. As I have pointed out, boys' performance on PISA is significantly lower than girls for all participating countries and economies. On its face, this finding strongly suggests that boys may lack the ability and drive to read as well as girls. However, researchers (Rauch & Hartig, 2010; Oddny & Lundetrae, 2016; Scwabe, McElvany, & Trentel, 2015) have found in separate analyses that PISA's item formats may indeed be favoring girls, as has been suspected. About half of the reading questions are open-response type, requiring answers of either short written explanations or longer constructed responses. In these empirical studies, the researchers determined that boys performed significantly less well than girls on these open-ended items, although boys were equally competent as girls on the closed-ended response items (e.g., multiple choice). This has led to speculation about whether the gender-based reading achievement gap is an artifact of item formatting on PISA rather than a genuine reflection of inherent differences in reading ability between boys and girls (Brozo et al., 2014). An extension of this logic suggests the potential diminution or outright disappearance of a gender gap on PISA if there were fewer or no constructed response items. I urge caution, however, when it comes to this interpretation, since questions requiring short and longer constructed-responses are designed to tap higher-level reading processes, which all of us would agree are as important to boys as to girls.

A related critique is that boys would likely demonstrate reading achievement levels comparable to girls on assessments like PISA if they were equally engaged as girls. There are data that seem to support this contention. Generally speaking, girls tend to have greater reading motivation than boys (Marinak & Gambrell, 2010; McGeown, Goodwin, Henderson, & Wright, 2012). Additionally, close analysis of PISA results shows that reading engagement is the variable with one of the strongest links to reading performance for all the countries participating, and girls have significantly higher indices of reading engagement than boys (Brozo et al., 2014). According to the OECD, boys' reading scores would be 23 points higher, on average across OECD countries, if they had the same value on the index of enjoyment of reading as girls (OECD, 2013b). However, it is important to point out that between PISA 2000 and 2009, countries that showed an increase in boys' reading enjoyment did not necessarily show a corresponding increase in boys' reading performance (Loveless, 2011). What this suggests is boys' self-reports of their own reading engagement may not be a very reliable indicator. Perhaps even more crucial to the improvement of reading ability is time spent reading outside school, and boys appear to fall far short of girls on that metric (OECD, 2015a). For example, surveys in the United States reveal that girls have more positive attitudes toward reading (McKenna et al., 2012) and are reading for pleasure daily at a percentage that is nearly twice as high as the percentage of boys (Common Sense Media, 2014; Rideout, Foehr, & Roberts, 2010).

Continuing to look on the testing front, challengers to the position I take in this book point out that males eventually catch up with and may even surpass their female counterparts as they enter and progress through adulthood. Support comes from findings on the Program for International Assessment of Adult Competencies or PIAAC, an international survey completed in 2012 by individuals age 16 to 65 in more than 30 countries across the globe. Overall test results revealed that men and women were statistically indistinguishable up to age 35, including countries like Germany, Finland, and the United States. After age 35, men's higher scores in reading, up to the oldest group, age 55 and beyond, were statistically significant. An important caveat to this trend in the PIAAC data is that in a PIAAC supplement assessment of US incarcerated (Rampey, Keiper et al., 2016) and unemployed (Rampey, Finnegan et al., 2016) adults there were virtually no differences between males and females on the literacy scale. Scores for both groups were many points below the overall US average of 272 and even lower for black and Hispanic adult males and females. This reminds us again of the need to parse large datasets for evidence of those males who exhibit the greatest need for extra literacy supports.

Another interesting challenge to my perspective about boys comes from those who see a kind of insidious sexism at play. Critics who hold this view argue that as girls make strides academically and professionally, which evidence suggests is occurring (Voyer & Voyer, 2014; Weber et al., 2014), advocates of boys' academic needs ensure males are given priority by regularly invoking "crisis" to rally popular support (Covert, 2014; Mead, 2006). The fact is that males continue to dominate political, corporate, and institutional life in the United States, Europe, and elsewhere in the world, for all the advances girls and women have made. In American society, it comes as a surprise to many to realize that, in more than a half century after the ratification of the Equal Rights Amendment, there remains a persistent underrepresentation of women in leadership positions. For instance, the United States ranks 71st worldwide in female legislative representation, as indicated by these facts: women occupy only 17 percent of Senate and House seats and 24 percent of seats in state legislatures, 9 percent of mayoral offices in the 100 largest cities, 12 percent of governors' office (6 out of 50), and fill three of nine seats on the Supreme Court (Re: Gender, www.wikigender.org/wiki/national-council-for-research-on-women/).

In another book on this topic, *Bright Beginnings for Boys*, which I co-wrote (Zambo & Brozo, 2009), an expression of the ultimate intent of that book matches well the goal I have for this book:

> Failing to meet the literacy needs of all . . . boys isn't so much a crisis as it is an imperative educational challenge. Furthermore, concerns about boys' reading attitudes and achievement should be framed around more responsive literacy instruction and interactions for all children. Boys need to be engaged and capable readers not solely to be as good as or better than girls, but to increase their educational, occupational, and civic opportunities and, above all, to become thoughtful and resourceful men (p. 3).

I see hope in the power of literacy for fostering enlightenment in boys. These same teen and preteen young men on whose behalf I devote this book will one day be living and working side by side with their female and LGBTQ colleagues and neighbors. Engaging them now in active literacy and doing all we can to sustain a lifelong literate consciousness can only improve the chances these boys, as they grow into adulthood, will embrace the merits of gender equity and social justice.

An additional critique of my goal of focusing attention on boys' literacy, learning, and life needs might be termed hegemonic masculinity (Morris, 2011). In this context, hegemonic refers to those who advocate a response to boys' lower levels of reading engagement and achievement by designing and implementing exclusively "boy friendly" curricular schemes (Hammett & Sanford, 2008; Martino & Kehler, 2007). This type of approach, it is argued, does little more than perpetuate gender myths and stereotypes by reinforcing binary notions of gender as a basis for literacy curricular decisions, which automatically excludes all the different ways of "being male" (Lingard, Martino, & Mills, 2009; Watson, Kehler, & Martino, 2010).

I am equally concerned about curricula and texts that cater to and promote a unidimensional conception of boys, males, and masculinity. Although certain boys may exhibit common characteristics, including shared preferences and dislikes, each boy must be regarded as an individual and, thus, I urge those who work with boys to learn about them as such. This means that for some struggling male readers, nurturing in them an enjoyment of reading may necessitate exposure to texts with traditional characters and themes. For other boys who are disengaged and challenged readers, it may be discovered that they become motivated to read texts with decidedly non-traditional characters and themes. In either case, as their tastes mature, so should the variety and themes of the texts made available to them. Above all, engaging teen and preteen boys in literacy should be the highest priority when developing reading curricula and seeking to foster independent reading habits. This is particularly critical for disaffected and struggling male readers. To achieve engaged reading, I propose the use of a great variety of texts and media along with a range of practices and programs that are likely to improve boys' thinking about what they read and increase their motivation to read.

What Does It Mean to Be a Reader in a Global Literacy Context?

Throughout this chapter, I have often referred to and drawn on findings from the three major international literacy surveys – PIRLS,

PISA, and PIAAC – for evidence of achievement disparities between boys and girls, males and females. This is because these assessments allow for direct comparisons within and across participating countries on a range of variables and performance levels. Thus, it is possible to interrogate the reading literacy assessment results for different subgroups within a single country, such as Germany or the United States, and also compare students' achievement with their national neighbors and across continents. Analyzing the findings for boys and older males of these major international literacy studies is important because of the ways in which reading literacy is defined and operationalized by their framers.

- **PIRLS** – "Reading literacy is the ability to understand and use those written language forms required by society and/or valued by the individual. Readers can construct meaning from texts in a variety of forms. They read to learn, to participate in communities of readers in school and everyday life, and for enjoyment" (Mullis, Martin, & Sainsbury, 2016, p. 12).
- **PISA** – "Reading literacy is understanding, using, evaluating, reflecting on and engaging with texts in order to achieve one's goals, to develop one's knowledge and potential and to participate in society" (OECD, 2016b, p. 11).
- **PIAAC** – "Understanding, evaluating, using and engaging with written text to participate in society, to achieve one's goals and to develop one's knowledge and potential" (OECD, 2012, p. 20).

What one immediately notices in these three definitions is, first, that reading is viewed as a complex ability that goes well beyond comprehending text, and, second, that there is a shared goal of assessing reading in such a way as to gain insight into readers' capacities for participation – in school, society, and everyday life. For boys who fail to develop expansive literacy abilities, full participation in an ever-increasingly demanding global society may be denied them.

Here is where I would like to make a broader case, rooted in a progressive vision of engaged citizenry of the twenty-first century, for ensuring all boys receive responsive reading literacy supports in and out of school. Each nation's success over the next decades will ultimately depend on economic growth. With greater economic opportunity comes improved levels of well-being for individuals and societies. Abundant evidence points to a direct relationship between economic growth and knowledge capital, or the skills of a country's population (Filmer, Hasan, & Pritchett, 2006). To realize these benefits, youth need to be able to demonstrate important skills and competencies (Hanushek & Woessmann, 2015). It is argued that when nations place emphasis on goals related to knowledge capital, their capacity to meet other important development goals is expanded, as well, such as ensuring equal sharing across society in the benefits of enhanced economic outcomes. Otherwise, those left behind, such as many of the boys and men I described previously, will continue to live with limited life and career options, as well as a galaxy of constraints associated with poverty, unemployment, and underemployment.

One of the most important cognitive skills all boys need, regardless of their ultimate career choice, in order to become effective problem solvers, flexible decision makers, and critical thinkers is skillful reading ability. Hanushek and Woessmann (2008, 2015) draw attention to the essential role cognitive skills, like reading, play in the lives of youth, stressing that skilled readers are far more likely to be successful in the workplace and in their communities than their unskilled peers. Male youth with low levels of literacy will be at a great and increasing disadvantage in today's society and modern workplace. In a world driven by information and knowledge, their skill deficiencies will limit access to the full range of opportunities enjoyed by their more literate peers (Bertschy, Cattaneo, & Wolter, 2009). Thus, the quality of literacy competence boys develop as young adults will impact their competence in personal, occupational, and community life as adults (Brozo & Crain, 2015).

Thus, changing workplace demands as well as the daily necessity to understand and evaluate competing media and information, and make critical decisions about what is best for one's personal, family, and community life underscore why boys need to become highly skillful readers. Although there may have always been a significant number of boys who were underachievers (Stroud & Lindquist, 1942; Gates, 1961) – leading some to charge that this proves there is no current boy crisis (Voyer & Voyer, 2014) – changes in today's workplace and the anticipated labor markets of the future have brought boys' underachievement into sharper focus. Up until the 1970s, in the United States, low academic qualifications were not necessarily a barrier to relatively well-paying jobs in manufacturing and industry. During that era, males with just a secondary school diploma, or even less, had the chance of earning high union-level wages (Western & Rosenfeld, 2011). Since the decline of industry and manufacturing in America, however, unskilled males have had far fewer options. As I have shown, there is a direct correlation between low qualifications and both joblessness and being trapped in low pay and unskilled work (Sum, Khatiwada, & McLaughlin, 2011).

Europeans are also grappling with challenges brought about by the mismatch between worker knowledge, skills, and competencies and jobs in the new economies of the twenty-first century. According to the European Commission (2016), as many as 70 million of its citizens struggle in their everyday lives with basic reading, writing, and digital literacy. Without these skills, they are at higher risk of unemployment, poverty, and social exclusion (UNESCO, 2014). To confront this knowledge divide, improving literacy and digital skills is considered the surest way to increase low-qualified people's life chances and employability.

Possessing sophisticated traditional and new literacy skills makes it possible for male youth to become, in adulthood, intellectual entrepreneurs, who are proactive in creating viable niches in global labor markets (Ananiadou & Claro, 2009). These literacy skills also make it possible for them to communicate, share, and use information to solve complex problems (Binkley et al., 2010). And facility with new literacies enables successful navigation and shaping of the "mediasphere" (Brozo, 2017).

Boys' Reading and Learning: A Coda

In UNESCO's report, *The Global Literacy Challenge* (Richmond, Robinson, & Sachs-Israel, 2008), the authors state:

> Literacy is about empowerment. It increases awareness and influences the behaviour of individuals, families and communities. It improves communication skills, gives access to knowledge and builds the self-confidence and self-esteem needed to make decisions ... Literacy is a process, not an endpoint. It is ... the passport to lifelong learning. We learn new ways to use literacy as we face new demands in work, study or our personal lives. Literacy is a necessary part of using new technologies, learning new languages, taking on new responsibilities and adapting to a changing workplace. (p. 21)

Indeed, this is the vision I have for boys as they learn to use literacy for gaining knowledge, effective communication, recreation and pleasure, and personal empowerment. The benefits of engaged literacy make it possible to successfully navigate through, and contribute significantly to, our modern world.

I have spent untold hours in general and remedial classrooms in numerous secondary schools around the United States, Europe, and across the globe, observing and learning from other teachers, conducting professional development, and gathering research data. The overwhelming impression I have been left with is that more must be done to reach the growing numbers of listless, detached, and struggling male readers. I have also found a clear and recurring pattern of concern among teachers and parents: Too many preteen and teen boys do not like to read, are choosing not to read, and are suffering academically, personally, and socially as a result.

Based on my own decades of experience, as well as a careful review of the ever-expanding evidence, I continue to hold the conviction that adolescent boys need special attention with respect to their literacy development and attitudes. Thus, I wrote this book based on an ongoing desire to share my experiences and ideas with the many teachers, parents, and others who are equally concerned about boys' literate futures. This book, then, is devoted to building an evidence-based case for the engaging texts, practices, and programs I share to help teen and preteen boys find entry points into literacy and stay the course as readers. Once entry points are found, boys increase their chances of developing a sense of self through active literacy and for an expansive intellectual journey throughout adolescence and beyond. This is critical because, as I have shown, possession of highly developed literacy abilities can ultimately lead to better lives for themselves and those around them.

Skillful and critical reading ability is an important tool that boys must have to become academically and personally successful. This tool, or its lack, can contribute to either a virtuous cycle of successful living or a grinding cycle of difficulty and failure. Good readers are better students in every subject area, and high academic achievement increases career and life options for youth. Superior students perform better on entrance examinations, making it easier for them to access postsecondary educational opportunities and, ultimately, find better jobs. But perhaps most critically, happier, healthier, and more successful people are, among other characteristics, active readers (Pearson, 2016). Moreover, those who achieve and exercise power over their lives, regardless of culture, spend more time reading than those who have less power or feel powerless (Hoffstetter, Sticht, & Hofstetter, 1999). Reading, it is asserted, leads to knowledge, which is associated with power regardless of other barriers that citizens face. People who practice active literacy acquire knowledge more readily than others, and knowledge is the great equalizer in terms of access to personal and professional power.

Those of us who are active readers already know that engaged reading directly contributes to our sophisticated literacy and thinking, which has also made our professional accomplishments possible. The purpose of this book is to help boys obtain the same benefits and pleasures we enjoy. Young men cannot bypass the path we have all traveled to become who we are as literate adults. We, however, can help make this journey possible for boys by providing them with engaging texts and meaningful experiences with those texts.

CHAPTER 2

Boys and Literacy: A Closer Look

> **In this chapter, I**
> - Explore what is known about literacy achievement and reading habits and their association with related factors (e.g., socioeconomic, immigrant, language learners, technology/new literacies, engagement, identities) for boys
> - Explain how gender differences in reading evolve and change in childhood and adolescence

In Chapter 1, I laid out in broad strokes much of what is known about boys' literacy achievement, their reading habits, and their literacy engagement. In this chapter, I explore in greater detail boys' reading achievement by way of several critical factors the research literature points to as having a significant influence on how well boys read, how interested they are in reading, what they read, and their self-perceptions as readers. By focusing on how factors such as socioeconomic or immigrant status, language learning, new technologies, engagement, and identity, I reveal how they shape boys' attitudes toward literacy, as well as their impact on boys' opportunities and facility with literacy tools. Each of these factors will be developed in depth from practical and programmatic perspectives in subsequent chapters.

Also in this chapter, I zero in on the developmental level of the boys of concern in this book to demonstrate how their reading achievement, reading habits, preferences, and attitudes evolve as they progress from childhood to adolescence. My many years of researching into the causes of boys' disaffection and struggles with reading and writing, as well as programs, practices, and texts that have been shown to increase literacy engagement and achievement for boys, leads me to urge educators to redouble their efforts to ensure that boys who bring the greatest challenges to our classrooms and schools receive responsive literacy texts and practices to increase their chances for academic, personal, and occupational success.

Evidence that emerges from studies like Robinson and Lubienski's (2011) longitudinal investigation of kindergarten through fifth-grade students shows girls are ahead of boys in reading right from the start. And though boys who are high achievers catch up with girls, boys at the lowest levels of achievement continue to fall significantly behind their female peers. Results such as these buttress my contention that we need to place special emphasis on those boys and male youth struggling the most with literacy. Moreover, this and other work (Brozo, 2010; Jyotsna & Pouezevara, 2016) point to a period in boys' development when literacy supports are especially critical. Thus, I focus my analysis of research and descriptions of successful and promising practices on the upper primary through secondary years.

Boys and Socioeconomic Factors

Socioeconomic status (SES) is a metric that combines economic and sociological factors to gauge a person's social position in relation to others. For individuals and families, factors typically included in SES are household or combined income, education attainment, and occupation. Individual and family economic well-being has been linked to a variety of benefits for children and youth, including overall academic achievement (Ladd, 2012), early word learning and language development (Farrant & Zubrick, 2012; Schiff & Lotem, 2011), reading achievement and growth (Aikens & Barbarin, 2010; Benson & Borman, 2010), and even physical and psychological health (Marmot, 2004).

Since societies around the world stand to benefit from increasing the SES for all its citizens, it is important to consider SES in relationship to cognitive skills in reading. Hanushek and Woessmann (2010) build a compelling case for leavening the economic health and overall well-being of a nation by raising PISA scores. They argue that "a modest goal of having all OECD countries boost their average PISA scores by 25 points over the next 20 years implies an aggregate gain of OECD GDP of USD 115 trillion over the lifetime of the generation born in 2010" (p. 6). The researchers further claim that GDP benefits up to 200 trillion dollars could accrue to the global economy if all students were brought to just a minimal level of proficiency (i.e., reaching a PISA score of 400).

The implications of Hanushek and Woesmann's analysis of reading literacy skills and the economy are staggering, particularly for the United States, which, according to the researchers, stands to make by far the most dramatic gain in GDP, over 40 trillion USD, as compared with other OECD countries.

Although state, district, and individual information related to SES is not available in the PISA databases, analysis of SES can be achieved using proxy variables. For instance, reading scores can be correlated to free and reduced-price lunch rates, which represent students' family income. Data from the PISA study confirm the linear relationship between these two variables. American students from the most privileged backgrounds, less than 10 percent of eligibility for free or reduced-price lunch, have an average PISA score (551) that is second in the world, just shy of the top performing jurisdiction, Shanghai-China (556). The score achieved by students who fall in the next category (10–29.9 percent free and reduced-price lunch) would rank them 5th in the world, just ahead of Singapore (526) and a few score points below Hong Kong China (533).

A very different outcome is evident for groups of students highly eligible for free and reduced-price lunches. At 50–74.9 percent, a score of 471 is comparable to a rank of about 31st among the 34 OECD countries participating in the 2009 assessment. The lowest score, 446, associated with students who are at least 75 percent eligible, ranks 33rd among the OECD countries, higher only than Mexico at 425.

Relating SES to reading ability of boys and male youth, the same patterns found among the general population of adolescents hold true for teen and preteen boys. Thus, boys in poverty are at the highest risk of reading failure (Payne & Slocumb, 2011). To be clear, I emphasized in Chapter 1 that each boy is unique, in spite of broad trends that emerge from large data sets. This means that poverty status alone does not mean, inevitably, a boy is a struggling reader any more than a boy from privilege is automatically a good reader. However, analysis of PISA results for bright boys from poor families in European countries such as England, Germany, and Denmark uncovered a gap of as much as 15 to 30 months between them and their high-achieving male classmates from the most economically privileged backgrounds (Jerrim, 2013). This finding points to the potency of poverty, which may act as a kind of weight holding back the reading achievement of even the brightest of boys from that economic stratum (Jerrim & Vignoles, 2013). The divide between those from poor backgrounds who are high achievers from their more privileged peers becomes more pronounced as they enter and progress through secondary school

(Crawford, Macmillan, & Vignoles, 2016), suggesting this developmental period may be critical for responsive interventions for particularly vulnerable boys.

Recent research in the United States adds to the picture of boys from the lowest rungs of the socioeconomic ladder. In communities where there are high rates of crime and incarceration, poverty, and single-parent families, all children struggle, though boys appear to be more susceptible than girls to the harmful effects of growing up in these unstable environments, according to Chetty and his colleagues (2016). Most notably, the researchers uncovered a persistent and generational pattern for boys who grow up in high-poverty areas – they are significantly less likely than their female counterparts to be employed in any type of work as adults. Out-of-work males translate into higher rates of crime in these communities, which contributes to unstable and stressful environmental circumstances for children.

The most seriously affected subset of all children by these conditions are black boys, Chetty's research team reports. Growing up in many American inner-cities and poor suburbs, black males find limited job opportunities, especially if they possess only a high school diploma or less. In some cases, the researchers found, earning money through criminal activity may be more accessible and more profitable than a regular job. If incarcerated and released, black males often have an even more difficult time finding gainful employment. The poverty that attends these conditions leads to food insecurity and malnutrition, which hits children especially hard. Add to this the stress of parental unemployment, depression, inadequate housing, and neighborhood violence and cognitive delays and other negative effects on brain development may result (Shanks & Robinson, 2012).

The research literature tells us the syndromes associated with poverty are especially harmful for boys, including their far greater chance of not acquiring expected reading competencies in primary school (Hernandez, 2012), failing to graduate from secondary school, falling into crime, and being jailed (Sum et al., 2009). On any given day in America, nearly 25 percent of young black males who dropped out of school are incarcerated or institutionalized (Styslinger, Gavigan, & Albright, 2017). And, as I noted in Chapter 1, the great majority of US inmates, including juvenile offenders, are either illiterate or have serious reading problems (Cohen, 2010). Most do not possess a high school diploma compared with their non-incarcerated cohorts, and their numbers have been growing (Pettit, 2012).

Immigrant Boys

The United States already has a majority-minority population of school children. According to National Center for Education Statistics (2014), less than 50 percent of students enrolled in American schools are white, a group that has been in decline for the past two decades. In contrast, there has been dramatic growth in the Latino population and a steady rise in the number of Asian-Americans. Meanwhile, African American growth has been mostly flat.

Morrell (2008) posits that one of the biggest challenges facing literacy educators in the United States today is finding effective ways to teach an increasingly diverse student population. At the heart of the challenge is the struggle to develop academic literacies through curricula and strategies that are inclusive and affirm the cultural value and individual identities of every adolescent (Freeman & Freeman, 2008; Janzen, 2008).

Regarding immigrant males in both the North American and European contexts, the evidence points to a number of ways they are doing less well both academically and socially than their female peers (Dumka et al., 2009; Gibson & Carrasco, 2009). Qin (2006) has urged theorizing of the role of gender in immigrant children's adaptations to and progress in American society, particularly because of the growing evidence that boys from many ethnic groups lag behind girls in terms of academic accomplishments. For example, according to the research findings of Villiger, Wandeler, and Niggli (2014), compared to immigrant girls, immigrant boys in Switzerland at the primary school level were significantly less motivated to read for enjoyment or out of curiosity and had significantly lower reading comprehension scores. In a related finding, Dronkers and Kornder's (2015) analysis of PISA reading scores for nearly nine thousand male and female migrant adolescents in 17 OECD destination countries uncovered an overall pattern of migrant daughters' superior performance as compared to migrant sons. The achievement gap was widest in favor of females who originated in countries and regions with higher gender equity levels. This female advantage appeared to carry over to school performance, as well.

Studies of gender differences among immigrants in the United States reinforce patterns observed in Europe (c.f., Loera, Rueda, & Nakamoto, 2011; Riegle-Crumb, 2010). Feliciano (2012) used data from the Children of Immigrants Longitudinal Study (CILS) to explore an increasingly substantiated immigrant female advantage in educational achievement in the United States, even if that advantage was not found in the immigrants' home countries. Compared with girls, immigrant boys had lower grades, spent less time on homework and more time watching television, had more negative perceptions of school and more negative experiences at school, and were less able to form positive school relationships. That these gender-based advantages for girls were most apparent for immigrant youth from lower socioeconomic levels demonstrates once again poverty's particularly detrimental effect on males. Santiago and her colleagues (Santiago et al., 2014) also investigated the academic achievement of immigrant adolescents, focusing on the differences between US-born and Latino youth. Among their many interesting findings was that English language proficiency and female gender were associated with higher grades in school, suggesting that male teens, both US-born and immigrant, who failed to develop their English were most at risk of school failure.

Suarez-Orozco and Qin (2005) targeted the experiences of immigrant boys' in US schools and found data that bolsters the trend that they underachieve relative to girls. The boys in their study performed less well than immigrant girls in reading and oral and written language. Whereas girls demonstrated better understanding of English, boys had poor to very poor written English skills. Additionally, the girls were more likely to commit to learning English and improve their reading and writing, while the boys were more distracted and tended to engage in anti-social behavior. Boys reported more conflict with administrators and teachers than girls, and perceived the American schools they attended, most of which were in high-poverty sections of the inner city, as "prisons" with their security guards and metal detectors. Furthermore, because the boys in the study were quicker to identify with neighborhood culture instead of school culture, they often avoided acting smart or carrying books for fear of not looking "cool" or being harassed.

One intriguing explanation for immigrant boys' inferior reading and academic performance focuses on the disjuncture between in- and out-of-school literacies and language competence. Souto-Manning, Dernikos, and Yu (2016) deconstructed normative discourses of literacy and learning in school to challenge how it shapes immigrant boys' self-perceptions as readers and learners. The researchers determined that many boys who were characterized as "at risk" and "struggling" readers actually possessed sophisticated communication skills, though these were deemed at odds with school norms and expectations. Findings like these point to the need to form bridges between boys' linguistic competencies and the literacy practices in school, especially for boys of color and immigrant boys who may have a history of academic failure.

Boys as Additional Language Learners

As we have seen, boys underperform relative to girls in North America and Europe on most measures of verbal ability (Loveless, 2015). Females also hold an enduring advantage over males in school marks and grade point average in language courses (Voyer & Voyer, 2014). So, it should not surprise anyone that females also outperform males on tests of language. For example, van der Slik, van Hout, and Schepens (2015) found that for students in Holland, from as many as 88 countries and 49 mother tongues, females had a significant advantage over males in their ability to acquire the Dutch language based on tests of language competency. Similarly, on the Test of English as a Foreign Language (TOEFL) non-native English-speaking women consistently score higher than their male counterparts (ETS, 2016).

Like other patterns of gender achievement in reading, female English language superiority is a global phenomenon (Education First, 2016). Throughout European countries and across North America, females are overrepresented in fields associated with traditional literacy, leading Goodman and Rogers (2010) to conclude that "language is the most feminized field in public secondary education" (p. 199). The implications of females' language-learning advantage echo those I have discussed previously in connection to reading literacy achievement in general.

English language competency, like reading literacy ability, is related to access to resources and opportunities denied those who fail to learn or develop English. In Education First's (2016) report of its global survey of proficiency in English as a non-native language, the importance of this lingua franca is expressed in this way:

> In a world where integration is the norm, English has become the medium of cross-cultural communication for a growing number of people in an increasingly diverse set of situations. No skill since literacy has held such potential to increase the efficiency and earning power of so many. The impact of English on the global economy is undeniable. English skills are a basic requirement in today's global economy. Mastery of a language is difficult and expensive, but parents and professionals understand the value of investing in English training, and companies and governments recognize the link between workforce English and long-term competitiveness in the 21st century. (p. 4)

These observations are reinforced by findings from the OECD studies related to integration of immigrants and global competencies that highlight the benefits of bilingualism (OECD, 2016). According to the OECD

(2015), the higher boys' PISA scores at age 15, the more likely they are to enroll in post-secondary education, choose more complex and higher-status major areas of study in post-secondary education, complete higher education, which slows skill loss as they age, have high earnings and low unemployment rates, and speak two languages resulting in a salary premium in adulthood.

In the United States, the fastest growing student subpopulation is English Learners (ELs) (Office of English Language Acquisition, 2017). Nearly 5 million students have been designated as ELs in K-12 US public schools, compromising almost 10 percent of the entire student population (US Department of Education the National Center for Educational Statistics, 2014). Although the mother tongues of ELs may number in the hundreds (Ryan, 2013), the dominant language by far is Spanish, with 38 million people indicating they speak it in the home, making the United States the 5th-largest Spanish-speaking country in the world (Ryan, 2013).

Generally speaking, ELs refer to a subgroup of students who are not "proficient" in English based on annual assessments given to determine their proficiency levels in reading, writing, listening, and speaking for both social and academic purposes (Baker & Wright, 2017). Within the EL subgroup of students, Long-Term ELs (LTELs) comprise the majority in the United States (Calderon & Minaya-Rowe, 2011). Long-Term ELs are typically students who are born and raised in the United States and have primarily attended US schools, yet, they continue to show consistent gaps in their education, primarily in areas of academic literacy (Olsen, 2012). I cannot emphasize this point too strongly: although some English Learners in the United States are newcomers, most of these students are by birth citizens of America. In fact, over 80 percent of primary-level and more than 60 percent of secondary-level English Learners are born in the United States (Zong & Batalova, 2015). Therefore, caution must be exercised when tempted to assume those facing challenges learning English come exclusively from immigrant populations.

Males comprise more than half of all English Learners in the United States and an even larger share of those who are identified as long-term (Brantmeier, Schueller, Wilde, & Kinginger, 2010). This means a considerable number of boys who come from homes where a language other than English is spoken continue to struggle with mastery of English at school with grim consequences (Menken, 2009). Data show that male English Learners, especially those whose language difficulties persist, are prone to exclusion from advanced placement courses, dropping out of school, finding only low-paying jobs, experiencing financial hardships in adulthood, as well as a host of other setbacks (Kanno & Kanagas, 2014; Mussman, 2013).

Boys in the Real World

"Dane"

Dane would rather play basketball than read. It is not that he dislikes reading and used to read enthusiastically when he was in elementary school. "Books just don't seem interesting anymore," he lamented, as compared with the other ways he likes to spend his time now that he is 16.

But when his history teacher incorporated a graphic novel, *Incognegro* (Johnson & Pleece, 2008), into a unit on the American civil rights movement, Dane was moved by the book and has become more eager to read further on the topic. The book is about how blacks in the south suffered the indignity and abuse of segregation and racism and were even lynched by the KKK and other vigilante groups. "My teacher told us that some blacks with real light skin who worked for newspapers in the North risked their lives to go South and write articles about lynchings. They called this going 'incognegro,'" recounted Dane. The main character, Zane Pinchback, is a reporter for a newspaper in Harlem. Because he is very light-skinned, he decides to go to Mississippi to investigate the murder of a white woman his own brother is accused of committing. Whites want to lynch Zane's brother, so he does everything he can to find out the truth and save his brother and himself from the lynch-minded mob.

Dane related to Pinchback because, like this character, he also has light skin from his white mother and father who is from Ethiopia. As Dane put it, "Some kids with tans look darker than me." Although his hair is curly it is not kinky and his skin is light brown, Dane nevertheless identifies as an African American, and all of his friends are black.

Dane is a struggling reader. School texts are difficult to understand and require a kind of stamina and skill he feels he does not possess. What made *Incognegro* comprehensible to him were the detailed and engrossing illustrations that accompanied the narration and speech. As Dane put, "I like this book because it's a graphic novel. For me, these kinds of books are a lot easier to read. I can read the words and if I'm not sure what's going on or if the dialogue isn't too interesting, I can also look at the illustrations. The illustrations in this book are awesome. They really help you get into the story."

Dane's history teacher asked his students to write a journal response to the graphic novel, and Dane was eager to share excerpts of his. He wrote, "I have a lot of respect for blacks who fought for civil rights. They risked their lives. Zane is afraid whites will figure out he's black, but he does what he can for his brother anyway. Reading about Zane and looking at the drawings of him, his brother, the angry whites, and the other people made the book so real."

And a final journal entry from Dane read, "Could I ever show the kind of courage Zane does or all those people who fought for their rights? I don't know. But I think I am strong enough and proud enough. There's one part of the book where Zane is looking right into your eyes. He is in Mississippi and he has found out who really killed the white woman. When I look into Zane's eyes in that picture, it's like I can see myself. He's scared but confident that he must do the right thing."

Discussion and Activities
- What recommendations can you offer to teachers working with Dane to help him develop the reading habit and improve his reading skills?
- How can Dane's interests in sports be exploited for further literacy development?
- In what ways can teachers take advantage of the kinds of topics and texts Dane enjoys to further his reading and writing abilities?

Identity Factors and Boys

Gender is directly linked to adolescent literacy identities. Recall from the PISA findings presented in the previous chapter, that boys are universally and significantly poorer achievers in reading and have lower levels of reading engagement than girls. Although these findings are based on overall averages, they suggest important patterns that merit scrutiny. Beyond the broad results of PISA and other large national and state assessments, there is ample evidence that too many boys in the United States do not possess positive literate identities (Boltz, 2007; Brozo, 2010; Husband, 2012; McNally, 2016). This is especially true of boys who come to school as struggling readers and for many boys from low-economic backgrounds (Anderson, Howard, & Graham, 2007; Kirkland, 2011; Schott Foundation for Public Education, 2012; Tatum, 2009).

Male youth, like all adolescents, increase their chances of developing the literate abilities and positive literate identities necessary for full participation as global citizens if they're exposed to and have meaningful and enjoyable literacy and learning experiences centered on texts of interest. In this book, I make repeated calls to know and learn to value adolescent boys' interests and literate practices beyond the school walls. The texts and literate practices boys already engage in outside of school can be honored in school to reinforce identities of competency, sustain their attention, and lead to more thoughtful reading and writing (Brozo, 2010; Haddix, 2009; Tatum & Muhammad, 2012).

Issues of gender, social class, and academic identity appear to be related in complex ways. For example, studies continue to affirm that making an effort to achieve academically has been found to be incompatible with working-class male identities (Abraham, 2008). Working-class and poor males have been documented describing boys who take school seriously in effeminate and unfavorable ways, such as wearing glasses and always with their head in a book, instead of being socially involved and "doing" things (Archer, Pratt, & Phillips, 2001). This perception by certain boys that positive academic identities are more in line with the ways girls behave presents many challenges for educators, parents, and community members. The implication that gender-normed behaviors for girls are more consistent with behaviors needed for reading and learning success invites a critical look into how teachers and school-based textual practices may feed these perceptions by boys and girls (Vantieghem, Vermeersch, & Van Houtte, 2014).

According to Bigler and her associates (2013), schools are critical venues for fostering gender stereotypes and engaging in gender policing. They urge boys' underachievement be viewed from the perspective of hegemonic masculinity, a concept I described in the first chapter. They see boys' literate and academic identities tied closely to dominant cultural notions of maleness that pressure boys to conform to particular ways of behaving and performing or else they may be isolated or even bullied. The authors point out how teachers communicate gender stereotypes explicitly and implicitly. For instance, while girls may pick up on implied and overt messages that reading is easier for them (Logan & Medford, 2011), boys may sense from comments, biased opportunities, and body language that math is easier for them (Riegle-Crumb & Humphries, 2012).

Empirical support for teachers' influence on girls' and boys' self-efficacy as readers comes from Retelsdorf, Schwartz, and Asbrock (2015) who sampled 54 teachers and over 1,300 students in a longitudinal study across two upper primary grades. The evidence showed that grade five teachers' gender stereotypes in relation to reading that favored girls was associated with boys' negative reading self-concept at the end of grade six. The authors argue that teachers, along with parents and peers, represent significant others in the lives of children and youth and can, by holding gender stereotype beliefs, affect students' sense of competence, achievement, and value. As concerns reading, teachers' gender biases appear to be particularly detrimental to boys. Parents as significant others can also shape boys' negative reading identities and achievement, as Rouland and her colleagues revealed (2013), through the ways they communicate their gender-based biases to their male and female children.

Elmore and Oyserman (2012) assert that boys may be rejecting reading because it does not feel "gender-congruent." Due to prevalence of gender stereotyping in schools, boys may perceive language arts and excelling in subjects that demand traditional textual reading and writing as "feminine." This kind of identity-based motivation might further explain how boys' reading skills can deteriorate over time. If language arts is perceived as something other than masculine, boys may choose to avoid reading and writing, especially outside of school, limiting their practice and experiences with text. As middle and high-schoolers, male youth also find peer acceptance policing their perceptions and behavior in school. Thus, male culture that regards literacy accomplishment and academic success as "not cool" can force even high-achieving boys to disengage (Vantieghem, Vermeersch, & Van Houtte, 2014). These findings remind us to be particularly sensitive to ways in which gender biases and stereotypes, whether directly or subtly, are being communicated to boys about reading and writing (Younger & Cobbett, 2014).

It may be that purposeful and inadvertent messages reinforcing gender bias position immigrant boys and boys of color in particularly vulnerable ways. In Harper and Williams' (2014) compelling report of black and Latino male youth in New York City, the authors sarcastically capture popular media's spin of inner-city boys of color by saying:

> Their futures are hopeless. All but a few will remain trapped in generational cycles of poverty and crime-infested neighborhoods. Their lazy, drug-addicted, government-dependent single parents care little about their schooling. Consequently, they inherit from their families and communities a staunch carelessness for learning and educational attainment. More appealing to them are guns, gangs, fast money, and one pair of career options (either becoming rappers or professional athletes). They are to be feared, stopped and frisked, and mass incarcerated, as they are the antithesis of law-abiding citizens. When they show up to school (which isn't very often), administrators and teachers should expect them to be disengaged, disrespectful, unprepared, underperforming, and violent. For sure, they are most likely to drop out of high school and least likely to enroll in college. This caricature of young men of color in urban contexts is both pervasive and longstanding. It also is one-sided, terribly racist, and far from universal. (p. 5)

The report goes on to document the academic success stories of adolescent males both black and Hispanic living in the various boroughs of New York City. Over 500 hours of interviews were conducted with 325 junior- and senior-high school students, many of whom had to overcome barriers such as single-parent and poverty-income households, gang violence, drug trafficking, as well as other neighborhood dangers. These boys of color who beat the odds and were college bound present a narrative of masculine identity that stands in sharp contrast to pervasive and essentialized media stereotypes of black and Latino urban youth.

The success stories of male youth of color in the Harper and Williams' report are all the more impressive given the identity formation challenges for immigrant adolescents reported by Qin (2009). She cites numerous sources of conflict in the lives of these adolescents due to the multiple cultural communities they must negotiate and the often dissonant expectations these communities hold for youth. On a daily basis, immigrant adolescents are pressured to adjust to new school and home environments and relationships, navigating between the attachment to their parents' culture, the lure of the adolescent peer culture, and aspirations to join the receiving society's mainstream culture. Inherent to these challenges are gender issues. According to Prieur (2002), "both in a process of labeling from the outside and in the construction of a subjective identity" (p. 53) gender shapes an immigrant students' formation of self.

In subsequent chapters, I discuss what teachers and parents can do to counteract the effects of their own gender stereotypes as directed to boys in particular. I also share successful and promising programs and practices that capitalize on the identities of boys to build bridges between their unique personal histories and the texts and practices validated by school.

Boys and Reading Engagement

Nobel Prize winning economist James Heckman argues in favor of what he refers to as "soft skills" – those personality traits that may be even more essential than cognitive abilities to successful learning and achievement inside and outside the classroom (Heckman & Kautz, 2012). According to Heckman and his colleagues (Heckman, Stixrud, & Urzua, 2006), traits such as curiosity and perseverance might have greater predictive power for success in life than cognitive skills.

Engagement for learning, like perseverance, is one of the soft skills that has been shown to be a potent predictor of academic success (Schunk, Meece, & Pintrich, 2013). Generally speaking, learning improves when students are inquisitive, interested, inspired, or otherwise "engaged."

Evidence for the benefits of engaged learning is quite compelling. We know that correlational data from the National Assessment of Educational Progress (NAEP) continue to show adolescents who identify themselves as being interested in reading not only achieve better scores on the NAEP but have better high school grade point averages than their less interested peers (Loveless, 2015). Even more convincing are data derived from the PISA, the global study of reading-literacy for 15-year-olds, I described in Chapter 1. Engagement is the variable above all others that has the strongest relationship to performance on PISA (OECD, 2013). Higher reading engagement, as indicated by reading enjoyment, extensive daily and weekly reading time, and reading a wide variety of fiction and nonfiction texts, was correlated to higher achievement (Brozo et al., 2014). Students who failed to do this, the highly disengaged readers, found themselves behind their highly engaged peers by nearly two years of schooling. Remarkably, that's like being absent from two years of instruction.

There is a well-documented slump in achievement and motivation during the upper-elementary and middle school years (Martin, 2009). Curiously, this phenomenon is not restricted to the United States. Youth from across the globe exhibit a similar decline in performance and interest as they move from primary to secondary school (Brozo et al., 2014). Some of our best thinkers and researchers in youth literacy have proposed that this decline in academic motivation results from a disjuncture between adolescents' need for content and learning experiences that are accessible and relevant, on the one hand, and traditional school-related reading, writing, and disciplinary practices, on the other (Alvermann & Eakle, 2007; Fecho, 2011; Thomson & Hall, 2008).

What is truly fascinating about the findings from PISA related to engagement is that youth from the lowest SES who were highly engaged readers performed as well on the assessment as youth from the middle SES group and cut in half the disparity between themselves and their high SES peers (Brozo, Shiel, & Topping, 2007). In other words, highly motivated adolescents made up for low family income and parents' limited educational attainment, two oft-considered risk factors in the school lives of students. This should be ground-shaking news, because it strongly suggests that if we can keep students engaged in reading and learning they may be able to overcome what might otherwise be insuperable barriers to academic success. Indeed, it has been shown that when girls and boys have similar levels of reading engagement, as measured by the amount of time spent reading, they have similar levels of achievement (Topping, Samuels, & Paul, 2008).

The PISA studies offer more important revelations about the gender factor in reading achievement and engagement. As might be expected, given their overall superior performance on most measures of verbal ability (Brozo, 2010), girls from the United States had significantly higher indices of reading engagement as compared with boys. Girls enjoyed reading more, spent a greater amount of time reading, and had a wider range of reading preferences as compared with their male peers (Brozo et al., 2014). So, it should not come as a surprise to learn that girls' higher levels of engagement contributed to their superior achievement to that of the boys.

This potency of engagement to performance on PISA reading has been reconfirmed in several studies. Lee (2014), using US data from the 2000 PISA study, looked at the scores of over three thousand 15-year-old students from 121 US schools and documented the significant predictive power of engagement with reading performance. Similarly, Chuy and Nitulescu's (2013) showed that girls outperformed boys on the 2009 PISA reading literacy assessment by the equivalent of one-half a reading-proficiency level, or one full year of formal schooling. The analysis revealed that enjoyment of reading has the strongest association with reading ability and dominates other factors.

The National Assessment of Educational Process (NAEP) results have also been analyzed to verify the association between engagement and reading achievement for boys and girls. Straus' (2011) investigation of eighth grade males and females' scores on NAEP reading and their levels of engagement uncovered a familiar pattern in which engaged reading, as a whole, was found to be a significant predictor of reading achievement.

In the European context, corroboration of the strong predictive power of engagement for gender-based academic achievement has been accumulating. German researchers, such as Kessels and her associates (2014), describe engagement as a kind of self-fulfilling prophecy wherein boys get rewarded for achievement in math and thus become increasingly engaged in math studies, while girls receive affirmation for demonstrations of reading competence, which reinforces their reading engagement. Researchers in Flanders tracking school engagement and achievement for nearly three thousand adolescents from grade seven through grade twelve concluded that girls were more engaged than boys and had higher academic achievement (Van de gaer, Pustjens, Van Damme, & De Munter,

2009). They also documented a general decline in academic engagement as both boys and girls progressed through the grades, though boys experienced a much steeper decline in engagement than girls. In a study of approximately 400 Dutch seventh graders, Lietaert et al. (2015) found boys were less engaged in school than girls and reported less support from their teachers. Additionally, the researchers learned that boys' level of academic engagement increased when they were allowed greater involvement in classroom lessons and given support for autonomous learning. In a related study conducted in Norway, Tonne and Pihl (2012) discovered that boys in multilingual classes were less engaged and were the lower reading achievers. However, the researchers observed a positive effect on engagement and reading achievement among the males and females in the study after two years in a special literature-based literacy program designed for these students. Finally, in the United Kingdom, Oakhill and Petrides (2007) analyzed an extant database of 10- and 11-year-old boys' and girls' performance on a reading test over two passages on different topics. The boys in the study scored higher on the assessment related to a passage for which they had higher interest and engagement, while the girls scored equally well on both passage assessments regardless of topic interest.

Boys and New Technologies/Literacies

Today's youth in North America and Europe might truly be called digital natives (Prensky, 2009). Consider that teens in America are spending almost nine hours daily viewing and interacting with digital media (Common Sense Media, 2015), leading researchers like Danah Boyd (2014), who undertook longitudinal case studies of adolescents and their digital media, to assert "these technologies – and the properties that go with them – are just an obvious part of life" (p. 42).

The spread of these new information and communication technologies has brought about a global shift from print to digital texts. For most American citizens, computers are now, after television, the second source of news, even more so than radio and printed newspapers and magazines (American Press Institute, 2014). British children and teenagers, too, appear to prefer digital texts over printed texts (Clark, 2014). And instead of inhibiting reading, a majority of users of mobile phone-based readers from several nations are more interested in reading and are spending more time reading now that it is possible to read on their smart phones (UNESCO, 2014).

Acquiring and expanding competence with these new literacies and technologies is forcing youth to stretch beyond foundational literacies that had been sufficient for past forms of reading and writing (Hartman, Morsink, & Zheng, 2010; International Reading Association, 2009). Many now claim that an essential twenty-first-century competence involves negotiating and creating new forms of text found in ever-new combinations of traditional offline environments with new online media (c.f. Dalton & Proctor, 2008; Wyatt-Smith & Elkins, 2008).

The realization that boys are likely the most active participants in the mediasphere (O'Brien, 2001) means the new forms of text they experience and create should be acknowledged and appreciated in school settings, since proficiency with these new literacies will serve them well in the constantly evolving digital age (Alvermann, 2010; Squire, 2011). One source of affirmation for boys' preference for and skill with electronic media comes from Wu's (2014) investigation of over 34 thousand PISA test takers from 19 countries. She affirmed boys' were equally as capable as girls on the electronic assessment, even while girls were superior with printed versions of the reading assessment.

I believe the digital discourse and new media worlds most boys inhabit, if validated in the public sphere of schools and classrooms, could narrow achievement gaps (Leu et al., 2015) and increase engagement in literacy and learning (Walsh, 2010). Primary and secondary schools are the settings where boys' interest and motivation in multiple literacies could find expression in the understanding, critical analysis, and reinterpretation of concepts and content (Leu et al., 2013; O'Brien & Scharber, 2008).

Boys' Literacy Needs from Childhood to Adolescents

Boys may be boys, but a boy at 8 years is not the same as a boy at 14 years. To appreciate this difference is critical to providing responsive literacy supports tailored to the skills, interests, and aspirations of boys across this age span. Many of the developmental differences among boys from childhood through teenage-hood parallel well-known human growth and development processes (Beckett & Taylor, 2016). Thus, boys, like girls, during this period change emotionally, physically, and cognitively in ways that can be characterized as general stages even while all youth, as I have advised, must be regarded as individuals who grow and change in their own distinctive ways.

Uniquely, however, boys in childhood through adolescence lag behind girls on a number of language development indices, which have been related to brain development (Rosselli, Ardila, Matute, & Velez-Uribe, 2014). For example, de Bellis and colleagues (2001) documented more rapid brain growth in areas associated with receptive and productive language among girls from childhood through young adulthood. Others have shown how boys' slower building up of certain brain structures related to language affects their cognitive performance (Ardila, Rosselli, Matute, & Inozemtseva, 2011; Gibson & Petersen, 2010; Kanaan et al., 2012).

It is important to remind ourselves here that although brain growth and cognitive development may progress in generally predictable ways for "normally" developing children and youth, these biological and neurological changes do not occur in isolation of the language and learning opportunities each boy encounters in his daily life. It is clear that brain structures involved in tasks like reading change in response to the environment (Hoff, 2009; Zambo & Brozo, 2009). Thus, a psychobiosocial theory of gender and learning, like that promoted by Halpern (2012), offers a more complete explanation of the interplay between changes in the brain and environmental stimulation. Consider how what boys learn modifies their brain structures, which in turn supports certain skills and abilities that impel boys to seek additional experiences consistent with those skills and abilities. At an early age for boys, these skills and abilities may not include reading and writing, though they may do so for girls. In this transactional way, according to Halpern, the environment and inherent processes of cognitive development interact to form the architecture of the reading brain.

The instructional implications of a psychobiosocial perspective of boys' reading development are many. First, it is critical that boys, particularly those who are struggling to acquire the skills of competent reading, be given accessible and motivating language and literacy experiences that promote and reinforce neural connections. If boys find the cognitive and dexterity challenges of reading and writing do not reinforce their developing skills and abilities because expectations are too high, the task is too difficult, or it fails to engage them, then they may seek activities more consistent with their burgeoning cognitive expertise, such as playing computer games, reading comic books and graphic novels, or writing song lyrics.

As boys grow as readers from their preteen to teen years, it is important to be aware of how the level of difficulty of texts on topics in which they continue to be interested will need to be adjusted. Thus, although a teenage boy may be just as interested in American baseball as he was when he was eight years old, his tastes for texts related to that topic will inevitably become more sophisticated, nuanced, and complex. For example, Mike's enjoyment of baseball as a third grader does not mean he reads the sports page in his local newspaper or that he follows team and player averages or that he delves into controversies about performance-enhancement drugs many baseball stars are putatively to have taken. Nonetheless, Mike could get excited about reading Ken Mochizuki's (1993) *Baseball Saved Us*, a primary-level picture book about a Japanese-American boy whose determination to become a good baseball player while in a World War II internment camp helps overcome lingering racial stereotypes and prejudices in post-war life. Ruben, on the other hand, as a teenager is not as likely to read Mochizuki's book in spite of his own strong interest in baseball. More in line with Ruben's age and skill level, would be a book like Zack Hample's (2011) *Baseball: Stunts, Scandals and Secrets Beneath the Stitches*, which is filled with insider trivia, anecdotes, fascinating illustrations, and advice for bringing home souvenir baseballs from stadiums.

In addition to making necessary adjustments to the level of difficulty of texts as boys mature as readers, it is equally important to be aware of how boys' interests in topics and texts may change over this timespan. The extant surveys and studies related to boys' interests and reading preferences are indicative of patterns for boys in general. Of course, to learn more about specific interests in reading and outside-of-school activity, it is essential to get to know boys on an individual level through interviews, surveys, and other means (see Chapter 6 for more information about assessing boys' interests and practical and programmatic approaches to supporting their literacy around those interests).

What the evidence points to is that, at the primary level, boys prefer texts of nonfiction, as well as adventure, humor, and fantasy texts (Boltz, 2007). We also learn that boys are more likely to read graphic novels and texts on such topics as sports, athletes, and cars (Bunn, 2012; Merisuo-Storm, 2006). In addition to information research has revealed about boys' preferences for text topics and genres, Canadian researchers Blair and Sanford (2004) have contributed to our understanding of what elementary school boys find engaging in terms of texts and related learning experiences. They tracked a group of boys over three years, observing them in their classrooms and conducting numerous interviews with them to determine literacy activities in which the boys were most engaged. Their analysis revealed five themes that included (1) texts and learning experiences with those texts that linked to their *personal interests*, (2) texts that described *action* and prompted active learning, (3) texts and related tasks that made them feel *successful*, (4) texts that were *fun* to read and spawned fun learning experiences, and (5) texts and tasks that were *purposeful* to boys' goals and desires. Armed with information like this, teachers put themselves in a much better position to support boys' own literacy practices as well as to incorporate activities to engage boys into their daily instruction.

For adolescent boys, we find similar trends to those for younger boys, as well as unique age-based differences. For instance, in a survey of leisure-time activity among middle school students, Sanford (2006) found that boys were far more likely than girls to (a) play sports, (b) build models, (c) ride bikes, (d) collect things, and (d) play video and computer games. Meanwhile, girls spent more time (a) talking to friends, (b) cooking, and (c) watching television. Most importantly, 66 percent of the girls in Sanford's study reported reading for enjoyment outside of school to boys' 21 percent, and only 7 percent of the boys indicated they spend time writing for leisure as compared to 40 percent for the girls. Similar results related to the gender disparity in reading for enjoyment were obtained by Hughes-Hassell and Rodge (2007) from their study of leisure reading habits of urban middle schoolers. Sixty-two percent of the girls reported they read for fun versus 54 percent of the boys. Furthermore, boys at this level said they would rather surf the web (34 percent to girls 24 percent) or play video games (35 percent to girls 15 percent) than read. The top choices for the boys who read for fun included magazines about sports, video games, and music.

Bozack (2011), in her study of ninth and tenth graders in an all-boys school, documents a critical developmental shift in reading motivation from elementary to secondary level. Unlike findings on reading motivation for younger readers (Wigfield, 1997), a key element of motivation for the adolescent boys in her investigation was Reader Identity. The high correlation between the two constructs suggests, as boys grow older, they need to braid literacy into their burgeoning adolescent and male identities. In other words, adolescent boys who "see" themselves as readers are more likely to be engaged, motivated readers. Bozack also reconfirmed the foundational nature of reading ability for overall academic achievement, as she found the boys' "reading scores (were) related to achievement across content areas" (2011, p. 70).

To be sure, a healthy reading identity should be fostered right from the start with boys, since belief in their own competency as readers is closely linked to their skill level and overall achievement in school (Logan & Medford, 2011). However, it appears that, as boys progress through primary school into secondary school, developing and maintaining a strong sense of reading identity is critical to helping them grow as independent readers and achieve academic success.

A Closer Look at Boys and Literacy: A Coda

The premise of this book is that our collective knowledge about boys and their literacy development is enriched by accumulating insights gained through quality research and practices (Hildreth & Kimble, 2004). In this chapter, I demonstrate the need to build a more complete understanding of boys and the critical factors that influence their growth as readers by considering a range of valuable evidence and insights.

In Michael Kennedy's (2015) profound treatise on the power of globalized knowledge, he describes those who accept its benefits by saying, "They appreciate how it increases the power and privilege of its patrons or augments the public good of the communities in which the knowledgeable and their institutions reside" (p. xii). My goal with this book is to expand the knowledge base related to understanding boys and their challenges with literacy, as well as ways of responding effectively to the challenges these boys present.

The sharing of knowledge about key correlates to boys' literacy achievement, including such factors as socioeconomics, immigrant status, language learning, technology/new literacies, engagement, and identities, is meant to better inform those stakeholders in boys' literacy development and enlarge our capacity to craft responsive programs and practices to meet the literacy needs of boys. Moreover, synthesizing salient knowledge about how boys' literate identities are shaped over time, as well as how their interests, desires, and goals evolve from childhood to adolescence and have been shown to differ from those of girls, offers further opportunities for ensuring male youth have engaging and meaningful literacy experiences in primary and secondary school.

CHAPTER 3

Boys' Masculinities and Identities: Evidence and Practice

> **In this chapter, I**
> - Demonstrate how theories of literacy identity can inform us about boys' attitudes and practices
> - Explain the importance of deconstructing hegemonic masculinity in conceptualizing and crafting literacy curriculum for boys
> - Describe the role of textual practices in constraining or expanding boys' literate identities
> - Describe successful and promising programs and practices

In the first two chapters, I laid out important foundational ideas about, and factors related to, boys' literacy growth. Germaine to this chapter are those issues I raised before that concern boys' perceptions of masculinity and identity and how these link to their engagement and achievement as readers. In this chapter, I provide additional ideas and information to further explain the linkages between boys' masculinities and identities and their literacy achievement. What receives emphasis, however, are practical envisionments of approaches and programs that promote a positive sense of male identity through reading and writing.

A Closer Look at Masculinities, Identities, and Boys' Literacy Achievement

In the first chapter, I also acknowledged the risks any of us confront when advocating for literacy curriculum and approaches that are based on gender. Among these is the proclivity to essentialize boys or reinforce binaries in regards boys' preferences and choices (Kehler & Martino, 2007). In response to these risks, I have urged a more nuanced perspective on the so-called "boy crisis" in literacy by stressing the need to first, gain an appreciation for each boy as an individual, and second, pay particular attention to boys who may exhibit challenges with reading, writing, and learning. Above all, I endorse the perspective that all boys benefit from responsive literacy instruction and programs designed to elevate their levels of engagement and expand their reading and writing abilities.

Where do masculine and literate identities come from? Researchers exploring this question have identified many interesting vehicles for identity formation for boys. For example, Rouland, Rowley, and Kurtz-Costes (2013), exploring how African American youth view themselves as readers and learners, discovered parents play a salient role. The stereotypes parents held for their seventh and eighth grade children contributed significantly to their domain-specific ability attributions and overall self-concepts. Thus, boys in their study who struggled with reading developed negative identities of themselves as readers that were reinforced by their parents, who generally held that girls were high achievers in reading. Digesting findings such as these remind us that, although our hands may be tied with respect to changing parent-student relationships and the unwanted messages parents could be sending their sons, there is much we can do to support positive literacy attitudes and genuine reading achievement while male youth are in school or under our supervision.

Even so, building engaged reading into the gendered identities of boys, especially those who routinely find themselves struggling with text, is no mean feat. This is because school-based literacy work does not occur within a vacuum. Boys interact with texts, teachers, and other students based on ever-evolving gendered identities that are interlaced with how they position themselves racially, culturally, and socioeconomically (Godley, 2003). The kinds of outside-of-school images boys hold for themselves – such as rapper, footballer, skateboarder, joker, stoic – constrain the textual practices they engage in within the classroom and the extent to which they benefit from such practices. Godley's work leads her to recommend that, when it comes to urban male youth, "educators must recognize that literacy learning, as a form of interpersonal communication, is not only an academic endeavor but also a negotiation of social identities and thus a social practice that can delimit or offer new possibilities for students' self images and life choices" (p. 273).

Working against or through stereotypic masculinity is certainly one of the significant goals I have for this book, because I know how resistant to change these rigid conceptions of gender identity are and how widespread they remain, even today, among certain groups of boys. Finnish researchers

Manninen, Huuki, and Sunnari (2011) learned this firsthand in their longitudinal study of how school boys use violence, physicality, materiality, and performances to achieve respect and establish power relationships. Their research was ultimately designed to foster a revised self-image among the male participants that excludes venerating stereotypic masculinity and instead values the exercise of power in fair and responsible ways.

It is reassuring to learn that in some school settings, boys' identities are evolving away from those characteristically associated with hegemonic masculinity. Exploring boys' perceptions of masculinity at a diverse "standard" secondary school in the United Kingdom, McCormack (2011) learned that homophobic, misogynistic, and aggressive attitudes were not as potent in regulating masculine behaviors or even achieving dominance. Instead, a range of masculine behaviors were associated with status. For instance, a couple of McCormack's interviewees, Sam and Jack, asserted that fighting, which once established one's position in the hierarchy, was no longer a defining characteristic of manhood. "Guys are now more laid back – they depend on their wit, rather than strength" (p. 91), claims Jack. McCormack identified charisma and authenticity as two prominent attributes of status among the boys in his study, though these were not exclusive of more traditional archetypes of maleness, such as sportiness and sexual freedom. In the end, results of this kind bolster our contention that teachers and other interested adults should gain an appreciation of each boy individually, which can lead to a widening of the possibilities for texts and textual practices made available to them.

What is apparent is that identity formation always occurs relationally (Chu, 2008). Adolescents' individual and cultural identities are formed within their social world (Jensen, 2008) and shape their sense of being literate (Akey, 2008). Akey witnessed this process with a group of secondary school students transitioning from a compensatory reading class to a mainstream English class. The study participants, particularly the boys, felt their sense of being literate was reshaped as a result of relationships with teachers and their more competent classmates, who helped them meet the more rigorous demands of the mainstream English class. These supportive interactions, cultivated as much by the boys as by their teacher and peers, helped them improve their reading and writing and gain acceptance as members of the classroom community. Through these relationships, their self-efficacy was enhanced and their literate identities improved. These results point to the salience of relationship building around texts and textual practices, both with teachers and classmates, in enhancing literate identities for boys.

Building relationships with boys to promote positive literate identities and expand consciousness about themselves as gendered beings is just part of the challenge for teachers. Another is ensuring textual work is engaging to listless male readers and those who already hold to rigid conceptions of masculinity. A tale from the field is instructive in this regard.

Some years ago, I was conducting an evaluation of a secondary reading program in a moderately affluent suburban school district near a large city in the southwestern region of the United States. As part of the evaluation process I spent many hours in reading teachers' classrooms documenting such things as the overall literate environment, the instructional strategies and materials, and the level of student engagement. Of particular concern to me was the gender ratio in these classes because students were placed in them based on low scores on the state-mandated reading achievement test. I was struck first, though not surprised, by the fact that every reading teacher in all five junior highs and the two high schools was female. Yet, the ratio of boys to girls in every classroom was approximately two to one, that is, twice as many boys as girls. Indeed, one class had 14 boys and only 1 girl!

Not only were males overrepresented as students in the reading classes, but so, too, were males of color. The district's demographics were rapidly shifting with a growing student population of ethnic minorities, predominantly African American, Hispanic American, and Asian-Indian American.

One lesson I witnessed during a week's worth of observations conducted in Ms. Willis's junior high reading classroom was revelatory. Ms. Willis was an experienced English teacher of 12 years, in her third year as a seventh- and eighth-grade reading teacher. Her classroom was adorned with popular posters of famous entertainment figures urging students to "read"; there were bookshelves and magazine racks; and the room was also decorated with a variety of colorful posters with information about class rules, grammar, and homework.

The lesson for the week involved reading a newspaper article orally, answering the teacher's whole-class questions, and then taking a quiz about the material. The article was a lengthy feature piece from the local newspaper about a woman who had been abused herself and who had set up a shelter for other abused women. This is important stuff. Students should be aware of social issues such as domestic violence. Boys, particularly, need to become sensitized to their own sexist attitudes and behaviors and how these might, if they go unchecked, place them at risk of becoming perpetrators of domestic violence.

But soon into the very first lesson on the material, it became clear to her that the 16 boys in the class of 22 students were just not engaged by this text or the topic. With a history of low performance in, and disaffection toward, reading, most of these adolescent males were barely able to muster even a modest level of classroom decorum during the reading of this newspaper article. Boys were repeatedly wandering off task, squirming, tapping their pencils, talking, yelling across the room, laughing, and generally finding every way possible to avoid the text. Ms. Willis's comments to the boys throughout the lessons were disciplinary in nature. When she asked a whole-group question, no one volunteered a response, not even the six girls in class, though when pressed, they were the ones likely to give an answer.

I read the article Ms. Willis had asked her class to read and found it very moving and powerful. I wanted Ms. Willis's students to read it and find it powerful as well. I am certain that as Ms. Willis was cutting the piece out of the paper and preparing it to be copied for her students that she desperately wanted them to connect with its message and have it serve as a catalyst for meaningful and critical dialogue. But that did not happen for the boys in her class; she was plainly unsuccessful in gaining their interest and consequently involving them in meaningful learning.

It's possible to envision greater student involvement had Ms. Willis employed more interesting teaching and learning strategies. But how can we ever hope to bring students to a level of critical awareness about an issue such as domestic abuse if we cannot get them to read and engage with a text on the topic in the first place? More pointedly, how can we expect boys who are struggling readers and are generally turned off to reading to become engaged in text that does not interest them – in spite of the fact that we know it should interest them? Simon (1987) warns us: "We cannot simply wish our stories prevail" (p. 374), adding further: "Our authoritative voice is not oppressive by the weight of our own experience and knowledge but if it unwittingly subjugates other voices" (p. 374).

To try to understand these other voices in Ms. Willis's reading class, I interviewed several of her students individually. Sitting in the hall, I heard comments like, "We never read anything interesting in here." "She never lets us read what we like." "The stories in our book are boring." One guy looked at me and with cold contempt said, "I hate this class."

"What would you prefer to read?" I asked. Responses in order of popularity were: sports, funny things, stories with lots of action, and scary stuff.

I am convinced that if we fail to listen to boys like those in Ms. Willis's class and provide them texts and experiences that they enjoy and that capture their imaginations, we may lose them for good. And, as we have already seen, boys of color, immigrant boys, and boys from poverty are far more likely to drop out of school than their more privileged peers. Boys such as these who check out mentally or even literally may find themselves seduced by a street narrative and popular media messages that perversely celebrate hyper-masculinity, misogyny, and violence (Common Sense Media, 2017; Hällgren, Dunkels, & Frånberg, 2015; Jolliffe, 2011; Miller, 2011).

As disappointing as the experience was in Ms. Willis's classroom, I have also been fortunate to witness the kind of responsiveness I am advocating for boys; an approach that meets them where they are, in terms of interest and skill, and then supports their literate journey to higher levels of ability and broader consciousness.

In a tenth-grade reading skills class taught by Hector, I got to know one of the students named Antonio, who could not spend enough time talking about bodybuilding during the first half of the new school year. Hector learned of Antonio's obsession with weight lifting after reviewing the interest inventory he completed early in September. So when Hector gave a book talk on Chris Crutcher's (1995) *Ironman*, you would have had to nail Antonio's feet to the floor to keep him from racing up to select that book for independent reading. By January, though, bodybuilding had been supplanted by wrestling as Antonio's new obsession. He had had such an enjoyable experience reading *Ironman* that he begged Hector to give him a good novel about wrestling. Hector was eager to oblige and plucked three books from his shelf for Antonio. One, Mark Kreidler's (2007) *Four Days to Glory: Wrestling with the Soul of the American Heartland*, is a story about the biggest high school wrestling tournament in the United States. Another book, Brian Shields and Kevin Sullivan's (2009) *WWE Encyclopedia*, showcases the pantheon of popular television wrestlers (with whom Antonio was familiar) with colorful photos and short biographies.

Hector's selection of narratives about wrestling, because they would seem to celebrate traditional or even stereotypical masculine behavior, may leave some people uncomfortable. Simon (1987) reminds us, however, that we should respect boys' reading preferences or "discourses of desire" to avoid demeaning their lives; furthermore, when helping boys find entry points into literacy, we should always bear in mind that we had modest beginnings on our own literacy paths. For example, some of the most renowned figures in the United States, from novelists to Supreme Court justices, found entry points into literacy with such "artless" texts as those from The Bobbsey Twins and Nancy Drew series (Cooper-Mullin & Coye, 1998). The point is this: Only after years of traditional print explorations do we come to pride ourselves on our sophisticated and flexible reading abilities. Teachers should, therefore, resist the tendency to withhold what young men desire to read, because boys already filled with disaffection toward books cannot bypass the journey that we have taken to arrive at a point of active literacy and expanded consciousness (Young & Brozo, 2001). Ultimately, no one knows where a young man's first exciting print experiences will lead him.

The other book that Hector gave Antonio was John Irving's (1997) *The Imaginary Girlfriend: A Memoir*. This book tells Irving's own story of college wrestling. Devoid of the smoke and mirrors, loud threats, and bizarre outfits and makeup seen in televised wrestling, Irving recounts his wrestling experiences in pure and vivid images. He captures the atmosphere of the wrestling room and reveals through anecdotes that he and his buddies were not a bunch of "dumb jocks"; intercollegiate wrestlers expend a great deal of physical and emotional energy to be successful. Irving shows the reader how common sports themes such as fair play, graciousness in victory, and cooperation really do apply to life. This is a splendid book for adolescent athletes to enjoy and appreciate for its portrayal of honorable masculinity.

Hector allowed Antonio to do his six-week project on the similarities and differences between professional and amateur wrestling. On a large poster board, Antonio created two columns. Each column listed information about the two forms of wrestling in parallel fashion. For example, a statement under the Professional Wrestling column read, "Every wrestler can fight any other wrestler." Directly across from this statement, in the Amateur-College Wrestling column, Antonio wrote, "Wrestlers are in weight classes and only wrestle guys in the same class."

Antonio's major breakthrough, however, was his acknowledgment of the disingenuous nature of professional wrestling. One of his entries read, "Pro wrestlers never act afraid and only talk about beating the other guy," whereas the other column read, "College wrestlers never brag in public and often get really nervous and sometimes even sick in the locker room before a match." On another line Antonio included the following statements for each column: "Pro wrestlers know how each match is going to go and who will win." "College wrestlers have to be ready for any move from the other guy, and nobody knows who's going to win the match."

How many teen and preteen boys are passing through life without knowing that outstanding fiction and nonfiction books that speak to their interests are readily available? Antonio is one of the lucky ones. Hector made it possible for at least one male teen to be introduced to exciting books directly related to his interests. As a result, Antonio read four books, which is more than what he might otherwise have done. The benefit of reading is well documented in the professional literature; however, the boost to his self-esteem and reaffirmation of a positive male identity that Antonio gained from reading is of incalculable value. The lesson here is that it is essential for teachers to discover male adolescents' interests and involve themselves in an ongoing search for quality texts that will capture boys' interests.

In the next section, I feature additional experiences I have had working with boys to elevate reading skill and nurture their positive self-images as readers as well as their masculine identities through a unit called "Real Men." The entire unit is described so readers can appreciate fully the challenges and successes as well as the specific strategies and practices employed throughout the eight weeks of this focused instructional activity.

Boys in the Real World

"Caleb"

Caleb is an African American senior at an inner-city high school where, like a majority of the students who attend his school, he qualifies for free and reduced lunch. The kinds of things Caleb does outside of school revolve around fitness, like running and working out with weights. He also tries to help his mother by doing chores around the house. And like most teens he enjoys "hanging out" with friends.

"Other than what teachers make me read, I don't do any extra reading," Caleb reports. Accordingly, he has little interest in traditional print reading and does not read books, magazines, or other similar texts recreationally. Even though Caleb is often texting and interacting on social media, he does not consider these activities "actual" reading or writing, because he is not "learning something."

Despite his disaffection with reading, Caleb sees himself as a "good" reader. His reading test scores as well as reports from his teachers indicate that Caleb is likely not achieving to his potential in reading and writing. He is able to express why reading is important, saying "you gotta know how to read to be able to do stuff in life," but feels it is not important to him now as a teenager nor relevant to his desired career as an actor. He has not read nor does he own any plays, scripts, or books about acting.

As with his attitudes toward reading, Caleb sees himself as a "good" writer, yet other than the essays and other compositions required in school he does not engage in traditional forms of writing at home or on his own. Texting and posting and exchanging messages on social media are not regarded as "real" writing by Caleb.

Discussion and Activities

- What recommendations can you offer to teachers working with Caleb to ensure his reading and writing interests are nurtured?
- How can Caleb's interests be exploited for further literacy skill and language development?
- Conduct an Internet search of apps for teens that support their playwriting and acting. Consider ways these apps could be used with and by boys to nurture their interest in drama and to expand their abilities as creative writers and readers.

Promising Programs and Practices

The Real Men Unit

Jamal's classmate Dwayne, who is taller and stronger, has been goading Jamal to fight him. Jamal knows the odds of getting beaten up are high unless he uses his newfound source of confidence – the handgun. I read just to the point before Jamal makes his decision, and then I abruptly closed the book. The students were disappointed; they asked me to read on, but I refused. The teachers, Patty and Teri, reminded their combined seventh grade classes that this was the kind of excitement they would experience over the next several weeks as we read *Scorpions* together.

The three of us were introducing a new unit that became affectionately known as "Real Men." I had just finished a brainstorming activity with the students, resulting in a web of popular images and stereotypes of men, which I had written on the board. We followed that activity with a book talk on *Scorpions*, Walter Dean Myers's gripping, pathos-filled tale of young boys and gangs in New York City. It was the beginning to an exciting critical study of men and boys in today's society.

The unit developed and taught by Patty, Teri, and me was built around the book's events and characters and was intended to help students reflect on their everyday experiences with other boys and men who accept violence and selfishness as inherent features of masculinity. We ultimately hoped that the students would become engaged readers and be more critical of their own attitudes about stereotypical masculinity. We discovered that careful instruction and interaction with an exciting young adult novel that speaks to traditional male interests helped the boys, as well as the two girls in the class, to become more engaged readers and learners (Brozo, 2010; Johnson & Gooliaff, 2013; Patterson, 2012).

The four students I highlight in my discussion of the Real Men unit are Ricardo, DeWayne, James, and Shantala. I included a female in this profile to make sure that teachers recognize the value of this unit (and others similar to it) for helping to clarify and transform girls' attitudes toward boys and men. Girls, especially those whose lives are filled with images of stereotypical masculinity, are also in desperate need of positive male images. The unit took place in a middle school in the barrio of a south Texas, USA, city. The following students who participated in the unit exemplify the worthwhile nature of our work.

Ricardo is a small-framed Hispanic-American boy who was living with his mother, grandmother, and two younger sisters. His father moved back to Matamoros, Mexico, and rarely visited the family. Ricardo and his family lived in a cramped two-bedroom apartment in federally subsidized housing. The apartment complex is notorious for high rates of teenage pregnancy, delinquency, and gang-related crime. Despite this atmosphere, Ricardo had managed to keep himself out of serious trouble, although other boys had begun pressuring him to join their gang. He had a desire to take on the roles of protector and supporter for the females in his life but was still too young and without the resources to really make this kind of contribution. In response to Jamal's dream of a better life, Ricardo wrote in his journal:

> For my future I want to live in a reg. hous [sic] and I don't know where I want to work. And my dream is to travel around the world.

DeWayne was a tall, lanky African American boy with alert eyes and a wide smile. DeWayne told us at the beginning of the unit that he lived with his mother, father, brothers and sisters. Within a few weeks, however, we discovered that DeWayne had actually been living for some time with a grandfather who was trying to care for all the kids. The grandfather characterized DeWayne's father as a "crack head," although he was eager to figure out a way to move DeWayne and his siblings out of his household. DeWayne's journal response reflected his desire for a carefree lifestyle with no restrictions:

> I want to have a nice car. I would put the top back and wear my shades and cruise for miles and miles. Maybe even right out of Texas.

James was a handsome, streetwise African American. He was the only student in the class whose father, although not his mother, lived with him; however, James's father, a hairdresser, wasn't often around during critical after-school and early evening hours to supervise his son. James told us about coming home from school one afternoon and mindlessly punching the power button on the television's remote control only to discover that the television, the stereo, and other household appliances had been stolen by his drug-addicted aunt, who had broken in through a window earlier that day. James's journal entry concerning his future reflected his dreams to become a high roller, surrounded by wealth and glitter:

> My dream is to become a business owner and have lots of money and a lot of sports cars. I would like to live in a manshion [sic] in Las Vegas. The kind of job I would want will be a casino owner.

Shantala was a tall, athletic African American girl. She was 13 years old at the time of our unit activities. Her mother lived in Houston, Texas. As a little girl, Shantala was given to a woman who was not a family member. There was no father in the home, and Shantala told us she does not know her real dad. She wrote the following about her dreams in her journal:

> What kind of future do I want? To be in the WNBA. In a big house. A good job, a job that pays a lot of money.

These four adolescents well represent the attitudes, desires, and lifeworlds of the seventh-grade classes. They were not unique in the sense that their home lives were not any better or worse than their 12 other classmates. Virtually all experienced the daily challenges that come with inadequate housing, not having two parents in the home, and limited financial resources. These factors, as we have advanced in the two previous chapters, clearly placed Ricardo, DeWayne, James, and Shantala at risk of failing to live out their dreams. We found, however, that by introducing them to activities and experiences designed to question masculine stereotypes spread by popular media, these students showed remarkable depth of sensitivity and understanding. They also demonstrated a heightened degree of enthusiasm for reading about issues of masculinity as well as crafting written and oral responses to what they were learning.

The Genesis of the Unit

My relationship with Patty dates back to graduate reading classes she had taken with me several years ago. We discovered a mutual interest in creating learning environments for secondary students that broke the mold. Patty's keen and critical mind, her sensitivity to adolescents' desires and needs, and her vast reserve of active language strategies (rooted in her background in theater) made her an ideal collaborator. Her school had coincidentally been the site of other research I had recently conducted. Teri had been an undergraduate student of mine, and I had not seen her for a few years until she was reintroduced to me during a teacher inservice workshop I had given at the same school. She had recently become a member of Patty's seventh-grade language arts team. When she showed up in one of my required reading classes for master's students, I immediately recognized in Teri another kindred spirit whose goals were to make learning for adolescents critical, stimulating, and personally meaningful.

By November of that school year, Patty, Teri, and I had agreed to teach a language unit for their seventh graders. Both Patty and Teri were well acquainted with my keen interest in boys' literacy development. They thought this should be the unit's focus because we shared concerns about their students' perceptions and misconceptions of masculinity as well as their challenges with reading. By a twist of good fortune, they were teaching the same reading course in adjacent classrooms during fifth period. The class was for seventh graders who had difficulty reading, and not surprising, boys far outnumbered girls in these classes. By combining the sections, we were able to expose a larger group of males to our readings and activities while coordinating instruction as a team.

Planning the Unit

We focused on the goals of the project at our initial meetings. After considerable discussion, we derived the following main thrusts for the Real Men unit:

- Use literature as a catalyst for critical explorations of masculinity
- Critically explore images of stereotypical masculinity in popular culture and media
- Foster engaged reading and learning

With these guidelines, we got down to the business of fleshing out a curriculum. We decided to devote the last eight weeks of the school year, two days per week, to the Real Men unit, and that it would be taught by the three of us. We also agreed that, in addition to the use of magazine articles, essays, and stories dealing with masculinity, a young adult novel would be used as the students' core literature source.

Finding an adolescent novel that would be just right for these unique seventh graders would take some time. We wanted to be certain whatever we used as the primary reading source would engage the students' imaginations throughout the eight weeks. We were fortunate to be living in a city with a wonderful bookstore specializing exclusively in children's and young adult books. The bookseller, a former elementary school teacher, had been a good friend and invaluable resource to me and many teachers in the area. With her help, we selected Walter Dean Myers's *Scorpions* to anchor the unit. This book was chosen primarily because, similar to our students, the two main characters in the story are in seventh grade, and as one is African American and the other Hispanic American, they were also ethnic matches with our guys; furthermore, the events in the story take place in a Harlem neighborhood, where events are similar to the daily events that take place on the streets and alleys of their barrio. We recognized the book's potential for providing our students with an excellent focus for critical exploration of masculinity, as it is perceived by adolescents of color living in poverty and without fathers or other positive male role models. Here was a book that could engage our youth, while offering countless opportunities to deconstruct the negative images of masculinity within its narrative through other readings and activities.

Using a small research grant, I was able to purchase a copy of *Scorpions* for each student participating in the Real Men unit. Gradually, Patty, Teri, and I began detailing the strategies we would use in the unit. We built our activities around events and characters from different chapters, striving to reveal how mass media, commercialism, and everyday experiences with other boys and men who were poor role models can distort perceptions of masculinity.

The next phase of planning involved making decisions about, and developing documentation methods to assess, the degree to which we achieved our goals for the unit. We agreed to gather data from several sources so we could determine the effectiveness of our project. These data sources are detailed in the following sections.

Responses to the "To Be a Man" Survey

We created the "To Be a Man" survey to have students reflect on statements based on issues and events from *Scorpions*. The students had to respond either yes, no, or unsure to the assertions about masculinity, particularly violent masculinity, inherent in each statement, then supply a reason for their choice. The survey, given to students before the readings began, served as a baseline for their attitudes on stereotypical masculinity and violence, which echo themes in *Scorpions*. The results of Ricardo's, DeWayne's, James's, and Shantala's pre-unit surveys are highlighted in Figure 3.1.

Teacher Anecdotal Logs

I have been involved in classroom-based research for many years, so I know that it is important for teachers to keep their own record of observations and perceptions of their work. This documentation serves as a reflection on teaching, offering crucial feedback on teacher instruction and student learning. Throughout the unit, Patty, Teri, and I used our own written records of classroom events and our responses to them as a focus for weekly discussions. The process of testing our perceptions against the students' perceptions ultimately led to a deeper understanding of individual student behavior, as well as greater sensitivity to classroom dynamics as a whole.

Student Work and Unit Projects

Student projects revealed a great deal about their level of involvement in the strategies and activities that prompted these projects, as well as their evolving sense of masculine identity. Some examples of unit projects included movie posters, scene reenactments, clay figurines with descriptions, life-size posters of characters with descriptions, and a three-dimensional model of a setting in the story.

Compare–Contrast Essay

Students wrote a compare–contrast essay when they finished reading *Scorpions*. It was intended to elicit their ideas about how Jamal is similar to and different from a "real man." As an end-of-unit activity, we wanted to discover whether students could analyze the behavior of a boy who chooses a form of destructive masculinity by comparing it to the expected behavior of a male who expresses his masculinity in honorable ways.

Week One: Introductions and Predictions

Patty, Teri, and I concluded our book talk on *Scorpions* and handed out copies of the book while telling the class that the tragedy of handgun violence is only one aspect they could expect to read about in this novel. After the students had received their copies, they began thumbing through the pages to locate the scene we had just simulated in our book talk, as well as to gain

1. When a man is being hassled by another man, he needs to fight to get the man to back off.
   Ricardo's response – "Yes."
   Ricardo's reason – "Because the guy will keep messing with him."
2. Men who walk away from fights are sissies.
   DeWayne's response – "Yes."
   DeWayne's reason – "When you got to fight, you got to fight."
3. Men need weapons like knives and guns to show how strong they are.
   James's response – "Unsure."
   James's reason – "Men should be able to have guns and knives."
4. You can't really be a man unless you are in a gang.
   Shantala's response – "Unsure."
   Shantala's reason – "You got to be really tough to be in a gang."
5. Men like to fight because that's just who they are.
   Ricardo's response – "Yes."
   Ricardo's reason – "We're stronger than girls, so we have to do the fighting."
6. Men who go to prison are real men.
   DeWayne's response – "Yes."
   DeWayne's reason – "My uncle knows this guy who was in prison because he killed someone, and he thinks he's cool."
7. If a man killed someone, other men would think he was really cool.
   James's response – "Yes."
   James's reason – "Where I live, you got to fight because people always messing with you."
8. Real men protect their families by fighting.
   Shantala's response – "Unsure."
   Shantala's reason – "If you don't want to get killed there, you better be a man."
9. As soon as a boy turns 13, he needs a gun.
   Ricardo's response – "Yes."
   Ricardo's reason – "People know you're serious with a gun."
10. Sometimes being violent is the only way for a man to make others understand he means business.
    DeWayne's response – "Yes."
    DeWayne's reason – "I've seen it."

Figure 3.1 Sample Pre-Unit Responses from "To Be a Man" Survey

a sense of the book's length. Prior to our book talk, we had administered the "To Be a Man" survey, asking both male and female students to complete it and to be completely honest in their responses. I present examples of post-unit survey responses later in this section of the chapter.

Following the book talk, the three of us explained the goals of the unit. I said we would be exploring the consequences of good and bad decisions through the novel, listening and conversing with guest speakers, writing, sharing, and reflecting. The ultimate intent of the unit, we stressed, was to help the class better understand and appreciate positive aspects of masculinity, so as to guide them in their own decision-making about who they wanted to be and with whom they wanted to associate. I told the class when the unit was completed I wanted them to be able to recognize what a "real man" was. To this statement, James replied, just loud enough for me to hear, "I am a real man." The boys around him chuckled. I smiled and did not challenge him.

I led the students in a group brainstorm to discuss their attitudes, perceptions, and experiences related to masculinity. I used the "Television Man" and "Real Man" as the central images for two large webs, which I displayed on poster board. By using television's portrayals of men, I knew it would be easier to draw out the numerous stereotypes of masculine behavior from these media-saturated youth. First, I asked students to turn to their neighbor, discuss what men on television are usually like, and jot down brief notes on these conversations. The class quickly fell into animated chatter about television personalities from sitcoms, commercials, sports teams, and music videos. When I opened the discussion to the entire class, nearly everyone was eager to provide input. Figure 3.2 illustrates the web brainstorm of some characteristics and images of the television man. James was quick to point out that they "have a lot of money ... they gotta be rich." Elton said a television man "always has a good car and a good job." "They're good looking and dress in suits," intoned Maria (to the hissing of several boys). James, in his supercilious and blasé manner, offered, "TV guys are tough; they use weapons like guns and do expensive drugs." Lalo, who often spoke with a sense of higher moral conscience, said flatly, "TV men are disrespectful of women and the law." Shantala's characterization of a television man was, "They immature, they always fighting and drinking, and they players, you know, they mess around on they women." Her last statement brought a great burst of laughter from the guys, although they did not deny that Shantala's perceptions were accurate.

Overall, I was impressed with the class's ability to think critically about stereotypical portrayals of males on television. To contrast these negative images, I asked the class to help me create another brainstormed web (see Figure 3.3) based on real men. Students were once again asked to talk it over first with a partner before they shared their ideas with the class.

Ricardo began with, "A real man is loyal and honest ... someone you can count on, you know, you can trust." These words have special importance because Ricardo's father had broken his promise to buy Ricardo a hunting rifle after Ricardo raised his grades. Ricardo's father did not live in the same household with his son and has never been the kind of adult male Ricardo could ever "count on." John, a strapping, brooding 13-year-old who also lives

Television Man — Web of Class Brainstorm

- Disrespects women
- Is a pimp/player
- Is a tough guy
- Has lots of money
- Disrespects the law
- Drinks beer and other alcohol
- Has a gun; uses weapons
- Is violent
- Does drugs
- Is immature
- Has a good car

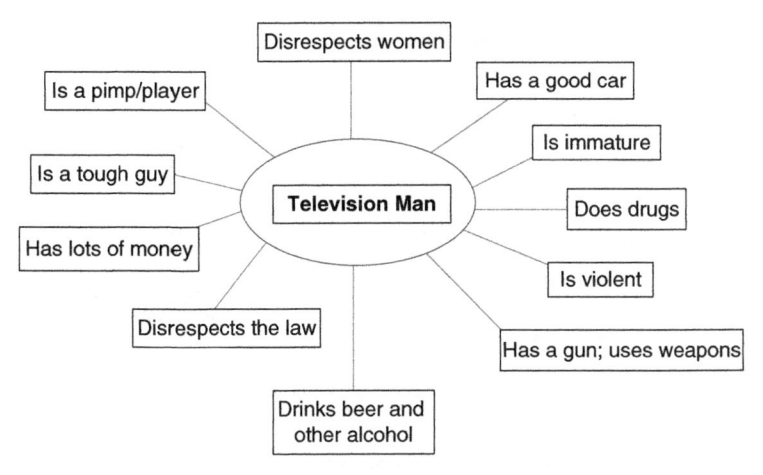

Figure 3.2 Web of Class Brainstorm of a Television Man

without a father, added, "He's gotta keep his word." Willis and DeWayne agreed that a good man should "have an education." Shantala rejoined, "A good man dresses nice and is polite. He opens a door for a woman, you know, shows respect." "He needs to have a steady relationship," stated James, whose father's womanizing had been a regular source of annoyance for the cool seventh grader. He recounted on several occasions how for each new "squeeze" his dad would bring home.

James was expected to act as though she might become his next "mom." Adding a last characteristic of a good man to our web, Tony suggested, "He should be able to find a pretty good job and keep it, so he can take care of his family and have a car." Tony's absent father had crashed and rendered inoperable his mother's car, which she depended on to go to the store, doctor's office, and the social service office. His father had neither insurance nor resources for acquiring another vehicle.

It became clear to Patty, Teri, and me that the seventh graders' perceptions of the qualities of real men reflected their own negative experiences with estranged fathers and other adult males. Fathers, and even mothers, behaving poorly were all too common in the students' daily lives.

Following the brainstorming activities, I shared a My Bag to give the students a fuller personal introduction. I have been using the My Bag strategy for many years as a way of getting to know students and for them to get to know me. The strategy involves placing items that symbolize strengths, loves, hobbies, experiences, and dreams in a bag or some other

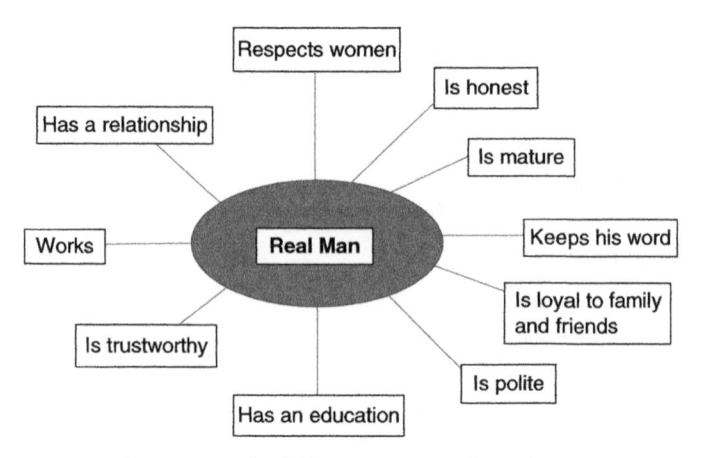

```
                    Respects women
                              Is honest
    Has a relationship
                              Is mature
    Works         Real Man   Keeps his word
                              Is loyal to family
                              and friends
    Is trustworthy
                              Is polite
                    Has an education
```

Figure 3.3 Web of Class Brainstorm of a Real Man

comparable container, such as a backpack. The decision-making process used to select items for the bag forces students to think critically about themselves. These items are then shared with other students and used to stimulate follow-up questions and conversation.

I included items that reflected my traditional interests and hobbies, as well as my devotion to personal and social literacy and my commitment to my family. Students were very inquisitive about each item; while passing around photographs of my daughter and wife, students wanted to know their names, ages, favorite things to do, schools attended, as well as how long I'd been married, if I had any other children, why we had only one, and so forth. The class showed particular interest in the various books I pulled out of my bag. The greatest response came when I passed around a textbook that I had authored. DeWayne was amazed that I had written "such a thick book!" We told students they would have the opportunity to put together and share their own My Bags over the next couple of class sessions, which clearly pleased most of them.

Before the period ended, we invited questions about the day's activities. Students were eager to know more about the novel, barraging us with questions about the characters and the plot. We did our best to respond with answers that revealed little yet continued to pique their interest in *Scorpions*.

At the beginning of the next session, I was greeted by the students with smiles, nods, fist bumps, and letters of introduction that they had written. That night I lay in bed reading about their lives and felt hollow inside. The comfort of my new four-bedroom suburban home, although a mere five miles from the barrio, must seem as far away and unattainable to them as Park Avenue appears to the characters of Jamal and Tito from their Harlem tenement. The crush of poverty, absent dads, and the dangers and discomforts that come with these conditions emerged from the still-awkward hands of our young students' letters. Although heartrending, their stories reinforced the legitimacy of my work with them. Consider how James described the way things are on the streets where he lives:

> One thing I do not like about my neighborhood is everybody is trying to kill everyone. What I mean by this is you can be walking down the road and a car is coming ... they will get in front of you and they won't move until you get close to them, and then they will move. Or they would carry guns or knifes [sic] around and threaten you, and the only thing you can do is run.

In her letter, Shantala included what had happened the afternoon and night before:

> I came home and my sister went in my room and pulled everything out of my dresser and my closet and messed up my bed, and I told my mom and she said don't worry about it and they will clean it up and they never did so I had to do it. And after I finisted [sic] I went in the kichen [sic] and their [sic] were no food left for me, and my dad made it worstest [sic] because he came over and it never got better.

Among the items in DeWayne's letter was this small but revealing anecdote from the day before:

> I was riding my bike and ran into a car. That was backing up and I hit it and I flew over the back end of the car. I hit the grown [sic] hard. Everybody was laughing at me, and they didn't help me up or nothing ...

Finally, Ricardo's letter made me realize that the fiction we had created in our book talk is perhaps too real for some students. His words made my skin tingle:

> I could relate to this book talk because it happened to my friend. He got shot sitting on the swings in the park. He was sitting on the swing with a gun in his pocket with the clip hanging out, and a gang drove by and saw it ... he got shoot [sic] with a 357 magnam [sic].

The students' letters reminded me that countless boys enter school classrooms each day wearing the psychic and physical scars of their harsh worlds. That is why we allowed the students in this unit the safety and freedom to interrogate their own and others' conceptions of masculinity, look critically at pop culture images of maleness, and consider other possibilities of masculinity characterized by positive male traits, such as caring, commitment, and intellectual prowess.

We spent most of this day getting through the first couple of chapters in *Scorpions*. Instead of round-robin oral reading, we employed a simplified Readers Theater, assigning the roles of narrator and the main characters in the novel – Jamal, Tito, Mama, Sassy, and Mack. We had created simple stage flats (recall Patty's theater background) of a cityscape on large sheets of poster board and attached them to one of the classroom walls. Here students took positions for reading their parts while employing simple gestures. We rotated the male roles, so every boy in class had a chance to participate. Shantala and Maria, our only girls, traded off taking on the persona of either Mama, Jamal's mother, or his sister, Sassy.

I was surprised to find students enthusiastically embracing their roles. I attributed this to the style of teaching the seventh graders had become used to with teachers like Patty and Teri, who exploited the theatricality of different novels and stories by having students participate in reenactments, impromptu dramatic interpretations, and Readers Theater.

At the end of the period, students had to summarize what they had learned and make predictions in their journals about the action in subsequent chapters. Ricardo predicted the following in his journal:

> Tomorrow Jamal will probably join a gang. The gang he will get in is called the Scorpions. After he is in the gang he will sell drugs and use the money to get his brother out of jail.

James speculated in his entry:

> What I think will happen is that Jamal is going to pressure Dwayne to join a gang, and Dwayne will. When he gets in the gang, he will start selling drugs. Dwayne will be making all the money, and he won't give it to Jamal. Jamal will kill him and brag about it.

DeWayne guessed,

> The problem will be about selling drugs. I think that Jamal will have pressure to join a gang. I think Jamal will join the gang and take a gun everywhere he goes. Jamal will probably kill someone and then go bragging to other people. He'll end up in prison like his brother.

The students' predictions reflect an uncomfortable level of familiarity with situations involving drugs, violence, gangs, and the criminal justice system. The students projected scenarios for the characters in *Scorpions* that approximated the lives of people who might live next door, down the street, or around the corner. These personal connections with the book's action and themes were what Patty, Teri, and I had hoped to achieve by using this novel. Another reason we chose the book was to have it serve as a reference for dishonorable forms of masculinity; that is, the central characters, seventh graders themselves, behave in ways we wanted our students to evaluate and ultimately disavow.

Week Two: Story Impression Writing and Skits

A strategy I found that worked extremely well with our seventh graders as a prereading motivator for the next chapter in *Scorpions* was story impression writing. Before students gathered their copies of the book, which were kept in a bookcase in the room, I wrote several words on the board. These words came directly from the pages we were about to read, and I asked students to use them in a short paragraph describing what was about to happen in the book. These story impression words helped the students form an idea about the action in the story, and their writing about that action served as a prediction of what they thought would happen next. As students read, they compared the actual events with their predictions. The aim of this strategy, then, is to hold students' interest for the duration of the reading and encourage careful reading.

The story impression words I gave the class in the order in which they appear in the chapter were *Jamal, bet, running, principal's office, Tito, boat basin,* and *yacht*. Then, I helped students find a partner and directed them to write journal entries using each of these words. Students got to work quickly and fell into animated discussion with their coauthors as they crafted their entries. When they finished, I asked the students to share what they had written with the class. This gives all students a chance to ruminate on plot possibilities before learning what actually happens. Here is Ricardo and John's story impression:

> *Jamal* and another student make a *bet* for money or something. Someone sees it and goes *running* to the *principal's office* to tell. *Tito* and Jamal get kicked out of school and go to the *boat basin*. They sneak onto a *yacht*.

DeWayne and James's story impression was by far the most elaborate and interesting; however, it revealed a knowledge about petty gambling and thievery that made me and the teachers uncomfortable.

> One day while *Jamal* was *running* to school he saw some kids in the back of the school rolling dice. They *bet* Jamal $5 that he couldn't roll a seven. Jamal said yes because he wanted to make some money to help his mama pay for Randy's new trial. As soon as Jamal picked up the

dice, the principal came. All the other kids ran and Jamal was stuck with the dice. The principal told him to come to the office after first period, Jamal said alright. When Jamal went to the *principal's office*, the principal said you should be suspended for betting and bringing dice to school. Jamal denied it and said the dice weren't his. The principal didn't know Jamal was telling the truth so he suspended him and made him leave. Jamal met up with *Tito* after school and walked down to the *boat basin*. Jamal asked Tito to look out while he snuck into a *yacht* to try to find something to hock so they could get some money for Randy's new trial.

My goal with this strategy was to create a heightened sense of eagerness in the students to read the chapter. As we progressed through it, I asked students to indicate whether they found corroboration for their story impressions.

When we finished reading, I directed the class's attention to one of Jamal's statements from the chapter. In this chapter, the reader learns something important about Jamal that Patty, Teri, and I decided would serve as a critical source of reflection on how males should behave in the face of taunting. In the story, Dwayne, a tall seventh grader, is egging Jamal on and seems to have it in for him. About Dwayne's persistent harassment, Jamal thinks, "The only way to deal with somebody stupid like Dwayne... was to punch him out" (Myers, 1990, p. 60). We formed groups of three students, presented the students with this quote, and directed them to create short skits showing how interpersonal conflict can be resolved without fighting. Felipé, James, and Maria's skit was typical of the performances by the class. Felipé introduced the scene as follows:

FELIPÉ: I'm asking a girl [Maria smiles coyly] to go to the movies with me, and this guy [James nods his head] says I'm messin' around with his girlfriend. So . . . .
FELIPÉ: Hey, Maria, you want to go to the movies with me?
MARIA: What's playin'?
FELIPÉ: It's a cool new Disney movie.
MARIA: OK. [James walks up, pulls Maria to the side, and confronts Felipé.]
JAMES: [with hostility] You messin' with my girl?
FELIPÉ: I wasn't tryin' to . . .
JAMES: Where you two goin'?
FELIPÉ AND MARIA: We're goin' to the movies. You wanna come?
JAMES: OK.

When the skit concluded, the class discussed how the three students were able to diffuse a potentially volatile situation by simply including James in their plans. James was angry and suspicious at first but was immediately calmed by Felipé and Maria's invitation to join them. In this way, James could see that Felipé and Maria were not attempting to conceal anything from him.

Another skit, however, was difficult for the class to accept as "something they would do." In the scene, John and Noe meet up after a football game; John challenges Noe to a fight. Noe walks away. John goads him by calling him a "sissy" and threatens to tell everyone that he "chickened out." In spite of these taunts, Noe keeps walking away until John eventually gives up. The male students could not believe the honorable way was to let John get away with his name-calling and threats. Noe best summed up this sentiment when he said, "He don't bother me in here, but if we were on the street, I'd jump him." With that, the two boys engaged in a mock fistfight.

Week Three: Anticipation Guide and Compare–Contrast Activity

I began the third week by taking the class through an anticipation guide for the chapter we were about to read. This strategy involves presenting students with statements related to the text they will read that day and asking them to guess whether the statements are true or false. This strategy increases students' interest and their desire to read the text closely to find support for pre-reading guesswork. Usually, as students read the text, they refer to their anticipation guide statements for possible connections. This time, however, students could amend their initial hunches if they found that they were incorrect, although they had to be prepared to defend their pre- and post-reading indications. Figure 3.4 shows the anticipation guide I presented the seventh graders. By taking a position on each of these statements about possible plot twists, the students were much more focused as we read the new chapter and eagerly checked their anticipation guides for accuracy or revision.

After rechecking students' anticipation guide responses in a class discussion, I pulled another line from the chapter to use in a compare–contrast activity of males who make good decisions and males who do not. In the book, Jamal, reflecting on his situation, reveals his sense of despair over the inevitability of a future marked by crime. He thinks, "If you were part of the life they were living, then after a while you did something and the police came and got you" (Myers, 1990, p. 117).

I asked students first to discuss these lines with their neighbors and think about whether people have control over their behavior and whether people (male and female, young and old) have the choice to make good decisions

Pre-reading			Post-reading	
T	F	1. Jamal and Tito throw the gun into the river.	T	F
T	F	2. Tito shoots the gun in the park.	T	F
T	F	3. Jamal lies to Mama about getting in a fight.	T	F
T	F	4. Dwayne tells the principal about the gun.	T	F
T	F	5. The police arrest Jamal at his apartment.	T	F
T	F	6. Dwayne fights Jamal again.	T	F

Figure 3.4 Anticipation Guide for Chapter 6 of Scorpions

or bad decisions. After a few minutes, Patty, Teri, and I led the class in a mini-debate. I was stunned to discover how many boys held sentiments similar to Jamal's. For instance, James commented that police stop people in cars just because they are black. Armando recounted a harrowing night when police with guns barged through his apartment's front door, believing the apartment was a crack house. They were all watching television, he said, and he was so scared he could hardly breathe.

We followed up the discussion by asking students to work in pairs to find pictures in magazines of males behaving in both admirable and reprehensible ways. Students made two columns on a piece of poster board and placed their pictures in the appropriate column labeled either "Positive" or "Negative." Not surprisingly, many students included a picture of a man and woman together, happy and in love, as positive. For example, Ricardo and John found a photo of smiling newlyweds and wrote beneath it, "This is a good man because he loves his wife." Lester and DeWayne also placed a picture of a bride and groom in their Positive column with the caption, "Is marrieing [sic] a woman he loves."

Other themes of honorable male behavior that the students chose included scenes of family life where the father is present. The caption of James and Felipé's picture of a father throwing a baseball around with his three sons read, "Good decision because the dad is spending time with his kids." Shantala and Maria also had a picture of a man holding his baby. They wrote beside it, "He is spending time with his child." Lester and DeWayne chose to portray positive male behavior through men who had jobs, particularly those with skilled professions. They attached a photo of a group of astronauts to their poster and wrote simply, "They have a good job." James and Felipé showed a man standing in the foreground with a proprietary look on his face, and a long cotton field and harvester behind him. They wrote underneath the picture, "Has a job and is a farmer."

Negative portrayals of men invariably involved guns and knives. There were several pictures of men and boys buying, holding, and shooting handguns and rifles. One ominous photo on Noe and John's poster was of a big man with his face in shadow; he was holding a pistol and his unbuttoned shirt revealed a long red scar running the length of his torso. They had written beside it, "He been cut so he have a gun." There were also pictures of men in prison garb. Shantala and Maria had a series of faces of infamous men, such as a mass murderer ("He killed over 30 boys"), a former athlete and movie star entering prison ("He killed his wife"), and even an American President ("He slept with another woman").

This activity and the mini-debate showed Patty, Teri, and me that the students could distinguish between the media's portrayal of positive and negative male images even though they had been exposed to many negative male role models in their own lives. Like Jamal from the novel, they had definite notions about what constituted positive and negative behavior of boys and men.

Week Four: University Field Trip

This was a special week for all of us. The seventh graders were given a field trip to the university to explore the campus, and most important, to spend time with undergraduates from a content area reading course I was teaching. The hour and a half was chock-full of activities, readings, and strategy demonstrations that kept everyone excited and involved.

Although only half a dozen miles from the junior high, this was the first time any of these adolescents had been on the campus of this or any university. I watched with delight as the seventh graders gazed in awe at the large buildings, the manicured grounds, the stream of students and faculty marching here and there, students singly and in pairs lounging in the shade of a live oak studying, and others throwing frisbees and footballs. This field trip was nothing short of an adventure for kids whose experiences were so circumscribed by their families' limited resources.

First, the students were to be guests in my university class. My undergraduate students had been prepared for their arrival, and as soon as the seventh graders entered the classroom, my university students greeted them, partnered off with them, and found a place to sit and visit. When everyone was settled, I introduced Patty and Teri. Patty reviewed what her students planned to do and gave directions to begin the first activity.

We began the class with companion introductions as a method of getting to know one another. Each junior high–undergraduate student pair first talked about their lives (family members, pets, role models, personal and career goals, proudest accomplishments, what they do for fun, and what they like most about school), and then took turns going to the front of the room to introduce each other. The unique aspect of this process came when personal introductions were made before the entire class. Students introduced their partners by role-playing one another. For example, when it was Ben, one of my undergraduate students, and Dwayne's turn,

Ben sat silently while Dwayne stood behind him and stated,

> Hello, I'm Ben. I'm a junior at this university. I am majoring in history. I was in the army for three years. I was in Kuwait during the Gulf War. I am married. My wife's name is Roseanne. My wife and I would like to have a child soon. I have a dog named Jack. I like football and to fish and hunt. I've been around the world with the Army. The person I admire most is my father. My goal is to be a high school history teacher and football coach. I'm proudest of my military record.

When my partner Noe finished, we changed places, and I introduced him:

> Hi, I'm Noe. I'm 13 years old and in the seventh grade. I have three sisters and one brother. I have a small dog named Pepe. I love basketball and play guard for my junior high. The person I look up to is my favorite basketball player, Carlos Arroyo. My goal is to make the high school basketball team and maybe go to college and play. My proudest accomplishment was scoring 18 points in one game. I like P.E. the best because I can give my brain a rest.

The next strategy began with the seventh graders assembling chairs in the middle of the room, where each took a seat. James suddenly stood up and said, "Jamal gets the job at Mr. Gonzalez's grocery store." Popping up right after him was Maria, who added, "He works after school and on weekends." She was followed by Noe, who contributed, "Jamal got paid after his first week and was real proud." John jumped up next and said, "Then Indian and Angel from the Scorpions came into the store, and Jamal got fired."

The students were demonstrating for my undergraduates a strategy known as popcorn review. Any student can begin the review by "popping" up to state a detail from the story. This detail begins a sequence of events, which entails the next person who pops up to correctly supply the following event and so on. Like popping corn, it is the random order in which students stand up to provide a brief description of the story's next event that gives the strategy its name. My undergraduate students were impressed, and we briefly discussed how they could use this strategy when teaching in science, history, English, and virtually any other subject area. The seventh graders invited the undergraduates to take their places and demonstrate a popcorn review of their new learning. The four students in my university class who were kinesiology majors decided to give it a try and showed the rest of us how they could use the strategy to review bone and muscle connections. For instance, the first student stood up and said "radius," the next student said "ulna," the next "metacarpus," and so on in reference to the complex of bones in the human wrist.

The following activity was the most enjoyable because it combined humor with review. Imagine a group of four students standing in a row in the front of the classroom. Each is wearing a long, white lab coat and a Groucho glasses with the attached fake eyebrows, big nose, and mustache. Here is the set-up for the strategy known as Professor Know-It-All. The sight of these students in their ridiculous costumes was enough to ensure that all of us were paying attention. A seventh grader sitting among us asked the Know-It-Alls, "Where did Jamal hide the gun?" With this, the "professors" huddled in consultation, then turned to the class. They provided an answer in a complete sentence with each student saying one word of the sentence, and the last student saying the appropriate end punctuation. To the preceding question, the student know-it-alls replied,

DEWAYNE: *Jamal*
RICARDO: *hid*
JOHN: *the*
SHANTALA: *gun*
DEWAYNE: *under*
RICARDO: *the*
JOHN: *cushions*
SHANTALA: *in*
DEWAYNE: *the*
RICARDO: *couch*
JOHN: *period.*

The Professor Know-It-Alls fielded several more questions before a new team was asked to take over. This form of review, along with the popcorn strategy, takes a process that is usually predictable and unimaginative and gives it a fresh, humorous twist. By reviewing story content or other subject matter in these ways, students prompt and monitor each other instead of passively waiting for the teacher to ask questions and call on someone for an answer. Giving students the responsibility for review creates conditions in which they can become more invested in the learning process; it also increases their level of engagement with the strategies.

When class concluded, several of my students and I accompanied Patty and Teri's seventh graders to the university student center for drinks and snacks. This extra time gave the adolescents a chance to fraternize with college students and talk about campus life.

Based on residual conversation with the undergraduates and the seventh graders, we all felt the afternoon had been a rousing success. One never knows the full impact of these kinds of encounters on either solidifying in a 21-year-old preservice teacher's mind that he or she chose a well-suited profession or exciting a 13-year-old's imagination to eventually realize a dream of attending college. Comments made to me by my university students, however, suggested a new resolve about teaching. One remarked, "I really enjoyed those kids. I know that's a tough place to teach, but it would be really rewarding to work with students like that." The seventh graders also used words like *cool* and *neat* to characterize their field trip to the university campus. Felipé asked me, "You think I could get a scholarship to go there?" and I overheard James tell Noe, "I could be doin' that in six years."

Week Five: A Tragedy at a Real School with Real Guns Strikes at Our Core

Dear Jamal,

I know your [sic] having some hard times but just solve it not by violence, comprimise [sic]. You don't need a gun to protect yourself; just have God in your heart. So just throw the gun away, okay.

Your friend,
Tito

The preceding letter was actually written by Ricardo after we prompted students with the following question, which we asked them to respond to in their journals: If you were Tito, what would you say in a letter to Jamal about what he should do with the gun? From the time Jamal receives the handgun from Mack, *Scorpions* deals with Jamal's dilemma about whether to use the gun in a way he thinks his older brother Randy would respect or get rid of it. Javier responded,

Dear Jamal,

I'm sorry I'm convicing [sic] you to throw away the gun, but I dont want you to get heart [sic], but now I think you should keep the gun for pretaction [sic].

Tito

With the issue over the handgun coming to a critical point in which Jamal either gives the gun back to Mack and disavows membership in the Scorpions or continues to hold on to it until real tragedy befalls him, we decided the opportunity was ripe for an extensive and critical exploration of gun violence among young people. Just as we were initiating discussion and activities to help the class better understand the seriousness of this topic, Ms. Guerra, the school's principal, announced over the intercom, "Teachers and students, I have terrible news to report to you. In a school not that different from our own, two teenagers have just shot and killed several of their classmates and they have killed themselves. I would like all of you to join me in a moment of silence for the victims. Thank you."

The news stunned all of us. It was one thing to talk about gun violence in our streets, homes, and schools, but it was something entirely different to have that reality thrust upon us in such a horrifying way that day. Patty immediately turned on the television. We spent the rest of the period watching the ongoing news coverage of the chilling events. In the years since that horrific event, numerous school shootings have occurred in the United States, with a limited number of such incidences elsewhere around the world (Younge, 2016). And with very few exceptions, the perpetrators have been males (Time Line of Worldwide School Shootings, 2016, www.infoplease.com/us/crime/timeline-worldwide-school-and-mass-shootings). The glaring and disturbing fact is that gun violence is a scourge of boys and men, who account for 86 percent of gun deaths in the United States (Dastiger, 2017). A recent outstanding novel for young adults on this topic is Marieke Nijkamp's (2016) *This Is Where It Ends*; and already a classic for teens, Todd Strasser's (2002) *Give a Boy a Gun*.

Patty, Teri, and I lingered in a stupor after the bell rang, and the students shuffled out of the room. We could hardly bring ourselves to talk. At that moment, our lessons seemed so trivial beside this palpable tragedy of horrific proportions. For me, it brought on an uncomfortable, almost eerie feeling of déjà vu. Five years earlier, I was in this same school doing a lesson with a group of eighth graders when Ms. Guerra interrupted class activities to announce the shooting death of Selena, who was perhaps the brightest and most promising Tejano music star ever, and whose parents still lived in our students' neighborhood, which made her death especially devastating.

Late on the night of the school shooting, I called Patty to commiserate and seek fortification. I wondered if we should not close down shop, if our efforts were too insignificant to matter, if mere words like the Reagan-era mantra "just say no" to guns and violence could ever be enough. Would this really make a difference in the lives of disturbed youth or youth living in grinding poverty or those with out-of-control adults who fail to provide any moral or behavioral compass for their children? Patty finally brought me out of my despicable state of self-pity by reminding me that our seventh graders were precisely the group in greatest need of our message of honorable masculinity. Incidents of gun violence, although increasing among white suburban youth, occur overwhelmingly in nonwhite, economically depressed communities like those where our students and families reside. She also reminded me that gun violence was hardly foreign to our students. Many of our students, like James who revealed the random shooting death of his best friend at the hands of local gang members, were already well acquainted with gun violence, crack houses, gang wars, and deadbeat dads. This incident of mass murder at a suburban high school would not change that. What might change that, she added, was our work in acquainting boys with positive masculinity to which they might aspire; thus, even if we gird just one young man with the confidence to stay clear of gangs and drugs, we might consider our work to have been a success.

With a new resolve, I began the next class session with a debate activity. The debate forced the students to focus on critical issues related to gun violence. I divided the class into two large groups, giving each instructions to adopt the perspective on their direction sheet and build an argument in defense of that perspective. The different perspectives were as follows:

> **Perspective 1** – You are a group of owners of gun stores. You have always followed the law, making sure the guns you sell go to people with proper identification and permits. A group of citizens wants to close your store because it feels your stores make it easy for criminals to get and use guns in crimes and homicides. Be prepared to defend your right to operate a gun store.
>
> **Perspective 2** – You are a group of citizens who wants to close local gun stores. You believe that because these stores make guns too easy to buy, guns

get into the hands of criminals. All of you have had loved ones killed by criminals with handguns. Be prepared to argue why the gun store owners should close their shops or leave town.

We reminded students that the handgun in Jamal's possession could have begun its journey at a gun store, then to a law-abiding citizen, then to a criminal in a robbery, then to a pawn shop dealer, then to a gang member like Mack, and finally to Jamal.

Students were directed first to brainstorm ideas in support of their perspectives by working in pairs. This way, all students were likely to have something to contribute when we opened the discussion to the larger group. We prodded Perspective 2 students to think about what they knew of guns from personal experiences. We challenged students working with Perspective 1 to consider a person's legal right to sell and buy guns, and whether that meant they should be held responsible for someone else's reckless use of a gun. As the groups consolidated their arguments, we asked that each select a spokesperson. Afterward, all students were told to be ready to join in the discussion.

The debate began slowly as each side stated its position. As spokesperson for the gun shop owners, DeWayne said, "No one could put them out of business just because they didn't like guns." He went on to say, "We don't like that people use guns to kill other people, but it's not our fault." As spokesperson for the antigun citizens, James countered, "We don't want to have to put you out of business either, but it's your guns that killed my son, so we don't have no choice." Members of each group angrily joined in after hearing this statement. The students argued over whether guns or people shooting the guns were responsible for murder when guns were used. James even used the incident of the school shooting to further his argument for the citizens.

After nearly everyone made at least one contribution to the debate, the dialogue wound down. We then asked group members to spend a few minutes talking among themselves about ways to reduce gun violence, assuming gun manufacturers and shops are not eliminated. Patty wrote students' ideas on the board as they shouted them out. The list of ideas included insightful recommendations:

- Parents should watch their kids, so they do not mess with guns.
- Parents should not leave guns lying around the house.
- Adults should help kids stay away from gangs because gang members always have guns.
- People who sell guns should be helped to make money some other way.
- Kids who bring guns to school should be kicked out for good.

- If kids kill someone with their parents' gun, the parents should have to go to jail too.

I reflected on our students' suggestions for reducing gun violence and wondered if any of them would fall victim to a criminal's bullets. Every day in the United States, children and young adults are killed by guns in homicides and in either purposeful or accidental self-infliction (Younge, 2016). These statistics rise precipitously in streets and alleys, tenements, and abandoned buildings of our inner cities, where poverty is high, education levels are low, and positive adult role models are scarce – situations similar to the lives of our seventh graders. Would James, for instance, one day find himself mistaken for a gang member and be gunned down while walking to the park? Would DeWayne awake one morning to find desperate crack heads pilfering his apartment and be forever silenced by a handgun? These unthinkable notions were always on my mind as I slapped hands with the guys exiting the classroom after another engaging lesson.

Week Six: Preparing for the Unit Projects

As we approached the conclusion of *Scorpions*, Patty and Teri began preparing the students for their unit projects. The students' options included movie posters, scene reenactments, clay figurines with descriptions, life-size posters of characters with descriptions, and a three-dimensional model of a setting in the story. Patty and Teri also invited students to propose their own projects, and at least a few students followed up on the offer. For instance, DeWayne asked if he could do an interview with a gang member or crack dealer (people from his neighborhood that he knew) and compare their lives with the life of either Randy or Mack from *Scorpions*. Teri was concerned about the liability for DeWayne's safety if something went wrong, especially if it were discovered that DeWayne was fulfilling a school assignment. I suggested that he might be able to get the information about a gang member through an Internet search, which he was able to conduct during class time, since his family did not have a computer at home. James, meanwhile, wondered if he could match words from popular rap songs to the novel's main characters. Patty thought this was an excellent way to demonstrate appreciation of character and gave immediate consent. Noe, the student in our unit with the most advanced knowledge about computers, proposed a PowerPoint presentation with photos, video, and graphics that covered the main story line, which was given quick approval. Once Patty, Teri, and I received commitments from every student to do a particular project, we stocked the classroom with necessary resources, such as poster board and paper, markers, variously colored clay bars, shoe boxes, and other material to help students complete the assignment. We also made available the two desktop computers in the room that were Internet ready. Part of each class session was reserved for work on the unit projects.

One of the activities the teachers and I used during this time involved revisiting the pop culture images of boys and men. I brought in a dozen or so copies of *Men's Health*, *Esquire*, and *GQ* magazines, Patty collected an assortment of teen music magazines and local newspapers, and Teri gathered photograph books of movies and films. We distributed these sources to students and had them pair up to review them. Each pair of students was given a wide piece of poster board and instructed to divide it into four columns. In the left column (labeled "Male Images"), we asked students to keep a running list of how these magazines and books portray males (for instance, what the males are doing and what they look like). In the second column (labeled "Interpretations"), students were to write what these male images suggested to them (e.g., physical strength, control, money, power, violence, authority with weapons, and lady's man). In the third column (labeled "Scorpions' Males"), students were to describe briefly similarities between boys from *Scorpions* and the male images in the first column. In the fourth and last column (labeled "My Behavior"), we asked the students to indicate their own behaviors or actions that coincided with male images in the first column. Before the period ended, the pairs shared their work with the rest of the class.

Exploring media portrayals of masculinity would appear to be an effective approach to take to help boys think critically about how gender is communicated on television and the Internet (Johnson, Richmond, & Kivel, 2008; Martin, 2008; The Opportunity Agenda, 2011), by video game producers (Mou & Peng, 2008), and by authors of literature written for youth (Bean & Harper, 2007; Harrison, 2010). Langker (1995), a teacher of media studies, reported on her success with junior high students as they deconstructed advertisers' images to reveal manipulations of young men. The students discovered that ads were replete with ethnic and gender stereotypes, portrayals of males as sexual objects, and messages that reinforced popular notions of the expendable man (such as fighting machine, soldier of fortune). In a similar vein, Ging (2005) was able to foster movement toward a critical sensibility about masculinity among teenage boys in Ireland through an analysis of how males were positioned as gendered beings in literature. And though the literature unit was not transformative, as gender stereotypes held by the boys proved resistant to change, there were, as Ging pointed out "cracks" in perception, suggesting value in challenging boys' fixed and narrow ideas of gender by critically examining how males are characterized in fictional texts.

Felipé and Ricardo were the first to share their work with the class. Felipé held up one end of the poster board as Ricardo held the other, and they explained what they had written in each of the columns. The first image of a man in their Male Images column was Clint Eastwood as Dirty Harry, which was taken from one of the movie books. In the photograph, Harry is holding his trademark long-barrel magnum with a caption that read, "Go ahead, make my day." Ricardo said,

> This is a man who thinks he's tough because he's got a gun. Mack and Jamal think they're tough too because they scare people with guns. Jamal scared Dwayne when he pointed it at him when they were fighting. I shot a rifle when I went hunting with my grandfather. I never pointed it at anyone.

Felipé and Ricardo both said they never shot a pistol, although they had both handled one.

DeWayne and John shared their poster and described an entry across all four columns. DeWayne explained,

> Here's a picture of a former NBA basketball player Charles Barkley, and it say next to him, "You gotta have protection." He so big he don't need no protection, so if you ain't big like him, you gotta get protection somewhere. In *Scorpions*, Mack says the same thing to Jamal when he give him the gun.

At this point, John broke in to say something about the last column. "My little brother, Carlos, was gettin' picked on by these older boys, so I had to walk him to school and tell them that if they messed with Carlos I would get 'em. They didn't touch him after that."

Shantala and Maria, who often worked together as they were the only females in class, had a different take on the assignment. Their poster identified several images of men either driving fast, expensive sports cars or in the company of adoring women. Describing one of the male images on their poster, Maria said,

> There's this man sitting at the table with a real pretty girl and some fancy food there. It say underneath "impress her with do-it-yourself gourmet." We thought this guy is only a player [slang for someone who selfishly uses girls and women] . . . he not cookin' to be nice but to get this girl 'cause she ain't got no ring on or nothin'. He just a phony. We couldn't think of

nothin' from *Scorpions* like this, but my mom told me my dad used to do stuff like that, you know, then he left us anyway.

James and Noe found a picture of a man in a red convertible. The man was wearing sunglasses and had a very attractive woman sitting next to him. James explained,

> He was going real fast because the road is all fuzzy and everything, so we thought guys like him have cool cars they can get pretty girls with. In the book no one has any money, but everyone tryin' to act cool anyway. There ain't no girls in there except Mama and Sassy. On my street, guys in low riders act real cool and always have girls hangin' around 'em.

When Patty, Teri, and I had the opportunity to reflect on that day's activities, we agreed that the students seemed to have a fairly critical understanding of the spurious nature of popular media's images of males. Talking about false men is one thing, avoiding the everyday traps that entice men to behave in false ways is something entirely different. This was also true for the two females in our class. It might be easy for Maria and Shantala to say to their teachers and fellow students that men who do things to impress women may have dishonorable motives. Will they, however, be able to resist the wiles of an insincere man? Young girls in neighborhoods like Maria's and Shantala's, marked by generational poverty, continue to get pregnant at alarming rates, with little expectation or hope for furthering their and the fathers' education or gaining secure and well-paying jobs (McCartney, 2014; Waddell, Orr, Sackoff, & Santelli, 2010). What does this say about Maria's and Shantala's futures?

We concluded our reflective session by ironing out the details on the end-of-unit activity – a school party to celebrate positive masculinity. It was only two weeks away. I had made arrangements with numerous male friends and colleagues to attend the celebration and share their personal feelings about being both men and readers. Patty and Teri were attempting to invite the students' fathers but held little hope that they would show up; after all, only James lived with his dad, and his father worked during the day. Teri would make arrangements for refreshments. Our agenda included teacher introductions, brief presentations by the male guests, one-on-one visits between students and guests, and student presentations of their projects, each of which would be displayed. Patty, Teri, and I also agreed to re-administer the "To Be a Man" survey after the party instead of at the book's conclusion.

Week Seven: End-of-Book Journal Entry

Students worked busily on their unit projects as they finished the last couple of chapters of *Scorpions*. Right after we read aloud the last word of the story, Patty asked students to open their journals and write a letter to Walter Dean Myers, telling him what they had learned as a result of reading his book. Ricardo wrote,

> Dear Walter Dean Myers,
>
> By reading your book named "Scorpions" I learned that life has many osticels [sic] like gangs, drugs, and other things. In the story Jamal is asked if he wants to be in a gang that his brother Randy was in. A friend of Randy's was named Mack and gave Jamal a gun. Just like in this story, I may or may not be asked to join a gang. But I am going to be on track and won't pick the same decission [sic] that Jamal had picked.
>
> Your reader, Ricardo

DeWayne reveals a very different reaction in his letter. His words left us all with the sinking feeling that despite what we had done in the unit, despite the message of honorable masculinity that pervaded the unit, despite the school's intolerance of fights and other violence, the logic of "street justice" may prevail for some of these kids.

> Dear Mr. Myers,
>
> I liked your book. I'm glad you had Jamal keep the gun. Dwayne could have messed with him again. The next time Dwayne might have a gun and try to scare Jamal and then Jamal could just pull out his gun and shoot Dwayne. Jamal needed the gun so the next time he go [sic] to the Scorpions hideout and a man tries to mess with him, he can either shoot the man or shoot at the man's ear.
>
> Your reader, DeWayne

The seventh graders pressed the issue of the surprise ending. Everyone sensed that Jamal's decision not to give the gun back to Mack or throw it in the river would lead to nothing but trouble. Jamal agrees to meet with the Scorpions in a remote area of the park late one night in what seems to be a bold statement, rejecting any thoughts that Jamal will be walking in his brother Randy's footsteps. Despite Tito's entreaties, he refuses to take the gun with him. This leads readers to conclude that if anyone gets shot, Jamal will not be the perpetrator. Two shots do pierce the air that night in the middle of a violent confrontation between Jamal and two members of the Scorpions. The students eagerly finished the last pages to find out which character had been holding the gun that fired those shots.

Week Eight: Real Men Finale

Although it all seemed to be over far too quickly, the unit's finale had arrived. The teachers and I had set up for the celebratory party in the back of the cafeteria. Student posters adorned the walls, and clay figurines and three-dimensional models covered a long table. Another table held several copies of *Scorpions* and a variety of student work created during the unit. Punch, cake, and cookies covered a third big table.

When I arrived, Patty pulled me aside and told me softly that Ricardo would not be joining us because he was suspended from school. She handed me a folder and said, "Read this." I tucked it into my briefcase. Later that morning, I opened the folder Patty had handed me, which held two pages of her project notes. I began reading and found that Ricardo apparently had been a lookout for a friend who had been caught stealing money from a teacher's desk. Soon after, Ricardo was in trouble again for hitting a boy in the jaw. His home life was not good either. Both his father and sister were in jail, and his grandmother, with whom he lived, had recently become ill. Patty spoke with Ricardo about this incident and discovered that Ricardo thought he had been justified in punching the boy.

Patty tried to reason with Ricardo by speaking about Jamal's actions in *Scorpions* and connecting Ricardo's actions to Jamal's. She asked Ricardo whether Jamal had been right to pull a gun and if Jamal could go to jail for his actions. Ricardo responded just as Patty thought he would because Ricardo knew Jamal's actions were wrong and knew the consequences Jamal could face because of these actions. She ended their conversation by asking Ricardo,

PATTY: So do you really think hitting that boy was the right thing to do?
RICARDO: [after a long pause] No, I guess not . . .
PATTY: What could you have done?
RICARDO: Told you or another teacher, or just ignored him . . .

Ricardo's behavior represents the difficulties of helping young men adopt new expressions of masculinity, which is a challenge everyone faces when trying to pry open the grip popular culture and media have on youth. Envisioning new ways of being boys and men was particularly challenging with our youth from the barrio because of their familiarity with the hegemonic masculinity that dominates their community and lives.

Patty did, however, seem to get through at some level with Ricardo. One of the more challenging boys in the seventh grade and growing up in circumstances that would require every bit of his willpower to surmount, he was brought to notice parallels between his troubles and those of Jamal. Ricardo seemed to understand that punching a classmate was a poor decision. This realization also acknowledges the emptiness of his own macho bravado toward the incident. His duplicity in stealing money was obviously very serious and demonstrated the fine line that Ricardo and many other seventh-grade boys walked daily between self-discipline and delinquency. I will always remember Ricardo for his ability to evaluate his actions and those of his partner critically – much the same way he learned to evaluate critically Jamal's behavior throughout the novel.

Patty's notes brought a kind of joy that reinforced the satisfaction I felt over the celebration of the unit's finale, which had just ended. The party in the cafeteria began with Patty speaking about the unit's goals, what we had done along the way, and what we hoped to accomplish within the next hour. With her cue, students approached our male guests to form teams for personal introductions. We allowed these groups to converse for a few minutes, then had the group share what they learned with the whole class. We chuckled as our adult guests stretched their short-term memories to introduce the seventh graders within their groups.

After companion introductions, the students presented their unit projects. DeWayne held up his three-dimensional model of Jamal's apartment and described the scene in which the preacher prays with Mama, Jamal, and Sassy for the older brother Randy, who was injured in a prison fight. James made clay figurines of the main characters. He displayed these while supplying character sketches of each, then answered questions about the characters. Ricardo's life-size poster advertising *Scorpions* was on the wall. Because of his suspension that day, Teri pointed it out to the group and explained what Ricardo had intended with his picture of a scorpion above the words *Scorpions are back!* Shantala and Noe reenacted the scene from the novel when Sassy discovers the hidden gun in the sofa cushions. They rewrote the book's dialogue and memorized their lines. They also used simple props, such as a picture of a handgun cut out from a magazine and a pillow on a folding chair.

When the students completed their presentations, Patty invited them to partake of the refreshments. Afterward, she asked our male guests to share some of their thoughts about being male and being a reader. Dr. Chuck Dugan, a kinesiology professor and former all-American gymnast, began by reading an excerpt from the poem "I Celebrate Myself," which is from one of his favorite books, *Leaves of Grass* by Walt Whitman (1993). He read the following lines:

> I celebrate myself, and sing myself,
> And what I assume you shall assume,
> For every atom belonging to me as good belongs to you.
> I loafe and invite my soul,
> I lean and loafe at my ease observing a spear of summer grass.
> My tongue, every atom of my blood, form'd from this soil, this air,
> Born here of parents born here from parents the same, and their parents the same.
> I, now thirty-seven years old in perfect health begin,
> Hoping to cease not till death.

Chuck went on to explain his philosophy about health: To be totally healthy, people must be both physically and intellectually active. He warned that the biggest mistake is to become imbalanced, forgetting to stimulate either the body or the mind. "Reading," continued Chuck, "is the best way to guarantee that our minds stay in great shape. That's why I read every day ... it's a kind of mental exercise."

Another marvelous male guest was Dr. Malcolm Booker, who candidly described his humble beginnings in rural Louisiana, his basketball scholarship to a state college, and, the pinnacle of his academic efforts, the completion of his doctoral degree in education at the University of Florida. He emphasized that life's circumstances give people plenty of reasons to avoid the difficult steps, to seek to "feel good" only for the moment, and to find excuses for bad behavior and decisions, which are truly within their own control. Despite the many questions students had about his exciting college basketball career, Malcolm adroitly refocused his answers on the importance of disciplining oneself, setting goals, and becoming as highly literate as possible. For example, after Felipé queried him about whether he ever played basketball with Michael Jordan, Malcolm laughed and responded, "I had dreams of playing big-time roundball, but when I broke my ankle in my junior year, and it never healed properly, my playing days were over." He went on to say,

> I knew many guys who were convinced that nothing would stop them from becoming pros ... but when they got injured or flunked out, they had no backup plan, no Plan B. My best advice to all of you, especially if you like sports and think you're really good: Keep playing hard, work on your game to become as good as you can, but work just as hard on your school lessons, so if one plan doesn't work out, you'll have another ready to go. The one sure way to be ready is to be a reader.

Malcolm concluded his presentation by reading passages from Martin Luther King Jr.'s "Letter from Birmingham Jail" from *Why We Can't Wait* (King, 1963). Looking out on the diverse group of young adults, he intoned,

> Moreover, I am cognizant of the interrelatedness of all communities and states. I cannot sit idly by in Atlanta and not be concerned about what happens in Birmingham. Injustice anywhere is a threat to justice everywhere. We are caught in an inescapable network of mutuality, tied in a single garment of destiny. Whatever affects one directly, affects all indirectly. Never again can we afford to live with the narrow, provincial "outside agitator" idea. Anyone who lives inside the United States can never be considered an outsider anywhere within its bounds. (p. 34)

After brief presentations from our last guests, the final day of our Real Men unit drew to a close. Rene Zamora, a successful investment banker, revealed his love of books from the thriller genre. Doug Horner, a local actor, read dialogue from *A New Way to Pay Old Debts* (Massinger, 1910), an Elizabethan play that was being staged in town. Doug said, "It has everything to do with choices young men make to be deceitful and unkind or decent and honorable." The lines he read that stuck out in my mind were those from Lady Allworth to her son:

> You are yet
> Like virgin parchment, capable of any
> Inscription, vicious or honourable. (p. 869)

The point, of course, Doug observed, is that even though boys are vulnerable to external influences, they must strive to reject the vicious and emulate the honorable.

All the guests were perfect. Each uniquely embodied the characteristics of a masculinity in sharp contrast to stereotypic forms pervasive in the lives of these and most youth today. Equally important was they clearly stressed how essential a life of active literacy had been in shaping their personal and professional identities. When the bell rang ending the class period, the finality of the moment hit me. I could only hope these young people might take the memory of this unit with them and make good decisions as they enter adulthood.

Revisiting the "To Be a Man" Survey

Although the unit officially ended, Patty, Teri, and I still had a great deal of work to finish. It was time to re-administer the "To Be a Man" survey to the students and compare the results from two months earlier to determine any self-reported changes in attitude toward stereotypical and hegemonic masculine behavior.

Documenting changes in attitude about hegemonic and even toxic masculinity (Pascoe, 2011) using self-report measures is similar to research conducted by Farrell and Meyer (1997). In their study, they examined the impact of a school-based curriculum designed to reduce violence for sixth-grade students from inner-city Richmond, Virginia, USA. At the beginning of the school year, students completed a survey reporting the number of incidences of assaultive violence in which they had engaged. Farrell and Meyer re-administered the survey after an 18-session violence prevention program. Results showed highly significant reduction in the frequency of violence and several other related problem behaviors for boys. Most of these differences were maintained through the end of the school year.

We were heartened after reading our students' responses to the post-unit survey. (The results of Ricardo's, DeWayne's, James's, and Shantala's surveys are highlighted in Figure 3.5.) Students' responses suggested that the unit was a success; however, it is impossible to know whether their responses reflected a genuine change in attitude or a desire to tell us what we wanted to hear.

Lessons Learned from the Real Men Unit

Now, from the perspective of several years on since the conduct of the Real Men unit, it is as helpful as ever to reflect on what the experience can tell us about boys' masculine and reading identities and the implications for teachers and other concerned adults.

Masculine Identity. Essential to the work with boys is moving them toward greater openness to masculinities and critical evaluation of their own self-images of masculine identity. As we learned, this goal must be approached with deftness, especially with boys who already hold rigid conceptions of gender. As Staples (2012) reminds us,

1. When a man is being hassled by another man, he needs to fight to get the man to back off.
   Ricardo's response – "No."
   Ricardo's reason – "Because they can talk it out."
2. Men who walk away from fights are sissies.
   DeWayne's response – "No."
   DeWayne's reason – "Even if you're stronger, what's the use of fighting."
3. Men need weapons like knives and guns to show how strong they are.
   James's response – "No."
   James's reason – "If they're going hunting or something, that's OK, but they don't have to use them [guns and knives] to fight."
4. You can't really be a man unless you are in a gang.
   Shantala's response – "No."
   Shantala's reason – "You're a man, staying out of gang."
5. Men like to fight because that's just who they are.
   Ricardo's response – "No."
   Ricardo's reason – "We have control of what we do."
6. Men who go to prison are real men.
   DeWayne's response – "No."
   DeWayne's reason – "That don't sound cool to me."
7. If a man killed someone, other men would think he was really cool.
   James's response – "No."
   James's reason – "You protect them better by having a good job and a good house."
8. Real men protect their families by fighting.
   Shantala's response – "No."
   Shantala's reason – "Prison ain't no place to prove you're a man."
9. As soon as a boy turns 13, he needs a gun.
   Ricardo's response – "No."
   Ricardo's reason – "A boy only needs a gun for hunting."
10. Sometimes being violent is the only way for a man to make others understand he means business.
    DeWayne's response – "No."
    DeWayne's reason – "There are other ways, like what you say that let's people know you ain't messing."

Figure 3.5 Sample Post-Unit Responses from "To Be a Man" Survey

"students' race and gender consciousness speak to and intermingle with intellectual work and literate abilities" (p. 55). Her case study of an urban African American adolescent boy demonstrates the power of exploiting favored popular cultural narratives as source material for critically articulating and questioning race and gender constructs. Staples' thick analysis of one boys' critical-identity journey reminds us of what was learned in our own work with male youth from a Texas barrio, that consciousness raising about masculine identity is a process that demands sensitivity to boys' histories, existential needs, and skill sets. It also requires texts and textual practices that are accessible and meaningful even while they are designed to challenge and extend boundaries of possible gendered selves. Thus, as was discovered with a book like *Scorpions*, because it was readable and relatable to the students in our Real Men project, we were able to keep them engaged while involving them in critical discursive practices around media, masculinity, and their own gendered identities. By honoring boys' "discourses of desire" (Simon, 1987), texts and related experiences that appeal can become the conduit for expanded consciousness.

Boys and Reading Identity. Some have theorized that the principle work during adolescence is identity development (Erikson, 1980; Steinberg, 2008). For boys to build reading into their burgeoning identities, they need to see reading as compatible with who they are as gendered beings. We know that for boys with entrenched views of stereotypical masculinity reading is regarded as a "girly" thing (Massoud & Sudic, 2014). This pervasive attitude may be contributing to boys' choosing not to read as often as girls and reading less in adulthood as compared with their female counterparts (Perrin, 2016; Sunderland, Dempster, & Thistlethwaite, 2016).

The evidence makes clear that youth, particularly those from marginalized groups, need literacy practices that foster success and learning communities that value their lived experiences (Alvermann, 2009; Cook-Sather, 2010; Sturtevant et al., 2006; Tatum, 2006). Indeed, when school curricula aligns with students' interests and outside-of-school competencies, the process of literacy learning itself should lead to changes in identity that are empowering and transformative (Brozo, 2017; Moje, 2007). The young adolescent boys in the Real Men unit were active contributors to the energy and value of the unit. The culturally relevant core text, *Scorpions*, anchoring the literacy work in the unit, as well as the numerous opportunities to link this narrative and other media texts to the boys' lifeworlds, engendered a community of readers and learners while enlarging the boundaries of possible gendered selves. Reflecting on her work with a preteen boy trying on forms of masculinity based on his fascination with World Federation Wrestling, Collier (2015) urges, "If the gendered identities for boys ... are complicated through the inclusion of everyday culture forms, productive spaces for exploration both inside and outside the classroom are born" (p. 221).

Boys' Masculinities and Identities: A Coda

The multidimensional nature of boys would seem to defy attempts to categorize them as a group or as a gender. Nonetheless, in this chapter we attempted to sort through some of the issues associated with masculinities and identities for male youth. What is gleaned from this effort is that, even while it must be acknowledged that every boy is unique in terms of his conception of his own masculine identity, it must also be recognized that large segments of the male student population struggle with aspects of literacy and language learning. How masculine identity relates to these literacy challenges is becoming increasingly understood.

Teachers and other concerned adults can foreground issues of identity and masculinity in discursive practices with boys to increase motivation and expand awareness of the importance of literacy as a tool for self-growth and social change. This was the hoped for outcome of the "Real Men" unit. It was a school-based, practical attempt to employ texts and literacy strategies to challenge stereotypes about masculinity and offer urban multicultural male youth struggling with literacy a counter-narrative to popular media and cultural constructions of boyhood and maleness. Boys who learn to deconstruct images of males as enemies of thoughtful, reflective reading and writing may be better positioned to gain important literacy skills and practices and use these in critical ways to shape themselves and their worlds.

CHAPTER 4

Socioeconomics and Boys: Evidence and Practice

> **In this chapter, I**
> - Relate socioeconomic factors to gender-based literacy achievement disparities
> - Explore the links between the underachievement of boys and the decline of industry and manufacturing
> - Draw attention to the relationship between low qualifications and both joblessness and low paying and unskilled work
> - Highlight the effects of class and status on boys' literacy engagement and achievement
> - Explain the relationship between school leaving, literacy skills, and SES
> - Describe successful and promising programs and practices

Reading literacy has a significant role to play in the economic health of individuals, families, and states. Raising a nation's reading achievement, according to Hanushek and Woessmann (2010), will increase the SES of all its citizens. Using PISA data, they document the potential gains to the economic health and overall well-being of a nation by increasing students' reading abilities. This is because advanced reading skill offers individuals possibilities for economic and social mobility, since it positions them for higher-status and higher-wage work. PISA results tell us that students from privilege have much higher reading scores than students from low-income backgrounds, suggesting convincingly that SES has a powerful effect on reading achievement (OECD, 2013). Thus, one can envision a kind of mutually supportive relationship between reading ability and SES. The better one reads, the more opportunities for advanced learning; the higher the levels of learning, the greater the chance for more lucrative employment. Children and youth who are the beneficiaries of this intergenerational cultural capital are then also likely to be academically successful, perpetuating a virtuous cycle (Morgan, Farkas, Hillemeier, & Maczuga, 2009).

The opposite to such virtuous cycles is what concerns me in my advocacy for male youth, because we know that inequalities of social position can have a cumulative effect, impacting opportunities for boys across generations. For example, the effect of large inequalities in parental educational attainment can lead to significant differences in their children's chances in school (Van de Werfhorst & Mijs, 2010). Furthermore, we must acknowledge that the influence of SES also extends to schools. Education systems in low-SES communities often lack the resources of their more privileged peers, which links directly to students' academic outcomes and progress (Aikens & Barbarin, 2008; Shanks & Robinson, 2012).

American educational psychologist David Berliner (2009) reminds us that, in the United States, "students spend about 1,150 waking hours a year in school versus about 4,700 more waking hours per year in their families and neighborhoods" (p. 3). He goes on to say, in sobering clarity, that "despite [school's] best efforts at reducing inequalities, inequalities do not easily go away, with the result that America's schools generally work less well for impoverished youth and much better for those more fortunate" (p. 4). The European Commission (2012) offers similar stark pronouncements about the effects of poverty on educational achievement for children and youth on that continent by reporting, "Children born into severe poverty are disproportionately exposed to factors that impede their psychomotor development, socio-emotional growth and cognitive processes. When linked with deprived or neglectful family backgrounds and poorly educated parents, poverty becomes the single greatest barrier to educational achievement" (p. 5).

In previous chapters, I have drawn attention to the impactful contribution a boys' SES makes to his academic development and literacy growth. In this chapter, I focus exclusively on socioeconomic factors, their relationship to literacy achievement, and proven or promising practices and programs designed to elevate the literacy achievement of boys who lack the benefits enjoyed by their more privileged peers.

The PISA results demonstrate convincingly the stark differences in reading achievement between boys from privilege and those from low-economy backgrounds (Brozo & Crain, 2015). The weight of growing up in poverty holds many children and youth down, according to Bracey (2011), who compares poverty to gravity, stating that it affects everything in a person's life, including conditions and dynamics that make it difficult to succeed in school. This is because being poor entails a syndrome of factors, including inadequate medical care, food insecurities, family stress, and crime-prone neighborhoods, all of which have been shown to bear directly on depressed academic performance (Berliner, 2009). Boys who are poor bring to school a range of poverty-induced problems such as neurological damage, attention disorders, excessive absenteeism, language delays, and anger management challenges (Kishiyama et al., 2009; Payne & Slocumb, 2011; Stevenson, 2004).

It is useful to remind ourselves that for many decades, perhaps as far back as the introduction of wide-scale testing in schools, there have been significant numbers of boys who are underachievers overall and in reading specifically. We know this to be true in the United States, where gender-based achievement disparities have been evident at least since the early 1940s (Stroud & Lindquist, 1942). This longstanding pattern notwithstanding, boys' underachievement, it is claimed, has become much more noticeable as industry and manufacturing in North America and Europe continue to decline (Lloyd, 2011). Up until the 1970s, low academic qualifications were not necessarily a barrier to relatively high-paying jobs on assembly lines and in mills. A young man right out of secondary school, or even an early leaver, might find employment in a unionized factory where he could earn a respectable wage and enjoy good benefits. Many such young men with low educational attainment could nonetheless buy a house, raise a family, and regularly purchase a new automobile on these blue-collar wages (Mirel, 1999). Opportunities like these are a distant memory. Today, limited educational attainment and low qualifications are more likely to lead to joblessness or being trapped in unskilled work with low pay.

And this brings us to the ways socioeconomic conditions influence boys' literacy achievement, their employment opportunities, and chances for a healthy, self-actualized adult life. As was pointed out in Chapter 1, boys who grow up in families and communities with high levels of class and status and the privileges that come with these, have financial and social protections against academic disengagement and low literacy achievement (Hill, 2014). Staying the course academically and developing complex literacy abilities all but ensures male youth of privileged background will also enjoy the benefits of higher education, positioning them for the better-wage and salaried jobs. By contrast, boys without these class and status protections will be vulnerable to the poverty-induced conditions already outlined.

Boys in the Real World

"Javier"

Javier is a ten-year-old fifth grader who attends his neighborhood school in a large urban area in the mid-Atlantic region of the United States. Javier has grown up in bilingual home where he speaks both English and Spanish. His mother can converse in both languages, whereas his father speaks predominantly Spanish, though he is studying English. At home, when Javier was young, his parents intentionally emphasized his learning Spanish before English. They knew he would learn English in school but were concerned that Spanish might not get emphasis once he got to school. Javier received English as an additional language service from kindergarten through third grade. At the end of third grade, he tested out of the English as an additional language program. He currently does not receive any extra services in his school.

Javier is a typical fifth-grade boys in many ways. Outside of school, he likes playing sports, such as soccer and football. What he really loves, though, is making comics. This activity helps define Javier's literate identity. Creating comics and writing dialog and captions for the illustrations are a source of immense pleasure and motivation for him both in and outside of school. Javier makes clear when he says, "I don't like to read them but I do them," that creating comics is what he finds fun, not necessarily reading comic books. His comics typically include super heroes and super villains who have special powers like speed, invisibility, or telekinesis. Javier uses popular culture, the Toontastic app (https://toontastic.withgoogle.com/), his own imagination, and research to create his comics.

Javier's research includes checking out books from the library specifically to help him get ideas and write his comics. Helpful resources for his comics are Stuart Gibbs' *Spy School* series and another Gibbs' book, *Spy Camp*. Javier also has multiple reading identities but he seems most engaged when creating comics and writing. He is very focused on the craft of writing and understands that to get better at writing comics he needs to find new sources for his comic stories and new ways of putting language together to make his stories more exciting.

Javier's literate identity includes confidence and pleasure reading historical fiction and non-fiction, particularly on his favorite topics, "The Civil War, World War Two, any war really." He also likes historical fiction in graphic novel formats about topics such as ancient Egypt. Javier also enjoys reading about sports, especially *The Guinness Book of Sports Records*. This is one of his favorite books, and he wishes he could find others like it in his school library.

Javier has multiple literate identities. He is most inclined to use writing and drawing in the creation of comics. He prefers writing to reading because he feels more creative and active. He also likes books about architecture and keeps a notebook of sketches of house designs. Javier uses books and other texts to inform his creative drawing and writing endeavors.

Discussion and Activities

- What recommendations can you offer to teachers working with Javier to ensure his reading and writing interests are nurtured?
- How can Javier's interests be exploited for further literacy skill and language development?
- Review Toontastic and other comic making apps to determine which ones might be most interesting and useful to boys in your classroom.

The Poverty Penalty for Boys

Surely, poverty is gender blind. Boys and girls alike fall prey to many of the same insidious and traumatic effects of being poor that often manifest themselves as truancy and absenteeism from school, maladaptive classroom behaviors, regular complaints of hunger, and exhibiting poor hygiene, lethargy, and anxiety (Najman et al., 2004). In addition to these injurious outcomes for both males and females, research is uncovering some important differential effects of growing up in high-poverty conditions. For example, in the United States, it is well known that, in general, men are more likely to work than women; however, boys from poor backgrounds are significantly less likely to find employment and work in adulthood than their female counterparts from similar backgrounds – this based on tax records of some 10 million Americans born between 1980 and 1982 (Chetty & Hendren, 2015). In other words, when it comes to joblessness, men from childhood poverty are hit the hardest. These negative effects of poverty on employment rates are particularly acute for African American boys and those raised by a single parent. Likewise, males who grow up in low-income families are more likely to drop out of school and less likely to attend college as compared to females (Payne & Slocumb, 2011).

Male youth from poverty who are early leavers or fail to attend college may be destined to remain in poverty as adults due to chronic unemployment or being consigned to minimum wage work. The transgenerational nature of SES explains how parental SES strongly predicts children's SES (Schoon, 2008). There are, of course, mediating factors, such as one's academic motivation and cognitive skills, both of which are associated with status mobility. Reading engagement, for example, emerged as one of the most potent predictors of reading literacy achievement on PISA. Thus, student participants from low-SES backgrounds and single-parent households who were otherwise highly engaged readers earned scores beyond what would have been expected (Brozo et al., 2014). Given their reading engagement and skill, these are students who stand a good chance of beating the odds stacked against them and moving into higher status groups as adults.

Documenting enduring links to SES across the lifespan, Ritchie and Bates (2013) explored whether reading and mathematics ability in childhood connected to SES in adulthood. United Kingdom age 7 students' reading and math achievement was found to have a significantly positive association with their SES by age 42. Reading and mathematics achievement in the study was also highly correlated to academic motivation and number of years of education. Another powerful finding was that SES at birth was a fairly potent predictor of adulthood SES, though mediated by reading and maths achievement levels. This implies that the more done to boost reading and math ability among students from lower SES groups at the earliest stages of schooling, the more chances improve for academic perseverance and success, as well as socioeconomic advancement in later life. Ritchie and Bates contend that SES is leavened by high mathematics and reading ability, which not only position one for higher status employment, but also improve health literacy and personal finance skills.

Schoon (2008) also investigated the mediating roles school motivation and persistence played in status attainment across generations. Analyzing extant data of over five thousand men and women who could be tracked from childhood to their mid thirties based on their participation in two major British longitudinal studies, the researcher found the most potent determinant of SES in adulthood was the number of years of full-time education. Those who remained motivated not to drop out of school and progress beyond the secondary level attained higher status than those who completed secondary school only or dropped out. The study's findings reinforce what we have learned from PISA data and the work of Ritchie and Bates in that participants from lower-SES groups achieved status mobility as a result of becoming academically engaged and staying the course in school.

Although boys and males are not singled out in the PISA findings reported above, nor in the Ritchie and Bates and Schoon studies, what is clear is that, regardless of sex, reading engagement, academic motivation, and persistence in school appear to be essential for overcoming socio-economic hardships in childhood. The challenge, therefore, is how to effect an attitude of academic engagement and perseverance in boys who come to school with all of the penalties and hardships of poverty and low SES. Because, as we have seen for boys from low-income backgrounds, they are less likely to be employed and experience upward status mobility compared with females from similar backgrounds. This challenge is all the more urgent because, it is suspected, too many boys growing up in high-poverty areas with limited educational attainment are shifting away from low-paying formal jobs, which may be all that is available to them, to seeking illicit means of making money (Chetty & Hendren, 2015).

Criminal activity and incarceration, as well as dropout rates in the United States, are already staggeringly high among boys and men from poor and high-minority backgrounds (Styslinger, Gavigan, & Albright, 2017). Indeed, on any given day, as many as 37 percent of African American males age 20 to 24 with less than a high school diploma are in jail or prison in the United States (The Pew Charitable Trusts, 2010). This is well above the rate for Hispanic males (12 percent) and white males (7 percent). With high recidivism rates and dwindling job options for males with criminal records, incarceration all but guarantees little if any economic mobility and lifelong entrapment at lower socioeconomic levels. A hopeful finding, though, echoes what we have learned from other studies cited here – the longer boys stay in school, the less likely they are to be incarcerated. A mere 2 percent of African American males with just some post-secondary education are imprisoned. And even a high school diploma lessens the chances of jail or prison by a wide margin (9 percent) as compared with early leavers.

Compounding the challenges American males from poor backgrounds face in seeking formal and legal work options for elevating status is the overall decline of the rate of employment for working-age men (between the ages of 25 and 54) that has been occurring for nearly five decades (Eberstadt, 2016). Well over 90 percent from the 1950s to the 1970s, employment rates among men have dropped steadily since to a current rate of about 85 percent. As pointed out earlier, manufacturing and industrial production saw its heyday during the immediate post – World War II period through at least the middle 70s. As these robust-paying jobs for a largely unskilled male workforce eroded, more and more men were compelled to make a choice – either take minimum-wage work or put themselves at the mercy of the state. Men and their families can survive on food stamps, housing assistance, Medicaid, and other federal benefits; however, without sophisticated skills and advance education, there is little hope for acquiring higher-paying jobs and moving out of low-socioeconomic conditions.

Quane, Wilson, and Hwang (2015) explain how poverty affects children, youth, and adults generationally. The authors describe low-income, inner-city black children, with a focus on males, as likely to attend challenged or failing schools from primary age onward, where they are apt to receive suspensions, be enrolled in special education classes, fail to graduate from secondary school on time, and be prone to leaving school early (Smiley, 2011). As a result, many young black males find themselves out of the workforce and unenrolled in postsecondary education institutions. In fact, since the 1970s, black males between 16 and 24 have been unemployed and unenrolled in school at rates ranging from 20 to 32 percent, higher than their Hispanic and white male peers.

Dropping out of school is one of the poverty penalties for boys that has its roots in their pre-school language and literacy experiences. A report sponsored by the Annie E. Casey Foundation in the United States identified oral language at age 5 as one of the three key predictors of school success and high school completion (Hernandez, 2012). Children at that age from low-income families, the report documents, typically exhibit underdeveloped oral language skills, limited expressive vocabularies, and even inaccurate alphabetic knowledge. An alarmingly predictable trajectory lies ahead of these kids, including, far too often, dropping out of school as adolescents. The report acknowledges the considerable impact schools and teachers can have on student achievement (Hattie, 2011); however, it makes clear that educational outcomes for children and youth will be influenced to varying degrees by homelife conditions (Berliner, 2009). Factors such as parental involvement, parent–child communication, and other forms of what Tramonte and Willms (2010) refer to as "relational cultural capital" (p. 203) have been shown to significantly affect students' reading achievement, as well as overall academic performance (Jeynes, 2005). This may be especially true for boys of color, who, according to the work of Harris and Graves (2010), are more likely to demonstrate increased reading achievement and positive academic development with parental involvement in their play and cultural activities.

Family, Community, and School Buffers for Boys

As we reflect on the scientific findings related to the daunting impact poverty has on boys, particularly males of color, it is important to remember, as Tamika Thompson (2011) reminds us:

> Behind every fact is a face. Behind every statistic is a story. Behind every catchy phrase is a young person [man] whose future will be lost if something is not done immediately to change his reality. And when it comes to young, African American men, the numbers are staggering and the reality is sobering. (para. 1)

What researchers have learned is, as the number of risk factors (e.g., substandard housing, noise, crowding, increased family conflicts, parental stress, community violence) decline for boys, there is a concomitant increase in their academic achievement, as well as a decrease in behavioral issues (Fantuzzo, 2009). The deleterious effects of low income and related risk factors for boys, however, have been shown to be buffered by early childhood education, such as Head Start, and a host of vital home and community interactions (Murry, Block, & Liu, 2016).

For example, it is reassuring to realize that when parents from typical risk environments create access to books in the home and regularly interact with boys around books, their sons' readiness for school improves and their reading scores are higher than peers who have not benefited from these kinds of academic socialization experiences (Baker, Cameron, Rimm-Kaufman, & Grissmer, 2012). Additionally, young African American boys who are exposed to culturally relevant toys, books, and conversations in the home demonstrate higher levels of academic competence than peers without similar opportunities (Caughy, O'Campo, Randolph, & Nickerson, 2002).

These findings are reminders of the impactful cultural capital all families and communities possess and how that capital can gird boys with the cognitive and behavioral armor to successfully confront challenging home, community, and school contexts. We see this again in boys of color who are imbued by parents and guardians with a sense of positive racial identity. African American male youth from modest household income families had higher levels of self-efficacy, elevated academic aspirations, and better school performance when they took pride in their racial/ethnic heritage

(Murry et al., 2009). Of particular significance was the sense of empowerment fostered among boys of color by their parents, in spite of material privations and financial hardship (Murry, Block, & Liu, 2016). Furthermore, African American adolescent males raised in families with high educational expectations, and where academic success was emphasized, had positive academic identities, healthy relationships with teachers and peers, and future-oriented educational expectations (Kerpelman, Eryigit, & Stephens, 2008). Significantly, boys from low-income urban settings who internalize these parental values are also less likely to engage in truant behaviors (Li, Feigelman, & Stanton, 2000). And as we have seen, the longer boys stay in school, the higher their achievement and potential (Harper & Williams, 2014).

I pointed out earlier that boys are especially vulnerable to the toxic effects of low-resource, high-crime communities. Their mortality rate is significantly higher than the general population of males (Miniño, 2013). They are far more likely to be suspended from school than their more privileged peers (Stetser & Stillwell, 2014). And males from poverty disproportionately represent the ranks of juvenile offenders and incarcerated youth (US Department of Justice, 2015). Many parents who raise sons in these challenging environments have had to find strategies to help protect boys from the injurious influences of high-poverty, high-crime communities, such as strictly controlling out-of-school time (Roche, Ensminger, & Cherlin, 2007), being involved, vigilant, and firm disciplinarians (Gaylord-Harden, Zakaryan, Bernard, & Pekoc, 2015), and creating an emotionally secure and supportive family environment (Gorman-Smith, Henry, & Tolan, 2004). In spite of the risks of living in low-resource communities, boys who feel family attachments and a sense of validation and worth are better able to respond adaptively to stressful circumstances outside the home (Murry, Block, & Liu, 2016). Moreover, Roche and colleagues (2007) found that male youth were less prone to gang and truancy activity when other adults in the neighborhood acted as additional mentors and proxy parents.

School conditions can also make a difference in the academic trajectories of males. For example, Gershenson and her colleagues (2017) report that black primary-school students matched to a same-race teacher perform better on standardized tests. More significantly, the researchers discovered that when a black male student in grades three to five is assigned a black teacher, the probability that he drops out of high school is significantly reduced, and this appears to be particularly true among the most economically disadvantaged black males. Having at least one black teacher in third through fifth grades reduced very-low-income black boys' probability of dropping out of school by 39 percent, the researchers found.

In the next section, I once again describe practices and programs that have shown promise in elevating literacy motivation and skill for boys. The approaches I share have been targeted at boys from lower socioeconomic groups or have included boys from this population.

Promising Programs and Practices

Cross-Age Reading Buddies: Elton and Angelo

Since the start of eleventh grade, Elton wanted to quit school. His older brother had dropped out, and his 17-year-old sister was receiving homebound instruction after having a baby. Ruby, the literacy coach at Elton's school, saw another possible future for this young man. She took particular notice of him while observing his history class one mid-September morning.

The class had been reading and learning about civil rights in America, and the history teacher had asked his students to find articles that dealt with some aspect of civil rights either in the United States or anywhere around the world. Students went to the long table in the back of the room that was stacked with newspapers and current events magazines and rummaged through them. Ruby watched as Elton spent more time than the others looking carefully for something that interested him. Back at his seat, Elton was reading very closely an article from *Jet* magazine as Ruby stopped by to visit with him. He explained to her in animated terms how the article was about white people who believed that, because Barack Obama was president, African Americans no longer have to struggle for civil rights. The author, Elton went on to say, was warning that blacks should not let down their guard or stop fighting for civil rights that are still being denied or infringed upon because of race. Ruby was impressed with Elton's passion for the topic and his sensitive, critical reading of the article. When it was his turn to give an oral encapsulation of his article for the class, he did so with the same level of enthusiasm he had exhibited when sharing his reactions with Ruby.

Elton was just the type of young man Ruby was hoping to recruit for a new cross-age tutoring program she was instituting, which targeted students at risk of dropping out due to poor academic performance, low ability levels, or difficult home circumstances. The overall goal of the program was to improve reading skills for struggling students and keep them in school by tapping into their sense of responsibility to younger students. Keeping boys like Elton in school and raising his academic performance and self-esteem were her highest priorities. She had made arrangements with the neighborhood elementary school, which was only a short walk away from the high school, to host tutorial sessions twice weekly involving second and third graders and high school reading buddies.

Ruby spoke with Elton and several other boys individually about participating in the program, and when she had commitments from eight of them, began preparing them for their roles. The students were all members of the same third-block English class, so Ruby was able to use that time for group training sessions. More important, the English teacher agreed to allow the tutoring activity to count toward students' grades. This would be an important recruitment incentive for Ruby. Elton and the other tutors learned techniques for finding out the children's interests. They were taught simple read-aloud and vocabulary strategies. They learned how to facilitate writing in response to reading, and how to make books. And reinforced throughout was the expectation that these male youth would be encouraging of their younger buddies' reading and writing efforts and would help them see that these activities can be enjoyable. Above all, Ruby hoped that by developing literacy strategies for helping younger male readers less able than themselves, these adolescent boys would, in fact, expand their own reading and writing skills. The literature, at least, leaves open this expectation (Brozo & Hargis, 2003; Hattie, 2006; Karcher, 2009; Paterson & Elliott, 2006; Van Keer & Vanderlinde, 2010; Wright & Cleary, 2006).

Elton's reading buddy was Angelo, a second grader, who was already experiencing difficulties with grade-appropriate reading materials. Elton was an ideal reading buddy for Angelo because it has been shown that gender- and culture-matched role models have the strongest positive effect on educational outcomes for their mentees (Zirkel, 2002).

In their first meeting, Elton discovered that Angelo lived in an adjacent apartment complex to his own building. He also learned that Angelo "loved" football and, because his father lived in New York, wanted to play for the New York Giants American football team when he grew up. Angelo also told Elton what he wanted most was a computer so he could play "cool games." Elton made sure to tell Angelo about his interest in football, too. After getting to know each other a little while longer, Elton read some pages he had practiced from a short biography about LeBron James. Before long it was time to walk back to the high school. Elton reassured his new younger buddy that he would return in a couple of days. It was a hopeful start of what was to become a significant experience for the two of them.

Over the next few months, the tutoring program experienced attrition of three boys who couldn't keep up the commitment. They became impatient or didn't want to plan reading and writing activities for their elementary partners or, in the case of two of the students, eventually dropped out. Elton didn't give up, however, and came to enjoy his newfound status as a role model and "expert" reader for Angelo.

Because Elton and Angelo both had a strong interest in American football, much of what they read and wrote about was on that topic. Ruby helped Elton find appropriately difficult, high-interest reading material. They enjoyed biographies of great New York Giants players from the past, such as Harry Carson, Frank Gifford, and Lawrence Taylor. They kept an electronic scrapbook of the Giants' performance that season, reading online newspaper stories and cutting and pasting pictures of their favorite players into the scrapbook. Along with these, they wrote captions, statistics, and bits of trivia from players' records.

While cutting out a photo of the Giants' premier linebacker, B.J. Goodson, also known to fans as The Ironman, Angelo seemed in awe about his powerful 6'1", 242-pound physique, wondering out loud how he got so muscular and strong. Using the Internet, Elton looked for more information on that topic. Because the cross-age tutoring sessions were held in the elementary school's media center, computers were available throughout the large open room.

Ruby helped get their search started using descriptors such as "football players training," and they found pages of sites concerned with bodybuilding and fitness. What caught Elton's eye, however, were references to performance-enhancement drugs. Ruby helped them locate sites with straightforward, objective information about these supplements, which they printed for reading later. Ruby made suggestions to Elton about the best way to share this information with Angelo. Her concern was that it wasn't presented in a way that could unintentionally glorify drug use. Elton assured her he was going to "set him straight about that junk."

Under Ruby's watchful eye, Elton planned how he would read, write, and talk about performance-enhancement drugs in the next few sessions. Her own research yielded a book on the topic for young adolescents titled *Dunks, Doubles, Doping: How Steroids Are Killing American Athletics* (Jendricks, 2006), which she found in the high school's library. The information in Jendricks's book is presented in a colorful, easy-to-understand format, with many illustrative photographs. She helped Elton develop strategies for sharing selected content from the book that would help Angelo begin to appreciate the drug-free ways of building muscle and stamina for athletic competition.

It was Elton, however, who came up with the idea of a digital activity related to the topic. Aware of Angelo's keen interest in computers, he developed a plan for taking a closer look at the characters from popular computer games. His plan was inspired by reading that one of the most common pastimes among many American football players when on the road or during the off-season was playing such games as "Manhunt" (Rockstar North), "Thrill Kill" (Virgin Interactive), "Gears of War" (Microsoft Corporation), and "Mortal Kombat" (Midway Games). Typically, the heroes and villains in these games are exaggeratedly muscled in ways that football players and bodybuilders must envy and, perhaps, strive to resemble. Demonstrating once again for Ruby his ability to reason critically, Elton saw how these images might influence certain athletes to do whatever it takes, including using drugs, to achieve unusual physiques.

With Ruby's help and assistance from the elementary school media specialist, Elton and Angelo used the Internet to find pictures of computer game figures from the games popular with football players. These pictures were then downloaded and altered using popular image-modification software. Elton and Angelo learned how to rework the main characters' physiques, reshaping them in ways that were more proportional to normal muscle development. They displayed their work in a slideshow presentation with "before" slides, accompanied by captions warning of the dangers of steroids and other illegal substances for building muscle, and "after" slides with statements about good health, diet, and fitness. Proud of the brief slideshow they had created, Elton and Angelo were given special opportunities to share the slides with other students in the cross-age tutoring program. The elementary school's principal was so impressed she made sure the slides were shown to the children during drug awareness events that year.

Ruby was pleased that the reading buddy relationship was a confirmed success for both Elton and Angelo. For Angelo, he gained valuable print experiences around purposeful, meaningful uses of literacy. In addition, he benefited from regular interaction with an older boy who, as a role model, helped Angelo recognize that reading and writing can be naturally integrated into a boy's male identity. At the same time, for Elton, agency and efficacy as a reader increased, factors that contributed to an overall improvement in his academic performance and his decision to remain in school that year. And in an interview with Ruby at the conclusion of the program, Elton even expressed possible interest in becoming a teacher – something unthinkable before his experiences as a reading buddy.

It has been shown that when boys' preferences for alternatives to traditionally formatted print texts are honored within the classroom, their engagement and achievement increases (Johnson & Gooliaff, 2013). Additionally, teachers have explored alternative ways of delivering literacy curricula to boys (Sanford & Madill, 2007). Teachers can discover the literate practices male youth engage in with alternative texts beyond the classroom walls and weave boys' interest in, and use of, these texts into their instructional routines (Van Duinen & Vriend Malu, 2015). Youth media, such as music, interactive websites, computer and video games, and graphic novels or comic books can be bridges to academic literacy and learning (Brozo, 2017; Diamond & Gaier Knapik, 2014; Guzzetti, Elliott, & Welsch, 2010). As a result, boys are more eager to read and respond to these texts.

Cross-Age Reading Buddies: Mando and Rickey

Think about how atypical the following scene is. Mando, a 15-year-old Hispanic American in a taut, white sleeveless undershirt that exposes his muscular shoulders and arms, and Rickey, a 6-year-old Latino child, sit on the front stoop of Rickey's house ... reading a book together. Mando has a crew cut, and his left forearm bears the name of his current or former sweetheart Delia. It is a muggy, hot summer morning in Corpus Christi, Texas, USA, but these boys are being real "cool" sharing Rickey's favorite story, *Where the Wild Things Are* (Sendak, 1988), which was also made into a feature motion picture (Jonze & Hanks, 2009). As Mando reads, with Rickey leaning in closely, he points to each word and invites Rickey to read along or say the words on his own. They soon finish the story for the second time, and Mando heads down the street to join his buddies, who are on their way to the park with a basketball. Rickey puts down the book and reaches for the large metal dump truck beside him, zooming it across the porch.

This is Molina, the same neighborhood with the middle school where the Real Men unit took place that I described in Chapter 3. Gangs are down the street, crack houses are around the corner, pit bulls pace menacingly behind chicken-wire fences, and some men sleep off drug or alcohol binges or congregate on street corners, throwing dice and drinking from bottles in paper bags. What makes Mando so special? He was in a buddy reading program the previous year. His English teacher, Maria, paired Mando with Rickey to help him learn to read; she also knew that they lived on the same block. Twice a week, Mando practiced his reading skills and thought more seriously about what it takes to be a good reader, while Rickey had the opportunity to see a "big, tough boy" reading, to read along with him, and to talk about stories with him. Mando, who also has three younger sisters, took a shine to this young *vato* (loosely translated as "close buddy").

Because Rickey lived nearby, Mando continued reading with him a couple of days a week during the summer. Mando knew Rickey's mother and realized she was trying to raise five children on her own while working as a waitress six days a week at Rinconcitos, a Mexican restaurant in Molina. Every concerned adult can exploit adolescent boys' desires to be respected by creating situations in which they can provide reading and learning guidance for younger boys.

Practical knowledge and research evidence lend credence to this learning-by-teaching model. Through years of scientific investigation, for example, it has been proven that when students generate their own learning, it is more permanent and meaningful (Hanke, 2012). In other words, when students become teachers, as in Mando's case, they generate learning for themselves and others.

Cross-Age Reading Buddies: Antoine and Thomas

In homes where the father is absent, older boys often take on the role of surrogate dad (Dance, 2001). Evidently, mothers who do not have husbands often groom their older sons for parent-like responsibilities to share the chores of raising other children (Silverstein & Rashbaum, 1995). Although child psychologists have voiced caution about mothers who expect their sons to be father substitutes, one extremely helpful role an adolescent boy can play in a single-parent household is that of a model and encourager of reading and learning. Teachers can work with concerned individuals outside of the family to help boys find buddies for shared reading opportunities. Coaches, pastors, and recreation counselors can bring older and younger boys together through reading.

This is precisely what Daniel, a youth center volunteer, was able to do after talking with a local junior high school teacher who made the suggestion. When the boys who showed up to use the basketball courts were forced indoors because of rain, wind, or chill, Daniel urged the older boys to read with the younger ones. The center has a television, shelves full of board games, and several portable tables. Daniel made certain that there were plenty of paperback books on hand as well. Although there is only one rickety bookcase, usually crammed with books, Daniel stores others in cardboard boxes and milk crates. Daniel explained how he kept such a steady supply of books for a relatively small cost: "I lose 10 or so books a month, but I consider that to be a good problem . . . It usually means kids are taking the books home and reading them. I buy them for almost nothing at garage sales and Goodwill stores. The library has donated discarded books . . . so most of them are giveaways anyway. Some of the guys will ask me if they can have a book, and I always say it's OK."

Daniel proceeded to describe how he encourages, but never forces, the children to read. He hopes to connect boys who are trying to make good choices with others, both young and old, doing the same. Daniel has watched many such relationships form. For example, 15-year-old Antoine is often seen playing with and mentoring 8-year-old Thomas. Both boys are growing up without their fathers. Their relationship started when they began reading *Trino's Choice* together (Gonzalez-Bertrand, 1999).

While monitoring the center, Daniel spends as much time as feasible reading. As he terms it, he is a "born-again" reader, and he wants the kids to see him enjoying books. He loved *Trino's Choice* because it takes place in San Antonio, the city of his birth. He was brought to remember many of the same troubles that Trino experiences, such as growing up without an adult male's guidance, living in poverty, being constantly threatened by gangs, and just squeaking by in school. As Daniel said, "It was easy for me to sell this book because I lived the life, and it was hard getting out. These boys around here, especially the teenagers, all have problems at home and at school. Most don't have dads living with them. They can barely pay their bills. They live in Section 8 housing [federally subsidized] that's crowded, noisy, and not the best place for a young man to feel good about himself."

Antoine and Thomas were hooked by the first chapter and returned to the center nearly every day for a while to read it. Antoine asked Daniel to keep the book with him, so it would be there when they came back. The book eventually disappeared from the center's collection altogether, but no one is complaining – except the other boys who have heard about it and now want to read it. Daniel plans to replace the missing copy because, "What's special about the story is it's realistic and it shows how a kid . . . can decide to stay out of trouble and make something of himself. I tell these kids that even if they feel they were born with bad luck, they can give themselves a chance for something better . . . but it's up to them. Being a good reader is the way I finally made it out, so I know it can really help." Because he stands up against criminality and turns courageously toward positive influences, Trino offers readers an image of masculinity sorely missing in the lives of too many male youth from low-income high-crime environments.

Family Book Club

Bargaining with after-dinner cleanup was worth it to single mom Roberta, whose three adolescent sons hated doing dishes more than any other household chore. Ever since they were old enough to help, Roberta had them clearing the table; wrapping leftovers; and washing, drying, and putting the dishes away. It was becoming more of a struggle every evening, though.

The boys fought her and each other over details and technicalities, made excuses, feigned illnesses, and procrastinated – all in an effort to either lessen the chore or get out of doing it entirely. Roberta was no pushover, however, and managed to get them to finish the job most evenings. Getting the boys to read was another matter altogether. Roberta was not winning this fight. The days when her sons sat on her lap and listened excitedly to stories or fell asleep in her arms to a bedtime story were a faint memory. The boys spurned the idea of leisure-time reading as emphatically as doing dishes. When Rashad, the youngest, was placed in a remedial reading class at the start of junior high, Roberta realized it was time to find ways to get him and his older brothers more involved with reading at home.

Although of modest means, Roberta held the family together on a nurse's income and had been fortunate to have a day shift for the past three years that gave her time in the late afternoons and evenings to be with her sons. She confided her concern about Rashad to a colleague whose son had been in a similar class the year before and had made rapid progress. This prompted Roberta to get in touch with Rashad's reading teacher.

When Lynn, the reading teacher, met Roberta she was immediately struck by her level of commitment to her boys and her dedication to rekindle their long-forgotten love of reading. During the course of their conversation, Lynn asked many questions about Rashad's out-of-school interests. It was then that she discovered Rashad's nemesis – doing dishes. After years of working with parents to find ways of linking literacy to home and community interests and activities, it did not take Lynn long to hit on the idea of offering the boys a reprieve from doing the dishes if they would agree to replace this activity with reading. Like most new ideas, it remained somewhat ill-defined until Roberta could experiment with possible options to see which worked best.

On her first attempt, Roberta had the guys simply read silently from any source they wanted while she did the dishes. This seemed to work for a week or so, but before long, they were finding ways around it by doing homework (which had always been an activity for after-dinner cleanup), complaining about not having anything good to read, or pretending to lose a favorite book, magazine, or newspaper section. Not to be taken advantage of, Roberta used a new strategy in which the boys took turns reading aloud, not unlike a teacher's old reliable, round-robin reading. This, however, could not be sustained for more than a couple of days before boredom set in or resulting in a ridicule match whenever one of them stumbled on a word.

Finally, Roberta decided she needed to be directly involved with the boys' reading and discussions to keep them attentive and involved. Her solution was to let the after-dinner cleanup wait for 30 minutes while she and her sons read together. It worked. The threats of reassigning after-dinner chores if they did not participate in reading dwindled and eventually disappeared as they rediscovered the pleasure of family reading. Before long, Roberta started referring to them as the "Cooper Book Club," and the name stuck.

Roberta found the material that brought out the best reading and discussion was what the boys selected themselves. Each had his turn, so no one felt left out. Roberta would occasionally introduce something for the boys to consider. Her material was often rejected, although there were significant exceptions. She managed to get articles on health, diet, and nutrition past the Cooper Book Club advisory board. The boys also agreed to read articles about God and spirituality, which were some of Roberta's favorites. In turn, Roberta read articles about sports figures, such as LeBron James and Kevin Durant, and musical stars, such as Drake, Future, and Rihanna. They read anything and everything that was mutually agreeable, regardless of the source. For example, new album notes and reviews from the Internet were often part of the after-dinner discussions, as were sports trading cards the boys would convince Roberta to buy when shopping at American discount department stores, such as Walmart or Target. No one would judge these sources as quality literature; however, simply getting her boys back into the habit of reading for enjoyment was most important to Roberta.

Roberta noticed other benefits that came with her boys' reading habits. For example, dinner conversation was usually centered on what the family was currently reading or about to read; thus, as a result of the Cooper Book Club, there was an increase in text-related conversation between the boys and their mother. This is not an insignificant aspect of Roberta's efforts. Schwarzschild (2000) says that, despite the seeming banality of family mealtime, "Quality mealtime conversation between parents and children has been shown to increase children's mental and verbal abilities ... develop important skills ... such as ... taking turns speaking, and listening to the person talking. Meals are one of the best times for children to pick up new words. Kids whose families chat most during mealtimes have larger word inventories" (p. 95). Similar language benefits of family mealtime have been reconfirmed in recent research (Fruh, Fulkerson, Kendrick, & Clanton, 2011).

In addition to increasing languaging about texts, quality mealtime conversation between parents and children has been shown to reinforce family unity (Fulkerson et al., 2009; Larson, Wiley, & Branscomb, 2006). Another potential bonus of the dinnertime book club is the way youth begin associating a pleasurable time in their day, in this case eating, with literacy (Hamilton & Wilson, 2009). In Roberta's sons' minds, the pleasing aromas, tastes, and general atmosphere of mealtime have become connected in a positive way to reading, discussing, and sharing. How different these connections are when compared with the all-too-frequent negative associations many boys have with school-based reading because of stale instruction, unappealing texts, or fear of humiliation in a setting that places their vulnerability on the line virtually every day.

The Cooper Book Club ultimately heightened the boys' awareness of books. In the past, for example, they would walk down the supermarket aisle that held books and magazines or past the entrance to a mall bookstore and not notice either. Roberta's sons were now giving these places a second glance. In fact, the family discovered the novel *Hoops* (Myers, 1999) as a result of a mall bookstore's display of Walter Dean Myers's (2000) novel *Monster*, which caught Rashad's eye. Roberta found *Hoops* to be a perfect match for her sons, who were basketball-playing, LeBron James wannabes. Rashad and his brothers could not get enough of this story and were ready to reread it as soon as they had finished. Roberta wisely acquiesced, reasoning that, like the desire to watch a great movie again, a great book deserves to be read more than once.

When Roberta had first come to Lynn about her concerns for Rashad, Lynn, a former student of mine, told Roberta about my reading clinic. Roberta did contact me about nine months before the clinic, but I did not have any openings for new clients. By the time I contacted her to let her know of an opening in the clinic, Roberta, to my delight, graciously turned down my offer for the best of reasons. She explained that Rashad was improving his reading scores, which Roberta credited in large part to the help he was getting from Lynn and his new recreational reading habit.

Socioeconomics and Boys: A Coda

What this chapter makes clear is that boys in poverty are at a particularly high risk of becoming struggling readers, losing their way academically, dropping out of school, becoming underemployed or unemployed, and finding themselves marginalized socially and economically throughout their lives. Although all children and youth suffer from the deleterious effects associated with growing up in low-income households and communities, boys appear to be the most vulnerable. As compared with their female counterparts, boys from poverty have a higher incidence of reading and learning problems, are more likely to drop out of school, have higher rates of incarceration, and are less likely to find gainful employment (Payne & Slocumb, 2011).

Given what we know about the constrained academic and life chances for boys from the lowest economic strata in society, it is essential that we do all we can to enrich their literacy development both at home and school. Encouraging parents and guardians to remain involved in boys' lives and creating frequent opportunities for boys to interact with mentors and reading buddies in school and outside of school hold promise for building reading and cognitive skills as well as instilling the motivation needed to achieve academically.

CHAPTER 5

Immigrant and New Language Learner Boys: Evidence and Practice

> **In this chapter, I**
> - Explore relevant findings from PIRLS and PISA related to immigrants, new language learners, and literacy challenges
> - Analyze evidence related to male youth who are immigrants and new language learners
> - Describe successful and promising programs and practices

I have emphasized throughout this book that certain boys and male youth are at a heightened risk of reading and academic failure. I assert, therefore, that it is on behalf of these vulnerable boys that we should exert our most strenuous efforts, even while remaining vigilant to ways of gaining and keeping all boys interested in reading. Male youth who are immigrants and who may be new learners of their host country's language present unique literacy needs that deserve special consideration. The academic well-being of immigrant youth, including boys, in the United States and Canada has been the focus of concern for many researchers and advocates (Gluszynski & Dhawan-Biswal, 2008; Leventhal, Xue, & Brooks-Gunn, 2006; Ma, 2003; Perriera, Kiang, & Potochnick, 2013; Qin, 2006; Santiago, Gudino, Baweja, & Nadeem, 2014; Suarez-Orozco & Qin, 2005). Moreover, the immigrant gap was identified by the High Level Group of Literacy Experts in Europe (2012) as one of the four major gaps that required narrowing, if the continent was to prosper in the twenty-first century.

In Chapter 2, I introduced evidence in support of the contention that boys who are learning another language exhibit more challenges and have lower performance on assessments of verbal ability than language learning girls. In this chapter, I take a deeper dive into this topic to explore further the nature and implications of these differences. I first lay out the case for devoting extra attention to the literacy development of immigrant and new language learner boys, and, like the two preceding chapters, follow this with descriptions of practical programs and practices targeted to these boys.

Immigrant Youth: Evidence from PISA and PIRLS

As I begin this section, it is important to remind ourselves that immigrant students often have needs in addition to those related to language learning. Beyond linguistic considerations, these students are equally likely to face challenges related to overall cultural adjustment, identity negotiation, peer group assimilation, economic hardship, and more (Compton-Lilly & Nayan, 2016; Hilburn, 2014; Yoon, 2012). Furthermore, studies of US native and foreign-born immigrant students demonstrate how these multiple challenges leave males particularly vulnerable to academic failure and dropping out (Roosa et al., 2009). This is an all-too-common phenomenon for Latino boys, who have higher rates of behavioral problems and are referred for disciplinary offenses far more often relative to girls while exhibiting poorer performance on most markers of educational achievement (American Psychological Association, Presidential Task Force on Educational Disparities, 2012). Latino boys, it would appear, seem to need to maintain connections to their culture of origin while learning to accommodate to and adopt dominant culture values (Gonzales et al., 2008). In addition, parental monitoring may be a critical factor in immigrant Latino boys' school-based achievement (Bacallao & Smokowski, 2005; Dennis, Basañez, & Farahmand, 2005).

It makes sense, then, for teachers and other concerned professionals to regard immigrant boys holistically and to pay attention to issues of personal, interpersonal, and acculturative stress, even while attempting to bolster their language and literacy skills and foster academic success.

With respect to PISA and PIRLS, major studies have been undertaken that unpack data from these two influential international assessments of reading literacy concerned specifically with the performance of immigrants, as well as variables with the strongest influence on their scores.

Andon (2012), for example, conducted a broad-level quantitative analysis of the immigrant achievement gap using data from PIRLS, involving multiple student, school, and country variables. One of her overarching findings that corroborates evidence from similar research for adolescent populations is that students who were native born, with native parents, whose parents had higher education levels and SES, and whose mother tongue was the same as the language of the test scored significantly better than their immigrant counterparts. Thus, it came as no surprise to discover that second generation immigrants outperformed first generation immigrants. The explanation is that, because those students' parents were native born and likely to be more fluent in the host country's language, they could transfer this competence to their children. An additional finding from Andon's comprehensive study points to the fact that immigrants were more likely than their native counterparts to attend lower-quality schools and this predicted lower reading literacy achievement. Conversely, those immigrants attending high-achieving schools were more likely to have higher achievement. Finally, and perhaps most disturbing, was the finding that countries with the least friendly immigrant policies and those with the greatest socioeconomic disparities tended to have larger immigrant achievement gaps.

In Chiu, Chow, and Mcbride-Chang's (2007) analysis of data from the PISA 2000 study, which included about 160 thousand participants, they discovered what has come to be a common theme: students who were native born, spoke the language of the country at home, came from higher SES families and attended school with higher SES students had significantly better reading literacy scores than those without these test-favorable characteristics.

A Canadian study of the differences in reading literacy achievement on PISA 2009 between immigrant and non-immigrant students found immigrant youth scored on average 24 points lower than their native Canadian counterparts (Gluszynski & Dhawan-Biswal, 2008). This translates into approximately one-half year of schooling. An encouraging result revealed in the analysis was that first generation students scored virtually as well as their native peers, suggesting that home and school supports in Canada are effective in elevating academic achievement for students from immigrant parents. Similar to Andon's finding, Canadian youth whose language spoken at home matched the language of the PISA test, regardless of their immigrant status, scored higher than those whose home language was not the same as the test language. The researchers identified Canadian students who were at the greatest disadvantage on PISA: those who were born outside of the country, who had lived in Canada for fewer than five years, and whose home language was not the test language. For this group, their average score was nearly 22 points below the OECD average of 500.

In another study of Canadian youths' performance on PISA, Ma (2003) analyzed data from the 2000 cycle and confirms findings from international literacy assessments in that country and elsewhere: non-immigrant students outperformed immigrant students in reading literacy. Ma also found school level variables, such as teacher-student ratio, teacher morale, and academic pressure were predictors of immigrant students' reading achievement. Important lessons might be drawn from these relationships. For instance, immigrant students are likely to perform best in classes with fewer students and where teachers can give them the extra attention they need. It also suggests when teachers exhibit positive attitudes about reading and create an atmosphere for learning that is appropriately challenging, immigrant students will achieve to their potential.

In virtually all European OECD countries, immigrant students had lower performance than native students in reading on PISA 2009 (OECD, 2012). The gap is as high as 60 points and even larger in countries like Finland, Austria, Belgium, Denmark, and France. This equates to at least a year and a half of schooling lag for immigrant students. Additionally, immigrant students comprise only 5 percent of the high-achievers on PISA reading, while representing a far greater percentage than their numbers should warrant among the low-achievers on the assessment. Indeed, for every non-immigrant low performer there are two low-performing immigrant students. Moreover, immigrant students who are late arrivals, in their host country for fewer than five years, suffer an additional penalty of 20 score points when compared with those in their adopted country for five or more years (Heath & Kilpi-Jakonen, 2012).

In reality, countries in Europe with increasing numbers of immigrants are facing unprecedented challenges (OECD, 2012). In Sweden today, for example, there has been a 5 percent increase in immigrant children, or over 70 thousand minors, among the 163,000 asylum seekers who have entered that country since 2006. Like so many other nations, Sweden has struggled to bring these non-native, non-host-language-speaking youth up to speed academically. And over the past ten years, Sweden's PISA reading scores have reflected these challenges, as the country has seen a drop of more than 20 points. The last decade also saw Sweden's overall reading score go from parity with the OECD average of 500 to 20 percent lower, resulting in a ranking of 27th in reading literacy among the 34 participating OECD countries.

Gender Differences in Academic Achievement for Immigrant Youth

In the United States, numerous studies have explored differences in language and reading ability among immigrant groups and between immigrant and native students. Leventhal and his colleagues (2006) compared verbal ability in English for students between the ages of 6 and 16 from various immigrant and non-immigrant groups. One overarching finding consistent with findings from the other research cited here is that immigrant students in the study had consistently lower verbal scores compared with their non-immigrant peers. And, not surprisingly, immigrant students' verbal scores were higher if from families with greater resources, another pattern often observed in the literature on this theme.

Evidence for immigrant girls' academic superiority over immigrant boys reminds us that the gender-based achievement gap appears to cut across racial/ethnic groups. Santiago and her colleagues (2014) looked at immigrant and non-immigrant Latino students and factors that either supported or placed at risk their academic achievement. Higher achievement was more likely for the females in the study, as well as those students with higher levels of English proficiency, and those with parents who closely monitored their outside-of-school time and behavior. Perriera, Kiang, and Potochnick (2013) also explored differences between Latino immigrant boys' and girls' academic achievement relative to perceived ethnic discrimination. The researchers documented the particularly potent effects perceived discrimination has on boys, though the effect was minimal or non-existent on girls, a finding consistent with previous research (Alfaro et al., 2009). Latino immigrant boys who felt discriminated against exhibited lower academic motivation and school-based performance compared to their female counterparts. Results such as these reinforce the need to focus special attention on boys' resiliency and their motivation for learning as these factors may contribute to their academic success.

Qin (2006) distilled the research evidence showing immigrant girls have superior educational achievement than immigrant boys. Four key variables were identified to explain gender differences favoring immigrant girls in academic performance. Qin asserts that after migration, parents set higher expectations for daughters to be successful at school. She also suggests boys experience more difficulty accommodating to the social culture of school. Furthermore, male immigrant students are more constrained by issues of gender identity formation than girls, which distracts them from, and may conflict with, focusing on their academic development. Qin expresses concern around this evidence, as she acknowledges gender may be a key factor in the future adaptation and mobility of new generations of immigrants. Qin's claims, based on analysis of the research literature, strongly suggest that immigrant boys' depressed educational achievement will put them at a disadvantage in adulthood by limiting their social and economic mobility.

Dronkers and Kornder (2014) analyzed the gender differences between the achievement of 15-year-old children of migrants from specific regions of origin countries living in different destination countries using the results from PISA 2009. The researchers were concerned about whether the pattern of gender differences among this group of migrant students differed from the pattern for native students in their destination country. Reading achievement data for 33 thousand male and female students of migrant parents were analyzed. The findings were consistent with the overall pattern on PISA of female superiority in reading. However, the gender differences in favor of females among migrant students was even larger than among comparable native students.

Gender Differences in New Language Learning

As Carr and Pauwels (2006) observe, in the English speaking nations of the world, where foreign language offerings in school are optional, boys are rare participants, indeed. This may not be a new situation, according to the authors, but the disappearance of boys in foreign language classrooms and programs dominated by female students and teachers has become increasingly concerning in our modern global society. Youth in the twenty-first century are expected to become global citizens with intercultural competencies, including multilingual skills. Those who are monolingual and monocultural could become the new "at risk" (Lapp & Fisher, 2011). Boys who fail to develop skills in an adopted nation's language or another dominant global language will find themselves at an increasing disadvantage. And there's an economic dimension to multilingualism, as Hogan-Brun (2017) points out. He describes a female Syrian refugee to Quebec, Canada, who quickly learns French to assimilate in the local culture, but also acquires English, the dominant language of Canada and the lingua franca of the world, to improve her position for academic and economic opportunities in the host country and beyond. Thus, boys who fail to expand their language repertoire to the same extent as girls will become increasingly marginalized in the new global economy (Carr & Pauwels, 2006). In the end, says Hogan-Brun (2017) and others (Edwards, 2012; Extra & Yagmur, 2012; Grin, Sfreddo, & Vaillancourt, 2010; Saiz & Zoido, 2005), linguistic diversity may require sizable effort on the policy and implementation fronts, but the opportunities it affords can be considerable.

Other studies of Canadian youth add to the case made by Carr and Pauwels (2006), who assert boys are far less likely than girls to study and develop fluency in another language. Kissau and Turnbull (2008) found males in their study were less motivated to study French, did not perform as well, and dropped out of French language courses at a much higher rate as compared with females.

These disparities in interest and engagement in language learning between boys and girls may be indicative of the traditional instructional routines employed by language teachers. Pavy (2006) reports on the results of studies exploring boys' lack of interest in language learning, and the boys' descriptions of the language classroom points to the likely cause – a highly traditional approach to teaching, dominated by grammar and translation, and textbook focused. This reality stands in sharp contrast to the kind of learning environment the boys preferred, such as learner-centered, contextualized learning, oriented around authentic communication and meaningful language activities. Thus, the author urges a closer exploration of the reasons young men are failing to be inspired to continue with language learning once it is no longer compulsory.

Whether boys are not putting in the necessary effort due to disinterest or, as we have seen, find language learning more challenging than other inside or outside school pursuits, data point to their generally lower levels of achievement. Studies of gender differences in learning English as an additional language demonstrate repeatedly girls' superior acquisition of vocabulary, greater oral and written fluency, and better reading comprehension (Abdorahimzadeh, 2014; Babayiğit, 2015; Brantmeier, 2003; Heinzmann, 2009). For example, gender was a key variable in learning English as a foreign language in Glowka's (2014) study of secondary school students in Poland. Arguing that girls possess something like a predisposition to accepting new linguistic forms in the target language that allows them to reconcile interlanguage differences (Ellis, 2012), the researcher gathered data showing girls had significantly higher achievement than their male counterparts. Based on the strength of the data, Glowka urges teachers of language to become more sensitive to the specific learning needs of boys. Specifically, she recommends the use of instructional practices that increase boys' motivation, confidence, and performance, such as helping boys develop organizational strategies and incorporating texts with everyday expressions and even slang for learning language. Recommendations are also offered to policy makers to officially acknowledge the role of gender in foreign language learning.

Rua (2006), too, finds empirical support for girls possessing neurological and cognitive tools that give them an edge in foreign language learning. It is posited that these advantages are enhanced by social and educational conditions that interact to produce higher achievement for girls. Thus, Rau asserts, "girls are equipped with a combined network of variables whose mutual influence is eventually responsible for their success in foreign language learning" (p. 99).

In general, researchers of vocabulary knowledge development for language learners have concluded that females are more capable than males of employing effective word-learning strategies, producing written texts with a wider lexical range, and generating contextual meanings of words (Jiménez & Ojeda, 2008; Sunderland, 2010). Typical of this line of research is the work of Llach and Gallego (2012), who determined the gender-based differential in acquisition of receptive vocabulary for Spanish students learning English. The longitudinal study spanned grades four through nine and tracked vocabulary growth of a single cohort of participants from year to year and between boys and girls. Both genders increased their word knowledge as they progressed through the grades, but the females demonstrated higher levels of vocabulary acquisition, especially for the first three years of the study.

Arellano's (2013) related study of Spanish adolescent boys and girls explored gender differences in reading comprehension of English at the conclusion of the study subjects' fourth and final year of compulsory secondary education. Using school-based test results and teacher marks, the author concluded that female ESL students had overall significantly higher comprehension achievement scores on English assessments compared with their male classmates. In addition, the females in the study showed superior performance in gathering specific and general information from English texts, understanding text structure, and inferring meaning from context.

In the United States, Martinez, Slate, and Martinez-Garcia (2014) tapped into the large Texas database of state reading test scores to examine whether there were significant differences in achievement between English language learner boys and girls from grades three to six. The researchers linked gender-based reading performance to the length of time students spent in bilingual programs, asserting, as others have (Tong et al., 2008), that developing English language proficiency and academic success for English learners requires years in these programs. Consistent with findings from most other related studies, Martinez and her colleagues found girls overwhelmingly outperformed their male peers on the reading portion of the state test. There were, however, no consistent patterns in favor of either an early-exit or late-exit bilingual education program, leading the researchers to conclude that, more than the length of time students are in these programs, programs must also be of high quality and responsive to the language development needs of both genders.

And even outside North America and Europe, research has produced results consistent with those cited here, namely, that boys underperform relative to girls in EFL programs and on related assessments (Mady & Seiling, 2017; Osman, 2012; Palancılar, 2017; Piasecka, 2010; Walczak & Geranpayeh, n.d.; Wang, 2015; Zoghi, Kazemi, & Kalani, 2013). Indeed, it appears the gender gap widens as students progress from primary to secondary level (Khamisi et al., 2016). It is important to reflect on how a global pattern of boys' lack of interest in and struggles with learning English is not unlike a global pattern of boy's inferior performance and lower levels of engagement in reading literacy, well documented in this and previous chapters.

The evidence, then, strongly suggests that these parallel challenges boys confront with reading literacy and language learning should lead to the establishment of educational policies that result in more responsive instructional practices and programs for language-learning boys.

In the next section, I share programs and practices designed specifically for immigrant boys and those who are acquiring an additional language or are part of a population of boys receiving targeted language instruction.

Promising Programs and Practices

Developing Language through Discussion

Additional language development, particularly for academic success, depends to a large extent on a foundation of oral language proficiency (Saunders & O'Brien, 2006; Soto-Hinman, 2011). Kieffer (2012) has shown for US Spanish-speaking students, English productive vocabulary in kindergarten predicted achievement levels in English reading through grade eight. Yet, evidence suggests English language learners in American schools receive a miniscule percentage of instruction in oral language development (August & Shanahan, 2006). What's more, this instruction often fails to focus on academic topics and rigorous content (Meltzer & Hamann, 2005; Zwiers & Crawford, 2011). Consequently, the daily language block many additional language learners receive in a typical school day is being seen as inadequate to the academic needs of these students. What makes more sense is to ensure these students experience language-rich instruction throughout the day. One form this can take is discussion around topics and content in every class ELLs have each day (Opitz & Guccione, 2009).

Value Line Discussion
Ruben's social studies class is comprised of students whose home language in Spanish. Several who are first-generation immigrants are receiving English language support from ESOL teachers. Ruben knows full well that his students need sustained opportunities to converse with teachers and peers about the academic content they are expected to learn in his class as well as in their other content area classrooms. To promote this level of focused academic conversation, Ruben employs a discussion activity called value lines (Brozo, 2017; Knight, 2013). This approach to discussion is especially useful when presenting students with content that evokes strong responses and controversy or when you want students to take a stand on an issue.

Ruben began by creating a symbolic line in the middle of the classroom by stretching a long strip of colored paper on the floor from one wall to the opposite wall. He told his students to listen to the statements he was about to read and asked them to move to the right side of the line if they agreed with it and the left side if they disagreed. Ruben's statements included the following:

- Cesar Chavez did the right thing by not using weapons and violence to lead our people.
- Good leaders like Cesar Chavez teach their people to fight with their minds, not their fists.
- When people are being treated badly by government or business they have a right to use nonviolent means to make things better.
- I have the kind of qualities that would make me a good leader of my people.

Once each statement was read, students moved to one side of the line or other. Then Ruben directed his students to face another person on their side of the line and discuss why they agreed or disagreed with the statement. After about a minute, he had students converse with someone across the line to share why they believed the way they did. At different times, Ruben asked pairs of opposing conversants to give their opinions and ideas for everyone to hear. As he monitored discussion, Ruben encouraged respectful disagreements and polite arguing.

Every statement spawned lively discussion in Ruben's classroom. For example, in response to the statement about possessing leadership qualities, Omar told Enrique, his partner across the value line, that because he led his gang in a war with a rival gang to settle a dispute over drug turf, and his gang won, he thought he could be a good leader Enrique countered that holding on to turf wasn't good for their people if it meant bad drugs stayed in the neighborhood and more kids got hooked. Overhearing this exchange, Ruben did not ridicule this pair of students, but redirected their discussion by asking Omar and Enrique whether Omar's gang activity would have been endorsed by someone like Chavez.

By using the value line discussion strategy, students in Ruben's class were able to look more critically at which of Chavez's qualities brought about nonviolent leadership and reflect on the appropriateness of their own leadership behaviors. More critically, these English language learners had engaging conversations about a complex topic, giving them all a chance to exercise and expand their speaking and listening vocabularies.

Another strategy Ruben employs to stimulate his students' productive vocabularies is to display additional books that depict characters from fiction or real life who are related to the social studies topics being explored in his class. These books typically vary in level of difficulty from easy (plenty of pictures and photographs) to more challenging (novels and historical biographies). Students are required to make oral presentations comparing and contrasting historical figures.

In one instance, after reading the short picture book *Jackie Robinson* (Schraff, 2008), Philipé, whose English language skills are at a basic level, shared how both Chavez and Robinson were told by Anglos they couldn't have what they had. And they both fought hard for their people and for respect. Robinson was black and Chavez was Mexican but the people looked up to them. After Robinson, black people could play baseball with white people. After Chavez, Mexicans had more rights.

Jiamé, one of the more accomplished readers in Ruben's class, took on a much longer biography – *The Tall Mexican: The Life of Hank Aguirre All-Star Pitcher, Businessman, Humanitarian* (Copley, 2000). Jaimé shared the following:

> Like Cesar Chavez, Hank Aguirre grew up in poverty. He had to make thousands of tortillas every day for his father's little restaurant. This must have given him a strong arm because he became a great pitcher. Aguirre was like Chavez because, even though he got famous, he never forgot about his people. This guy, Robert Copley, who wrote the book was a good friend of Aguirre, and he told a lot of really neat things about him. When Aguirre quit

playing baseball, he wanted to help our people, so he set up a business called Mexican Industries. It made a lot of money, and he gave jobs to Latinos, blacks, and people of other minorities.

Academic discussions such as those prompted and supported by content area teachers like Ruben are an important facet of effective instruction for all students but especially for those first- and second-generation boys acquiring an additional language, because, as we have seen, their struggles with language development are well documented. These students need opportunities throughout the school day to hear more proficient language users like teachers and advanced peers and express their own understandings and perspectives with meaningful and content-specific vocabulary (Lesaux, Kieffer, Faller, & Kelley, 2010; Proctor, Dalton, & Grisham, 2007; Taboada & Rutherford, 2011).

Boys in the Real World

"Ahmed"

Ahmed is a ten-year-old boy in fourth grade. He was born in the United States and his parents immigrated from Morocco. He has grown up bilingual speaking both Arabic at home and English at school. Ahmed has received services to support him in learning English at school. In his early education – in kindergarten, first, and second grade – Ahmed struggled with reading but he is now reading on grade level and really enjoys reading.

Outside of school Ahmed likes to play sports and read. He says he enjoys basketball, swimming, and soccer. He reports enjoying books about adventure. He said there was a specific book called *My Brother's a Superhero*. He explained that the book was about a boy who was kind of jealous of his brother and related to this because he said he sometimes felt jealous of his sister. He really related to the main character in this book and he lit up as he described his connection to the character. Ahmed said one of his favorite sports outside of school was going swimming with his dad.

Ahmed went on to describe how he finds a quiet corner in his house to read. He described reading adventure stories that made him feel like he was experiencing what the characters experience in the stories he reads. He said with excitement that, for example, in one story he read, he felt like a dinosaur was chasing him. Ahmed said when he reads, "I feel like I'm inside the story running with him," as he referred to a character running from a dinosaur.

Ahmed described himself as a good reader who likes to read books about adventures. Ahmed did not report doing any reading on-line. He said reading is not hard or easy but that he likes reading when it is just right. He

also said he thinks reading is important. He said he reads at home when he thinks he has played too many video games or watched too much TV.
I asked Ahmed about what video games he liked to play and he reported liking a game called Slither.io where, as a worm, you tried to avoid being eaten.

When I asked Ahmed to tell me about a book he got really excited about he went to the superhero book mentioned earlier. He said there was a second book, *My Gym Teacher Is a Superhero*. He said he saved some money and asked his dad to buy him this book from the school book fair. He said he was super excited to get this book. He said he likes to read by himself and that he and his friends don't talk about books at school. He said, at school, if he is reading next to friends and they are talking, he tells them to be quiet so he can read.

Ahmad said he loves to write. He said, "when I read stories I imagine the stories coming all together and that's how I write my story." He talked about a story called *Stone Rabbit* and he tied that story to another story. He explained he "Tried to picture the new story in his head." He also said he like to write mystery stories and that in his stories you would know what would happen next and that "You'd be on the edge of your seat." He also said, "It feels nice when I just sit down and write. I get to put what I imagine on the page."

Discussion and Activities

- What recommendations can you offer to teachers working with Ahmed to ensure his enthusiasm for reading and writing continue to be nurtured?
- How can Ahmed's interests in sports be exploited for further literacy skill and vocabulary development?
- In what ways can teachers take advantage of the kinds of books Ahmed enjoys to further his reading and writing abilities?

Texts Related to Immigrant and Language Learning Boys' Outside-of-School Interests

Guthrie (2008) points to a number of causes for student antipathy toward learning, such as lack of intellectual challenge or lack of understanding about how to apply their learning. Teachers who are able to reverse academic antipathy champion classrooms that promote active learning, employ a student-centered curriculum, and, above all, capitalize on student interests. Teachers will never make significant progress eradicating boys' difficulty with reading and language development unless they dedicate themselves to discovering boys' interests and acquainting boys with quality and accessible texts related to those interests.

For teachers working with boys who are new language learners and who are likely struggling to read and comprehend texts in the adopted country's language, it may be unproductive to ask them a question like "What do you like to read?" More often than not, these male youth will have very little to say to such a question. Why? The majority of them would not be receiving special reading and TESOL services if they were avid and engaged readers of their adopted country's texts. Thus, this direct approach to discovering what new language learners who may be struggling readers like to read may do little more than reconfirm their status as a weak reader or a nonreader. An oblique approach to finding appropriate texts for boys who are additional language learners that involves first discovering what their interests are outside of school and then introducing them to reading materials related to those interests is likely to be better. One such approach is called the *My Bag*.

Using the My Bag to Match Boys with Text

The Texas Coastal Bend is not known for its beaches the way California, Hawaii, or Florida is. To a hardcore group of young sailboarding junkies, however, the wind-tossed waters off Padre and Mustang Islands offer an undiscovered paradise. Delfino's interest in windsurfing came to my attention when he shared his My Bag with me on the night when his reading tutor was absent. At the time, I was director of the reading center at Texas A&M University in Corpus Christi, Texas, USA, which provided diagnostic and tutorial services to children and adolescents from the local community.

Delfino, I learned from conversations with him and from his file, came from a family of Mexican immigrants who arrived in south Texas from Monterey when he was 12. His parents only spoke Spanish. They lived with an uncle who had been in the United States for many years and had started his own landscaping business. Four years later, Delfino was still receiving TESOL services at his school. Although his English conversational skills had progressed rapidly, his reading and academic language skills lagged behind. For these reasons, his TESOL teacher recommended him for participation in our reading center.

I've been using the My Bag strategy for many years as a way of getting to know students. It allows them to showcase their strengths, loves, hobbies, and dreams. The strategy involves placing items in a bag or some other comparable container (Delfino used his backpack.). The decision-making process used to select items for the bag forces students to think critically about themselves and about how certain items symbolize different aspects of their life. An alternative is to create a digital My Bag with personal and Internet-available photos, symbols, emojis, illustrations, and even video links.

I began working with Delfino that evening by sharing items from the My Bag that I keep in my office and update regularly. My approach is to take items from the bag and use them as prompts for other students to ask questions. I do this instead of a show-and-tell, to build questioning strategies and encourage students' displays of genuine interest in their classmates. Delfino asked me several questions when I showed my guitar pick, such as how long I had been playing, what kind of music I played and liked, and if I played in a band. He was especially curious about a photo of me running on the beach. After brief conversation that revealed how I try to stay fit by jogging and my fondness for jogging along the Mustang Island shore, Delfino said he knew that beach like the back of his hand. To prove it, he rummaged through his backpack and pulled out a photograph of four teenage boys in wetsuits, standing next to a sailboard. Behind them was Bob Hall Pier, a landmark of that beach. Delfino was one of the boys in the picture. He told me that the other boys were his cousins, who owned the sailboard and had taught him how to windsurf. What happened with Delfino over the course of the semester only reinforces the power of the My Bag strategy to reveal personal information so critical in matching boys' interests with good books and other reading material.

Once I found out how enthusiastic Delfino was about windsurfing, I knew the book he would have to read: *Lockie Leonard, Human Torpedo* (Winton, 1991). The remainder of items from Delfino's My Bag did not include a single book or magazine. In spite of his intense attraction to his hobby, he was not reading about it. I probed Delfino for details about his school life, as I do most young adults who came to the reading center, only to discover that he could not remember a single teacher ever recommending a book for him to read besides his required reading. This is not an isolated story.

I have evaluated numerous reading programs around the United States and have found (particularly at the secondary level where the problem is most acute) that it is rare for students to (a) use school libraries except for required projects, (b) be exposed to alternative text sources beyond the core textbook, and (c) be encouraged simply to read a book for pleasure.

When Delfino returned the following week, I had already decided that I would continue working with him. The anticipation of reading *Lockie*

Leonard together, as a way of garnering Delfino's interest in reading, building his vocabulary and comprehension skills, and deconstructing aspects of teenage masculinity, was too much to pass up. I started by asking Delfino to keep a journal to track his responses to our discussions, as well as his personal reactions, questions, and connections, resulting in a kind of "my life–his life" analysis. Before we even began reading, we both responded to the following journal prompt: When do we feel happiest and most in control? I no sooner got these words out of my mouth before Delfino started writing. He wrote the following in a stream-of-consciousness format:

> That's easy ... for me there's nothing like boarding .... I don't like school that much and I don't like all this football and basketball jock stuff ... but I love being on my board ... there's nothing like it ... you should try it Dr. Brozo ... it's like nothing else matters when you're out there .... You know you can get up to 30 or 40 miles an hour ... that's really fast and you feel it in every part of you .... But sometimes when the water and wind are just right, you could be floating on a magic carpet ... that's what I'm going to name my board and rig when I save enough to buy one, you know, Magic Carpet.

I handed Delfino his copy of *Lockie*, which had Lockie on the cover "hanging ten." A smile came over Delfino's face, acknowledging an instant connection with the book's theme. We read the inside cover together:

> The sun was almost down as he caught his last wave, leaning and cutting across its orange glistening surface as it rolled toward the beach like the twist in a great monster's tail. It hissed behind him. His hand trailed in the smooth, faceless wall; he tossed his head back and hooted as the whole pitching funnel of his insides shot him down the line. He wasn't thinking of anything. He didn't need to. (Winton, 1991)

I then asked Delfino to compare what he had written with this description of Lockie's boarding experiences. He immediately drew a comparison between himself and Lockie by pointing out how he had written "nothing else matters when you're out there," whereas Lockie "wasn't thinking of anything. He didn't need to." "Only those of us who get out on the water on boards understand what we're talking about," Delfino said. Before we had read the first page, he was bonding with his water buddy, Lockie Leonard. Winton (1999) has reprised this character in at least two other novels and *Lockie* was made into a popular television series in Australia. Other teachers and researchers have made *Lockie Leonard* books available to boys and have reported on the life-changing impact the books have had on them (Harders & Macken-Horarik, 2009; Sanderson, 1995).

As we progressed through the book, I asked Delfino to point out passages that resonated for him. For example, in the first chapter he read to me:

> No joke. Lockie Leonard could surf. He was lousy at football. He could be counted on to entirely screw up a cricket match, and he wasn't even any good at Monopoly, but he could sure ride a board. Genuine surf rat ... (p. 12)

Delfino drew my attention to his journal entry again, pointing out how both he and Lockie felt disinterested in popular sports but knew they could handle their boards.

We spent a considerable amount of time each week critiquing other male images in the book. These males included Lockie's father, Sarge, and a variety of "bogans," which is Australian slang for teenage tough guys. We generated a variety of responses with these male characters: we listed their behaviors and qualities; we identified people we personally knew and people we knew from history and popular culture who were similar; and we discussed whether their male behavioral traits were worthy of emulation. Delfino characterized Lockie as wanting to be wild and free, much like himself, and not too complicated. I helped Delfino see that there was more to Lockie than this. For instance, Lockie demonstrates honorable qualities when he refuses to fight with the bogans, escorts his girlfriend away from trouble on the beach, and exercises self-control in the face of his girlfriend's sexual overtures.

When I think back to Delfino and our time with Lockie Leonard, I cannot help but reflect on the importance of connecting boys to books related to their interests. The eighteenth-century French philosopher Rousseau (1979) says in *Emile, or on Education,*

> Reading is the curse of childhood ... A child has no great wish to perfect himself in the use of an instrument of torture, but make it a means to his pleasure, and soon you will not be able to keep him from it ... Present interest, that is the motive power, the only motive power that takes us far and safely. (p. 213)

Delfino, the adolescent boy who had little interest in anything but windsurfing, became reacquainted with books after being introduced to the kindred spirit, Lockie Leonard. Delfino also discovered honesty, humility, and innocence in this fictional character – admirable qualities that he thought worthy of imitation.

Delfino's final journal entry epitomizes the power of books with characters and themes that interest the male reader. Delfino constantly mentioned how he was more eager to read Lockie each week than any other book he had ever encountered. This permeates his final response to the book:

> I still don't like to read much . . . but after *Lockie Leonard*, I like it more than I used to. This was the best book I ever read in my life. It was so cool to read about someone that was a lot like me. Lockie never made a big deal about how much he loved surfing and how good he was at it, but kids gave him a hard time anyway. Only my friends know I windsurf. Even my p.e. [physical education] coach thinks I'm no good at any sport . . . he hasn't seen me on the bay. I wish teachers would let students read stuff they're interested in. If when I was a kid teachers let me read books about surfing and stuff I think I would be a better reader now. I'm going to look for other books about surfing and also tell our librarian to get books on surfing. The next book I'm going to read is the other Lockie Leonard book.

I have shared my experiences with Delfino to demonstrate how I selected *Lockie Leonard, Human Torpedo* through the My Bag strategy. Delfino had already told me that he disliked reading, had low grades in English and most of his other classes, and did not read for pleasure. To have asked Delfino what he likes to read would have yielded little more than negative responses. With the My Bag strategy, however, I discovered that flying through the surf on a sailboard in the Texas Gulf was what made Delfino proud and happy. Only teachers who are concerned about boys' lives outside of the classroom have a chance of successfully engaging them with text, because the texts these teachers choose will directly relate to the boys' life worlds(Baxter & Kochel, 2010; www.guysread.com/). This is particularly important for language learners like Delfino, as they need sustained encounters with the adopted country's language texts in order to expand their word knowledge and understanding of linguistic forms.

Another successful My Bag story involves Paul, a high school reading teacher, and Mario, one of his students. Mario had been living in the United States for only one year when he was placed in Paul's high school reading course. Where he resided in Bolivia his parents were able to send him to a school that included regular English language lessons. Thus, Mario brought a foundation of English skills to his new American school experiences. Nonetheless, like many of his recent immigrant peers, he needed extra support in increasing his vocabulary, improving his reading comprehension, and, above all, having plenty of additional print experiences with English texts that were accessible but also stretched his abilities.

In the course, designed for students who failed to meet certain benchmarks on the state reading test, Paul made room in his daily lessons for students to read freely on a topic of interest. To discover these interests, Paul had his students create digital My Bags – similar in composition to an actual physical My Bag, like the one described above compiled by me and Delfino, but designed as a collage of personal and web-based photos, symbols, illustrations, emojis, and hyperlinks with video.

In reviewing Mario's digital My Bag, it became immediately clear to Paul that Mario had an obsession with bodybuilding and wrestling, which was prominently represented in photos and video. So Paul searched the school library and found Dave Batista's (Batista & Roberts, 2007) *Batista Unleashed*, a book he was sure would be ideal as independent reading for Mario. In this autobiography of a World Wrestling Entertainment heavyweight champion known as "the Animal," Batista, a Hispanic American, tells about growing up in one of the most impoverished areas of Washington, DC, and being raised by a single mother determined to keep the family together. Batista had to overcome his own criminal past, including a drug conviction and an assault charge. His message is that bodybuilding literally saved his life, because it helped him channel his rage and physical prowess in socially acceptable ways – as a bouncer and lifeguard. Without bodybuilding, Batista felt he was veering toward a life of crime. An "Animal" in the ring, Batista, as he characterizes himself, has learned to be an honest and even humble man outside the ring.

With the Batista book, Paul provided one-on-one support and scaffolding for Mario during free reading time in the class. Paul also helped Mario create an animated presentation of the book for the class employing PowToon (www.powtoon.com/home/) software available in the school. For example, Mario's superimposed head on an animated presenter within the PowToon frames writes on a whiteboard key questions about Dave Batista's life and professional career followed by the brawny professional wrestler character who enters the scene and delivers the answer as Batista.

Mario read another book about wrestling he found among Paul's classroom collection. This one was on the exciting Mexican wrestler, Rey Mysterio (Roberts, 2009), who always wears a mask. Mysterio grew up in tough circumstances in Mexico, was not physically imposing like most World Federation wrestlers, but popularized for American audiences a wild and anything-goes form of wrestling style from Mexico called lucha libra. Mario, an improving English learner, pored over this book like the others on the topic, giving him additional valuable opportunities to encounter new vocabulary and grammatical forms within a text of high interest.

Evidence shows boys, including English language learning Latino boys, are more likely to persevere with challenging reading material if it is highly engaging (Shaffer, 2015).

Popular Music as a Medium for Content and Language Learning

The eight boys in Marta's fifth-period business class were the toughest to keep on task, and she was always on the lookout for approaches that would be especially appealing to them. Marta employed an informal dual-language approach to teach the course, since several of these students were more fluent in Spanish than English. These language accommodations were necessary to ensure students understood content and directions.

One day, when she observed her male students enter the classroom, she became inspired by an obvious way the topic of writing business contracts could be linked to their real-world interests and desires. Many had Tejano music pulsing from their earbuds, which led Marta to consider how her students' love of this Mexican American musical hybrid could form the basis of a fun and meaningful lesson.

Marta formed pairs of students, one to represent a recording artist and another a record company. Each pair was asked to create a fictitious name for both the company and the artist. For example, two students created the Tejano singer, Lil' Mario, and recording company, Sanchez Records. Marta sent students to the computer lab with links to access required Internet sites. At these sites, students obtained background on the language and format of contracts in the music recording business, as well as actual business contract templates for recording artists.

Students had to download templates of recording contracts and negotiate the details from the perspectives of recording artists and record companies. Marta provided the class with a series of questions they would need to address to satisfactorily complete the contracts; these included such matters as the effective dates of the contract, the deliverables by the artist and the company, compensation, and contingencies.

Student pairs completed their contracts in preparation for a fishbowl discussion activity. With this technique, a small group of students goes into the "fishbowl" to discuss an issue or problem while the other students look on. The outside group must listen but not contribute to the deliberations of the students in the fishbowl. When the fishbowl discussants conclude, students looking in can ask questions and react to the discussion they observed. When finished, another group of discussants can enter the fishbowl to start the process over again.

While one pair of Marta's students demonstrated how they hammered out a contract, her other students looked on; then the roles were switched. At regular intervals, student observers were given the opportunity to share reactions to, and ask questions of, the pair of negotiators they were observing. Contract contingencies seemed to bring out the most animated discussion. For instance, Lil' Mario wondered what would happen if just before a big concert he broke his fingers and couldn't play his guitar or lost his voice due to a cold and couldn't sing.

Once Marta's students completed the business contract activity, she held a small reception in class, with Tejano music on the CD player, fruit juice, and pan dulce (traditional sweet breads), before continuing to explore information in the textbook on business contracts. The boys in her class were very enthusiastic about this activity and performed well on her unit test.

Book Club as Reading Curriculum for Language Learning Boys

Middle school teacher, Jeanne, had become frustrated with the growing number of male students entering her remedial reading classes. She noticed in her classes a trend that has been occurring nationwide – boys are three to five times more likely than girls to have a learning or reading disabilities placement (Zambo & Brozo, 2009). She was convinced their reluctance to participate, disinterest in the stories and books offered, and even hostility toward her would only be reversed if big changes were made.

During Jeanne's search for ideas and suggestions that would help her improve boys' reading skills and attitudes, she came upon a couple of articles I had written (Brozo & Schmelzer, 1997; Brozo, Walter, & Placker, 2002) and the first edition of my book, *To Be a Boy, To Be a Reader* (Brozo, 2002). Before long, I found myself exchanging e-mails with her to answer questions about my research into literacy and masculinity, and share strategies that might improve her male students' literacy.

In the end, Jeanne decided to organize a book club comprised of seven seventh-grade boys, whom she selected based on her experiences with them in sixth grade. Each was reading two or more years below grade level and had negative attitudes toward reading. Five had varying levels of competence with English and were receiving TESOL services. With the help of the guidance counselor and TESOL teacher, Jeanne managed to place all seven boys into her second period remedial reading class. Nara, Colin, Ricardo, Jaimi, Michael, Renard, and Esteban represented a similar ethnic mix to the overall school population, which was 46 percent Hispanic, 22 percent African American, 22 percent Caucasian, and 9 percent Asian.

Jeanne's decision to form a book club with these boys was well founded. Book clubs have been documented to increase student motivation and foster positive reading attitudes (Whittingham & Huffman, 2009), increase engagement and literacy achievement for culturally and linguistically diverse students (Kong & Fitch, 2002), as well as expand competencies with new literacies (Scharber, 2009).

Jeanne then invited me to participate in the club as a cyber member. From over 600 miles away in another state, I read the books the boys read, contributed my responses to the books, and engaged in electronic discussions with the boys in the club. My participation in the book club taught me three important lessons: (1) focus on boys' interests, (2) give boys options for responding to books, and (3) have fun with books.

Link Book Club Selections to Members' Interests. Student book clubs should determine selection of reading material solely on the basis of what club members like. The quickest way to undermine enthusiasm is to assume the book club serves as a mere proxy for the regular reading curriculum. The material really does matter and can make or break a successful book club experience. Boys who are disaffected readers in part because of the kinds of books and other print material they're required to read in reading class and the narrow response options allowed, will need much greater freedom with respect to what will be read in a book club context and the parameters for responding to these sources (Appleman, 2006; Bond, 2001; Lattanzi, 2014).

To ensure she was making the most interesting possible books available to her boys, Jeanne gave them a questionnaire to determine their outside-of-school interests. The most popular activities were (a) playing on the computer, (b) playing sports, (c) watching TV, (d) making things, and (e) telling jokes. Along with this questionnaire, Jeanne also asked the boys what they would like to read, and their responses were (a) books that are funny, (b) books that are action-packed, (c) mysteries, (d) books about "boys like us," and (e) books that tell you how to do things. These patterns of interest are not unlike those for male youth documented by others (Farris, Werderich, Nelson, & Fuhler, 2009; Hebert & Pagnani, 2010; Weih, 2007).

Armed with this knowledge, Jeanne and I were able to identify various books that would match the interests and book genres the boys revealed through the questionnaires. For example, to connect with the strong interest the boys had in computers, we introduced them to, and had enjoyable reading experiences with, *ChaseR: A Novel in E-Mails* (Rosen, 2002). In it, Chase's family moves to the country, but he remains in touch with his friends back in Columbus, Ohio, USA, by exchanging funny e-mails. Chase learns to create pictographs through the clever combination of various keyboard symbols. The boys in book club had fun reproducing these interesting keyboard figures while conversing with me via e-mail. Esteban, who was living with an aunt from Guatemala, wrote to tell me about *ChaseR* and the book club:

> I'm very happy to be in this class. The thing about a class full of boys is a good thing because we talk about our things, like girls and basketball and stuff. Not saying having Ms. C [Jeanne] is a bad thing but it is hard to like talk about boy stuff. I like the computer so my favorite book was *ChaseR* by Michael J. Rosen. It's about a boy who moved from the city to the country. He lived 60 miles from the city. The book is about e-mail messages that Chase writes to his new and old friends. Chase has a sense of humor because he expresses it in his e-mails because of his signs, and Jokes.
>
> When he writes he writes about what's happening in the country and what he hates about the country. My favorite part is when he makes signs. Here are some examples. \o/ / / / / / > that's a Cicada. It's weird. He says cicadas are very loud and annoying. They make a lot of noise with there [sic] wings by pushing them together. At the end of the book Chase writes about what he likes about the country. So he changes. But he keeps his friends by writing to them on e-mail. I miss my friends in Mexico but they don't have computers. If they did I would write e-mails to them.

Allow Book Club Members Multiple Modes of Expression. Typically, students are allowed a limited range of response options based on what they read. Answering the teacher's or the anthology's questions is most common. To help reluctant male readers become more engaged with text, creative response formats should be made available to them. These might include drama, electronic presentations, art, and making real-world connections. Michael, an African American struggling reader, wrote to tell me how much he had enjoyed *Death Walk* (Morey, 1993), the book the club just completed, and to get my reaction to an idea he had for a project.

> *Death Walk* is my favorite book so far. Do you like it? I thought it was so weird how Joel gets into a fight at school. Then because he was so afraid of his father, he ran away from home and ended up in Alaska. Then he has the snowmobile accident. Did the book make you feel helpless like Joel who is stuck up there because it snows all the time and the planes can't fly. That's how I felt. I thought Donovan was a cool trapper. He saved Joel. But Joel has to walk all those miles in the snow to that house where the guy has

a radio. This book made me think if I could survive a long trip by myself. It is the coolest adventure. Mrs. C. [Jeanne] says we have to talk about the book in some interesting way. I'm glad because last year all we could do were book reports. I'm thinking about doing this project on *Death Walk* using the computer. I want to show the route Joel takes from Seattle to Alaska and then to the cabin of the radio operator. I was going to read a little bit from the book that describes the places Joel goes. What do you think?

In subsequent e-mail exchanges with Michael, I offered suggestions for his project, such as useful websites and downloadable software, to enhance the presentation. Jeanne told me she had never seen him more enthusiastic in reading class than while preparing for and delivering his book project. One obvious explanation for Michael's enthusiasm is choice – choice of books to read and choice in deciding how to respond to gratifying books (Fisher & Frey, 2012). This holds true for most reluctant and struggling readers, boys and girls.

Make Having Fun with Books a High Priority in Book Clubs. When reading is difficult and unappealing for boys, one of the best antidotes is to immerse them in experiences with simply told stories that are very funny (Scieszka, 2003). To make sure the boys never grew too weary of the selections for the book club, even when they were related to their interests, Jeanne made humorous books available throughout the year. After reading the first in the series of Jon Scieszka's *Time Warp Trio* books, the boys couldn't get enough of them. During conversation about the Trio books we read in the club, Colin, a low-achieving reader and English learner, effused,

Hi, Dr. B. How do you like the Time Trio series books? I read three already. That's really good for me because I don't finish many books. There [sic] really exciting, aren't they? My favorite book is *Viking It Liking It*. I can't read fast like Nara but I don't care if books are long when there [sic] good. The Time Trio books make me think about how fun it would be to travel in time. I like to dream about neat things like that.

Nara, who began reading books from the series on his own, wrote to tell me,

I have read another book written by Jon Scieszka. The book's name was *2095*. It was funny. *The Time Warp Trio* meet their great-grandchildren. I like the part when they didn't have the number to pass the robot. His books are good. I really like his books. They are also funny.

Humorous books helped Jeanne's book club members sustain their efforts to read, discuss, and respond to all selections. Exposure to this genre also impelled some of the boys to seek similarly zany books to read on their own.

This book club experience reinforced my convictions about the kinds of books adolescent boys will read and why, when given the prerogative and support. When Renard, a genuine nonreader at the outset of the year, wrote me in May to say, "It's like okay to read even if other kids don't because reading is only one thing you do," I realized just how successful the boys book club had been. The book club, as an alternative to the traditional remedial reading context, offered Jeanne a way of honoring boys' unique literacy needs. And when her boys found entry points to literacy because their interests were matched with pleasurable books, their reading and language skills improved, too. Five out of the seven boys passed the state test for reading that year. Jeanne was disappointed she couldn't take all seven over the top but was cheered by the very real hope that her boys will remain engaged readers throughout their lives.

Expanding Word Knowledge through Morphological Analysis with Language Learning Boys

Verna embeds morphological analysis skill development within a broader instructional approach to expanding strategic reading and metacognitive thinking for her English learners. This approach stemmed from her dissatisfaction with not finding answers to her questions about how to address the serious needs of her culturally and linguistically diverse students who were striving readers. Her fellow eighth grade English teacher colleagues said intensive phonics was the only way two of her male students who scored at the third grade level on an informal reading inventory could ever hope to improve their reading skills. But Verna was dubious. She had become well-acquainted with her striving middle graders and their disaffection for reading the stories, poems, and essays in the class anthology. She wisely reasoned that an approach based exclusively on skill and drill could alienate them further from books and print. But what was the alternative? The evidence was clear; the boys' demonstrated a significant need for word attack skills and vocabulary development on the school district's reading test. And these issues appeared to be the primary reasons for their limited overall comprehension of the test passages as well as the class readings.

At a professional development workshop, Verna had a chance to explain her concerns to the district literacy specialist, who suggested an alternative to programmed and systematic phonics instruction.

The specialist agreed with Verna that her eighth graders were not likely to enjoy or stick with an approach that forced them to review basic letter–sound relationships. Instead, she recommended the skills these students needed be embedded within meaningful and authentic literacy practices. With interesting and accessible texts Verna's striving readers might come to recognize the value and rewards of learning word attack skills. Following up on email, Verna wrote to and acquired further specific ideas from the specialist. Soon, she had a coherent set of activities for building word attack skills ready to try out with her diverse and striving readers.

The most important realization for Verna was that two of her male students, who were the most seriously striving readers in her class, were not going to be able to make much if any meaning from the stories, poems, and plays in the literature anthology unless she provided major scaffolding. The students had developed excellent listening skills to compensate for their inability to read most course material, which was a strength on which Verna thought she could build. They also had a rich background of experiences. Emilio was born in Guatemala, Qasim in Sudan. Both had journeyed with their parents as young children to the United States. Both were proud of their culture and, with their families, continued to celebrate holidays and traditions brought from their heritage countries.

When the rest of the class was involved in independent reading, Verna used the time to work with Emilio and Qasim on building vocabulary and fluency through an apprenticeship approach. Verna, as a knowledgeable and sophisticated role model, provided explicit instruction and created productive opportunities for Emilio and Qasim to develop familiarity with, and control of, critical word level skills. She worked reciprocally – an approach that has shown promise with language learners (Fung, Wilkinson, & Moore, 2003; Williams, 2010) – by modeling strategies and reading behaviors and then eliciting those same strategies and behaviors from the boys.

Many of the readings in the class literature anthology were too difficult for Emilio and Qasim, but some were within their instructional range. She found, for example, the Robert Frost poem "The Road Not Taken" was comprised of only a few words that were difficult for the boys, making it ideal for the focus of her apprenticeship teaching approach. The ensuing discussion illustrates the productive modeling and eliciting practices Verna employed for developing the boys' word attack and word learning strategies.

VERNA: Okay, I'll read the entire poem first like we've done before then we'll go through it together more slowly. (She reads "The Road Not Taken" aloud.) Now, who wants to read from the beginning? Qasim?

QASIM: Two roads di ...

VERNA: Let's skip that word for now and go back to it after this line and the next one.

QASIM: Okay, Two roads ... blank ... in a yellow wood, and sorry I could not travel both ...

VERNA: Great, okay, let's stop for a minute. Have you ever taken a walk In the woods? You know there are footpaths and sometimes you go down one and then another one might go off from it to.

EMILIO: Yeah, I go walking with my cousin near his house and there's a field with all these trails going through it where you can walk one way or another.

VERNA: Good. See how you can think about what you already know or the things you do that are like what you're reading about? So where is the poet, I mean the person in the poem? What's he doing?

EMILIO: He's in the woods.

QASIM: And there are two roads.

VERNA: Is he going to walk down both roads?

QASIM No ... he says he's sorry he can't take both.

VERNA: Yes, so he's in a yellow wood ... Why does he say yellow? (The boys are unsure and shrug their shoulders.) Well, forests and woods can be different colors depending on the season, right? Like in the summer, the woods are usually what color?

EMILIO: Green. Oh, I think I know, it's fall and the leaves have turned yellow.

VERNA: Do you see that, Qasim? Here look at this picture. (They turn the page in their literature books to look at a picture of a forest of bright yellow leaves with a road covered in leaves running down the center.) Now, let's take another look at the word in the first line that begins with the letter "d." The first thing I would do to figure it out is look for little parts. I see "di." You know the word from math "divide." What does that mean? What happens when you divide something?

QASIM: To break into two pieces ...

VERNA: Yes. So this word also has "ver" ...

EMILIO: That's ver.

VERNA: And the "ged" gets a soft /j'd/ sound like aged or large. So let's see if we can say the word now ... (Qasim and Emilio say diverged along with Verna.) Great! Now, if two roads diverge in the woods what kind of word is "diverge" ... I mean by where it is in the line is it another noun, a verb? As I look at it, it's telling me the roads are doing something, so what kind of words do that?

QASIM: Verbs?

VERNA: Right. "Diverge" is a verb ... and knowing that can help you figure out what it could mean. Try to do that when you get stumped by a word; see if you can't figure out how it's used in the sentence. Okay, so now where do you think

the narrator of the poem is? Let's look at the first two lines of poem for hints again.
EMILIO: He's right there where the two roads come together and you can't go down both at the same time.
VERNA: Excellent. Do you see that, Qasim? So what do you think diverge means? Is it where two things come together or . . .
QASIM: Where two things divide or go different ways.
VERNA: Perfect!

Verna went on to review strategies for attacking pronunciations and meanings of unfamiliar words. (See below for helpful independent word learning prompts and strategies.) She reminded Emilio and Qasim of the steps they went through to figure out the pronunciation and meaning of "diverged." Notice how Verna focused the boys' attention on the various cueing systems for word learning. She modeled the use of grapho-phonic cues by drawing their attention to the sounds of individual letters and syllables. She demonstrated the utility of syntactic cues by helping the boys figure out the way "diverge" was used in the sentence of the poem or its part of speech. And she invoked the semantic cueing system by reminding the boys of their prior knowledge about seasons and forests, relating the prefix "di" to a related word from math, and rereading the couple of lines of the poem to put the word "diverge" in context. As Verna continued the model/elicit process, she had the boys demonstrate these same word-learning strategies with new unfamiliar vocabulary they came upon in the poem. She made sure they applied the practices she modeled for them and talked out loud about what they did, so as to reinforce their strategic and metacognitive thinking.

Independent Word Learning Prompts and Strategies

When striving readers come to an unfamiliar word, have them ask and try to answer the following questions:
1. What is the purpose of the word? Does it name something? Show action? Describe something?
2. What clues are in the sentence? Is there a common expression, a synonym, a definition, extra description?
3. Are there any clues in the sentences before and after the sentence containing the word?
4. What things in my life can I connect with the text and the word?
5. Can I pronounce the word? Does the pronunciation give me any clues about what the word might mean?

6. Does the word have smaller parts? Do they tell me something about the word?
7. Is this word so important I need to use the dictionary to look it up?
8. If I look up the word in the dictionary, can I say the meaning in a way that makes sense in the text?

To build fluency, Verna ensured Qasim and Emilio had multiple opportunities to read and reread familiar text. For instance, after working reciprocally through the entire Robert Frost poem, "The Road Not Taken," she had the boys practice reading it silently, then orally several times until they could get through it without any interruptions or miscues and with appropriate expression. To guide them through oral reading, Verna took the lead while the boys echoed her words. As fluency further developed, the three read the poem together in choral fashion. Finally, the boys read the poem aloud on their own. Once Emilio and Qasim felt totally comfortable with the poem, she invited them to give their oral rendition for the entire class. They particularly enjoyed demonstrating their competence with a reading from the class anthology because it was the same text all of their classmates had to read, too.

Immigrant and New Language Learning Boys: A Coda

Employing responsive instructional approaches for male youth who are learning an additional language and struggling with reading is a demanding task. It is well documented that boys experience greater challenges with language learning than girls, and immigrant boys may have more difficulty adjusting to new cultural expectations of their schools and communities as compared with their female counterparts. To be successful, a total commitment is required of all teachers with whom these youth interact during the course of a school day. Literacy growth may not always be as rapid as would be hoped but is far more likely to occur when teachers, administrators, and support staff dedicate themselves to responsive and culturally sensitive practices for male language learners.

When reflecting on the unique and complex nature of these boys, it is important to bear in mind that they will need the best of what we know about language development, literacy, and youth culture. They will need engaging and meaningful skill development that expands interest, builds competence, and promotes a sense of agency and independence. They will need highly knowledgeable and flexible teachers as well as comprehensive literacy programs that offer opportunities for encounters with accessible texts, frequent experiences for learning new words and generating language in meaningful contexts, and multiple options for reflecting newly gained skills and knowledge. Perhaps most critically, boys who are striving to acquire a new language and become competent readers will need teachers and school personnel interested in forming close and supportive relationships with them as a context for literacy and language growth.

CHAPTER 6

Literacy Engagement and Boys: Evidence and Practice

In this chapter, I
- Explore relevant findings from PISA on boys' reading literacy achievement and engagement
- Analyze theories and research relevant to reading and literacy engagement that can inform curriculum development and instructional practices for boys
- Provide a rationale for the importance of sustaining engagement in literacy for boys
- Describe successful and promising programs and practices

What really motivates a boy to read and learn? As we have seen in connection to other factors related to boys' literacy and learning, answering this question involves an appreciation of boys as individuals each with their own unique needs, desires, and aspirations, on the one hand, but also an understanding of boys as gendered beings, on the other. Thus, one might answer this question with evidence from the research literature that shows, in general, boys and male youth are more motivated to read with certain types of texts, when texts portray particular types of characters, and when boys are given options for choosing, responding to, and using what is learned through reading. Another approach to this question is to seek ways of learning about what motivates boys outside of school in order to introduce them to texts that match. Stocking classroom and school libraries with books that are humorous, books about sports, and adventure books is consistent with the former approach. The My Bag described in Chapter 5 is a strategy for discovering what motivates boys to read that is consistent with the latter approach. Either way, these efforts are likely to offer valuable insights into what motivates boys to read, as well as the kind of texts to sustain the reading habit.

As adult experienced readers, when we reflect on the question for ourselves, we quickly realize that what motivates us to choose certain texts for pleasure reading, for self-improvement, to satisfy a curiosity, or to solve a problem are unique to each of us. It stands to reason, then, that our decisions to read and the types of texts we choose are based on our experiences, needs, and goals. This, of course, also applies to boys and male youth.

When I was a boy growing up on the east side of Detroit, Michigan, USA, I had little time for reading. What really motivated me were sports and games. The day was not long enough to contain my boundless energy for baseball, football, and hockey. And many a summer night, I recall, begrudgingly heading back to my house wondering why a wonderful game of hide-and-seek or one-catch-all had to end, just because it was getting dark. And, then one July morning, everything changed. None of my friends were around and after walking aimlessly through the neighborhood for a time, I found myself directly in front of a branch of the Detroit public library. Although, the library was literally just down a short block and across the street from my house, I had never really paid much attention to it. It had started to rain, so I stepped inside.

People often talk about pivotal events that shift their life's trajectory, and walking into the Montieth branch of the Detroit public library was such an event for me. Little did I know then that reading would become my life's project; but I remember a certain giddiness that struck me as I gazed at the rows of shelved books and magazines. I was attending a very modestly appointed Catholic school that had nothing like this. Within minutes a librarian – whose name, Mrs. Oshob, I can still remember – approached me and guided me to a section of children's books and magazines. She asked me what I was interested in and what I liked to do. Once she learned that I was a sports-nut and that I wished I could spend time wandering the countryside (a place very unlike where I lived in the middle of a large city), the librarian pulled several selections for me to peruse. I settled on *Boys' Life* magazines and quite literally reading about surviving in the wilderness, making a fire with wooden tools and stones, eating wild berries and mushrooms, and making a compass with water and toothpicks was how I took my first tentative steps down the path of lifelong literacy.

From *Boys' Life* the librarian encouraged me to read "juvenile" novels by American authors like Stephen Meader, who wrote amazing tales of young boys about my age sailing on whaling ships, working in lumberjack camps, and wandering the countryside in one of my favorites, *Boy with a Pack*, a Newberry Honor book. In reflecting on my own literate journey, I now know these entry point texts had a profound influence on my reading skills and identity as a reader (Brozo, 2013, 2018; Thomas, 2011). For the first time, I began to see myself as a reader with no loss of enthusiasm for sports. And the journey was launched by a caring and sensitive librarian who understood that introducing a young man to texts that are engaging is the key.

Within the past couple of decades, volumes have been written about student motivation and engagement, including how to motivate reluctant male readers to engage with text (Atkinson, 2009; Bozack, 2011; Brozo & Gaskins, 2009; Fingon, 2012; Kirkland, 2011). Yet, teachers have an ongoing interest in acquiring more information about how and employing ever more responsive practices to motivate students (Andermann, Andrezejewski, & Allen, 2011; Yonezawa, Jones, & Joselowsky, 2009), especially male youth (Love & Hamston, 2003; Marinak & Gambrell, 2010; Merisuo-Storm, 2006; Oakhill & Petrides, 2007; Van De Gaer, Pustjens, Van Damme, & De Munter, 2007, 2009), to read and learn. And there is evidence that justifies this interest. A well-documented slump in achievement and motivation appears to occur during the upper-primary and lower-secondary years for all students (Martin, 2009) and for boys in particular (Osman, 2012; Robinson & Lubienski, 2011). This phenomenon, moreover, is not restricted to the United States and Europe. Boys from across the globe exhibit a similar decline in performance and interest as they move from primary to secondary school (Brozo et al., 2014; Van Langen, Bosker, & Dekkers, 2006). Some of our best thinkers and researchers in youth literacy have proposed that this decline in academic motivation results from a disjuncture between adolescents' need for content and learning experiences that are accessible and relevant, on the one hand, and traditional school-related reading, writing, and disciplinary practices, on the other (Alvermann & Eakle, 2007; Fecho, 2011).

What we do know is there is strong relationship between boys' attitudes toward reading and their reading comprehension performance (Logan & Johnston, 2009; Shaffer, 2015). Boys' feelings about reading are also closely linked to how frequently they read. Boys who have negative perceptions of reading are unmotivated to read in school and for leisure. Resisting reading acts to further diminish skills, which shows up on reading assessments (Mol & Jolles, 2014). Unfortunately, many boys and male youth can find themselves in a downward cycle of diminishing interest resulting in diminishing skill resulting in a further decline in reading motivation and so on. The challenge for teachers is to do everything possible to prevent young boys from losing interest in reading and keeping boys as they progress through the grades motivated to read.

We also know that literacy motivation for boys cannot be detached from social contexts, such as classrooms, families, and communities (Love & Hamston, 2003). An individual male youth's motivation to read and learn is linked closely to the social worlds that are part of his daily life (Brozo, 2018). And while teachers may have little influence on the social worlds youth navigate outside of school, they have a great deal of control over the arrangement of conditions within the classroom that can effect positive academic and reading motivation for boys.

Not only should boys be engaged in interesting experiences related to *what* they learn but, more important, *why* the content is being discussed and studied. To tell boys, "You must learn this because it's in our curriculum guide" may be the truth, but does little to motivate them to become active readers and knowledge seekers. Instead, by linking reading to boys' own needs, issues, concerns, and interests inside and outside of school, we increase engagement while helping them discover real-world purposes for reading (Brozo & Gaskins, 2009). Greenleaf, Jimenez, and Roller (2002) put it this way: "Only when adolescents read material that is important to them will they understand why one uses . . . reading strategies and skills, [and] only if adolescents understand why they might want to use these skills will they master them and use them" (p. 490). Simply put, teachers must look to male youths' own reasons to learn as the source for motivational strategies.

Nobel Prize winning economist James Heckman argues in favor of what he refers to as "soft skills" – those personality traits that may be even more essential than cognitive abilities when it comes to successful learning and achievement inside and outside the classroom (Heckman & Kautz, 2012). According to Heckman and his colleagues (Heckman, Stixrud, & Urzua, 2006), traits such as curiosity and perseverance are thought to have greater predictive power for success in life than cognitive skills. Engagement for reading and learning, like perseverance, is one of the soft skills that has been shown to be a potent predictor of academic success (Schunk, Meece, & Pintrich, 2013).

Evidence for the benefits of engaged reading is quite compelling. We know that correlational data from the National Assessment of Educational Progress (NAEP) continue to show male youth who identify themselves as being interested in reading not only achieve better scores on the NAEP but have better high school grade point averages than their less interested peers (Loveless, 2015). Even more convincing are data derived from the PISA. Engagement is the variable, above all others, that has the strongest relationship to performance on PISA (OECD, 2013). As might be expected, given their overall superior performance on most measures of verbal ability (Brozo, 2010), girls from the United States and across Europe had significantly higher indices of reading engagement as compared with boys. Girls enjoyed reading more, spent a greater amount of time reading, and had a wider range of reading preferences as compared with their male peers (Brozo et al., 2014). So, it should not come as a surprise to learn that girls' higher levels of engagement contributed to their superior achievement to that of the boys (Marks, 2008). PISA data further indicates that, on average, boys who failed to acquire the habits of engaged readers found themselves lagging behind their highly engaged peers by nearly two years of schooling. Remarkably, that's like being absent from two years of instruction (Brozo et al., 2014).

Given these stark reminders in the literature about boys' eroding motivation to read and their depressed reading performance, we should take heart in what is truly a fascinating finding from PISA related to reading engagement. Analysis of youth from the lowest SES who were highly engaged readers performed as well on the assessment as youth from the middle SES group and cut in half the disparity between themselves and their high SES peers. In other words, highly motivated adolescents made up for low family income and parents' limited educational attainment, two oft-considered risk factors in the school lives of students (Brozo, Shiel, & Topping, 2007). This should be ground-shaking news, because it strongly suggests that if we can keep boys engaged in reading and learning they may be able to overcome what might otherwise be insuperable barriers to academic success.

Factors Influencing Boys' Reading Motivation

Due to the ongoing scholarly and practical interest in better understanding motivation for reading and how it can be elevated for disengaged learners, several critical factors have been identified in the literature that appear to positively influence reading motivation. These factors should be accounted for when crafting literacy curriculum and practices for male youth to ensure they become and remain active engaged readers in school and in their personal lives.

Self-Efficacy

The research literature makes evident that students with high, school-related self-efficacy – the belief and confidence that they have the capacity to accomplish meaningful tasks and produce a desired result in academic settings – are more engaged and motivated than students with low self-efficacy (Pajares & Urdan, 2006). Teachers can create the conditions for male youth that are associated with increased perceptions of competence and, consequently, a willingness to sustain effort to be successful (Schunk, Meece, & Pintrich, 2013). These conditions are created with such practices as introducing new content in engaging ways (Brozo, 2004), making a variety of accessible texts available (Brozo & Hargis, 2003; Ivey, 2011), giving youth choices (Ho & Guthrie, 2013), exploiting youths' everyday literacies (Moje & Tysvaer, 2010), and creating multiple opportunities for collaborative learning (Guthrie, Wigfield, & You, 2012). These practices are described in more detail within the next few pages and embodied in the strategies presented later in the chapter.

Interest

A self-evident and empirically grounded truth about learning is that students will expend the energy necessary to read if they are interested in the material (Hulleman et al., 2010; Guthrie & Klauda, 2014). This is certainly not a recent revelation. Over 300 years ago, the philosopher Rousseau (1979) made a compelling case for exploiting "present interest" as the single best way to motivate students to read and learn. John Dewey, in the early twentieth century, promoted the idea that when students are interested in a topic or activity they will learn "in a whole-hearted way" (1913, p. 65). Today, the desire among educational researchers and practitioners to know more about the influence of interest on student literacy and learning is as strong as ever (Gambrell, 2011). The realization that students must have both the skill and the will to learn has led to a variety of instructional practices designed to support the affective as well as the cognitive aspects of literacy development and school achievement.

Teachers of male youth who understand the importance of interest in motivating reading and learning do not automatically assume each of their male students eagerly desires to read and learn course content (Brozo, 2005). Instead, they prepare boys for reading by helping them become active participants in the reading process (Wigfield et al., 2008), demonstrating how the reading material can relate to their lives and concerns (Alvermann & Eakle, 2007), and providing opportunities for boys to enjoy reading and learning (Brozo & Flynt, 2008).

Boys in the Real World

"Joshua"

Joshua is an African American eleventh grader who lives with both of his parents in a suburb near the District of Columbia in the United States. His parents hold graduate degrees and have worked with school-age children for many years in different occupations and capacities. Despite the emphasis on education in the household, Joshua still struggles in school. He underwent a psychoeducational evaluation during the ninth grade. His scores ranged from very low to low average.

Outside of school, Joshua enjoys playing sports, especially basketball, his favorite leisure time activity. He also spends time playing video games, hanging out with his friends, and being on his phone. Twitter, SnapChat and Instagram are his favorite social media activities, and he also texts often.

Joshua's describes himself as a "pretty good reader," who understands the importance of reading, such as improving vocabulary and the ability to "talk better," but reading is not a high priority. Joshua understands the importance of reading, but finds reading boring, and therefore avoids it. He gets enthusiastic about reading when reading about all things basketball from the magazines that come to the house in the mail. He especially enjoys reading about LeBron James, his favorite basketball player.

When it comes to school-based writing, Joshua tends to receive positive feedback and acceptable grades on his writing homework and essays; nevertheless, he does not enjoy writing outside of school and does not recognize that tweeting, texting and communicating on various other social media platforms is, indeed, writing. Joshua does not seem to see the relationship between the writing he does on a daily basis and the importance of writing. As he indicated, writing "does not fit into his life at all" and is "not as important as reading."

Discussion and Activities

- What recommendations can you offer to teachers working with Joshua to ensure his reading and writing interests are nurtured?
- How can Joshua's interests be exploited for further literacy skill and vocabulary development?
- In what ways can teachers exploit the social media Joshua enjoys to further his reading and writing abilities?

Local Interest

Even if boys are generally interested in a topic, this does not diminish the need to employ practices that capture their attention and motivate them to read and learn for a particular day and lesson (Rotgans & Schmidt, 2014). For example, a tenth-grade boy who finds the topic of the American Civil War interesting may not stay focused in class nor be eager to read on the topic without specific strategies that gain and hold his attention. Even worse, the student's interest might fade if his teacher does little more than lecture or require oral reading from the textbook. Many boys are going into language, history, science, math, and other classrooms without a general interest in any of the texts and topics to be studied. For these students, local, daily strategies for helping them sustain effort are essential (Rotgans & Schmidt, 2011).

Thankfully, there are a variety of engaging strategies teachers can apply to any text and information source that will often entice even the most reluctant males to play more active roles in their reading and learning (Del Favero et al., 2007; Holstermann, Grube, & Bögeholz, 2010; Long et al., 2007; Palmer, 2009). If we can spark an interest in reading for just one day, the experience acquired that day may make it easier to continue reading and gaining new skills and knowledge the next day (Guthrie et al., 2006).

Outside-School Literacies

The same boys who may be disconnected from academic life and are unmotivated to read school-related texts may also be active readers and users of new media at home and in their communities (Alvermann, 2011; Brozo, 2018; Skerrett & Bomer, 2011). Many boys of the Net Generation and Generation Z (IRA, 2012) who may find little motivation for traditional print-based textbook and other academic reading, are nonetheless engaging in literate practices such as texting, networking through social media, and consulting online computer and video game magazines for strategies (Gee & Hayes, 2011). Motivating these students to read and learn may be possible by tapping into their everyday, multiliteracy practices (Agee & Altarriba, 2009; Hinchman et al., 2003/2004; Kajder, 2010).

Primary and secondary school teachers can create the space for boys to find and make connections between school topics and the media they use to know their worlds (Clarke & Besnoy, 2010; Williams, 2004). By motivating male youth to become academically engaged by linking their everyday literacies with traditional textbook reading and print media, teachers will also build their capacity and efficacy as learners (Dredger et al., 2010; Moje & Tysvaer, 2010).

Accessible and Interesting Texts

When eighth graders across the United States were asked on the NAEP how often they read for enjoyment, only 19 percent reported doing so every day (National Center for Education Statistics, 2012). For twelfth graders, the figure was about the same. Of even more concern were the sizable percentages of students who reported reading for fun on only a monthly or yearly basis, or not at all. Why are such large numbers of students turning off to traditional print media? One explanation, of course, is that they are turning to other media with which they engage in alternative literacy practices, no less enjoyable than traditional print, but not easily accounted for on surveys like the one used for NAEP.

Another possible explanation requires a closer look at the types of texts youth encounter in school and how this might influence attitudes toward reading. For example, books and texts that may have appealed to youth of previous generations are still all-too-common in classrooms today (Fisher & Ivey, 2007). It has also been found that the books youth would prefer to read are often scarce to non-existent in school (Baines & Fisher, 2013). When this is the case, students' only print encounters in school may be with the texts they are required to read. Boys who find school-related texts difficult and uninspiring are likely to develop negative attitudes toward reading (Gavigan, 2010; Lattanzi, 2014; Lenters, 2007). These negative feelings may turn boys into resistant readers and become generalizable to all types of text, including texts that might otherwise be enjoyable to them. If reading is seen by many boys as unpleasurable, it becomes easier to understand why so many indicated on the NAEP survey that they read for enjoyment so infrequently.

In the United States, a Gates Foundation-commissioned survey of some 40 thousand teachers (www.scholastic.com/primarysources/PrimarySources-2014update.pdf) found few believe traditional textbooks can engage today's digitally facile youth and prepare them for success in college and the workplace. Teachers in the survey said they prefer digital resources or alternatives to textbooks, such as magazines, newspapers, primary documents, information books, and even picture books. In fact, only 12 percent surveyed said textbooks help students achieve, while only 6 percent said textbooks engage their students in learning.

If you spend any time working with textbooks, you will soon notice that invariably the prose is abstract, formal, and lifeless (Thomas Fordham Institute, 2004). These features of textbook prose are surely contributing to boys' disaffection with school-based reading. It is imperative therefore that teachers make every effort to get students, especially disengaged male youth, interested in classroom topics through the use of alternative texts, such as fictional works, graphic novels, and new media (Baines & Fisher, 2013; Brozo, Moorman, & Meyer, 2014; Hebert & Pagnani, 2010; Simon, 2012).

In my own experience, I have found that when schools and classroom teachers make a total commitment to ensuring every student has readable and engaging texts within easy access, then motivation for and attitudes toward reading improve (Brozo & Flynt, 2008). In order to become enthusiastic readers and learners, boys need to see firsthand the value their teachers and other school staff place on reading for personal pleasure and growth. Valuing this type of reading should take the form of strategies and programs that include stocking school and classroom libraries with a variety of interesting texts related to a host of topics at a range of difficulty levels, creating opportunities for self-selection of texts, and structuring time for sustained print encounters (Brozo & Hargis, 2003; Lapp & Fisher, 2009).

Choices and Options

Choice may be one of the most critical elements of motivation (Guthrie, Wigfield, & You, 2012; Patall, Cooper, & Wynn, 2010). As students progress through primary and secondary school, their choices about many things outside of school increase significantly, yet options in school remain limited. For instance, teachers may require students to answer a question in only one way or read just the assigned texts.

From a developmental perspective, allowing youth more input into what and how they read could help increase their sense of autonomy and agency, while building academic competence and identities (Vieira & Grantham, 2011; Wilhelm, 2016). We know from good evidence that students in primary school (Freeman, McPhail, & Berndt, 2002) and secondary school (Moley, Bandre, & George, 2011; Patall, Cooper, & Wynn, 2010), when given the choice, are quite capable of identifying reading materials and activities they believe are helpful to their skill development and learning. Many have documented the benefits of acquiring students' input into classroom practices and materials and then giving them choices based on this input. Youth feel empowered and motivated to participate constructively in their literacy learning when invited to help choose how and what they read, write, and learn (Aboudan, 2011). Boys from all ability levels can be informants to help bring about more motivating literacy practices (Brozo, 2018).

Collaboration

Vygotsky (1978) reminds us that learning is, above all, a social process. Thus, when teachers create opportunities for boys to work together in the pursuit of new knowledge, they are taking advantage of the social nature of learning. An added benefit to boys is the sense of belonging that grows out of cooperative and collaborative engagement in the classroom (Juvonen, Espinoza, & Knifsend, 2009). This sense of belonging for boys has been associated with an increase in motivation for reading and learning (Ivey & Broaddus, 2007; Malloy, Marinak, & Gambrell, 2010).

Boys can be unmotivated for many reasons, but it seems clear that disengagement is as much a social challenge as it is any other (Brozo & Gaskins, 2009). Consequently, teachers will be more successful in motivating male youth if they employ practices consistent with those surveyed by Cambria and Guthrie (2011), who found that students are generally more motivated when they are allowed to sit with someone who will help them read and learn, work in cooperative reading and learning groups, and choose a project to do with another student.

A great variety of strategies and practices based on these guidelines have been shown to be useful in motivating boys to read and learn. As with previous chapters, the balance of this chapter will be devoted to describing successful motivational strategies and programs for boys. We have often witnessed a rarely accounted for benefit of teachers' efforts to develop imaginative, motivational activities. As teachers observe an increase in engagement among their students, they became more interested in, and excited about, teaching as well. And the more enthusiastic teachers are about reading and learning, the greater the chance of awakening interest in their students (Flynt & Brozo, 2009; McKool & Gespass, 2009; Powell-Brown, 2003/2004).

Promising Programs and Practices

Kicking and Reading

Combining sports and reading has proven to be an effective approach to increasing boys' engagement in books and other texts while improving skill

(Brozo, 2018; Senn, 2012). An example of this salutary combination in the United States is an initiative like "Books and Balls" that involves boys who play on Little League and community baseball teams to also participate in book club activity after practices and games.

In Germany, a similarly designed initiative exploits boys' interest in playing soccer to provide literacy supports and nurture the reading habit. The program, called *Kicking and Reading*, has as its overarching goal to engage lower secondary boys in literacy. It achieves this goal by interlacing training in soccer and reading. Additional objectives of the program include improving boys' reading skills, helping boys develop healthy self-concepts as readers, ensuring boys experience reading for pleasure, and, above all, demonstrating for boys that reading can be an attractive cultural practice for males.

Schools that commit to the year-long *Kicking and Reading* program are obliged to contribute teachers, staff, and physical resources, though no financial commitments are necessary. Participating teachers are provided a one-day seminar of initial training before the project begins, and then receive required in-service training of 90 minutes weekly in specific reading supports for boys throughout the year. These teacher professional development sessions are given by project staff with expertise in reading and by a noted children's book author. The participating teachers are also given the opportunity to engage in regular feedback meetings and exchanges among colleagues to discuss challenges and successes as well as to problem solve and help build curriculum. Teachers are given a manual containing plans and methodological advice targeting struggling male readers.

Boys from the participating schools are clustered into groups of about 15. Their literacy training consists of focused reading support based on individual needs. Practices such as repeated and paired reading, reading aloud, and free reading time occur with a colorful mixture of books at three different reading levels. Book genres include crime, fantasy, adventure, science fiction, football stories, and a variety of non-fiction topics.

On the soccer side, the boys have regular training days with professional German footballers helping develop technique and skill while emphasizing teamwork and sportsmanship. Matches and competitions are staged, as well. The *Kicking and Reading* project is also structured to involve the boys in fun excursions and reading events. For example, boys have made visits to local TV and radio stations, where they have been interviewed and given demonstrations. They have gone on fieldtrips to author-reading events, a sports museum, soccer autograph sessions, and to watch a professional soccer match and meet the players.

A culminating event of the project is a book slam in which the boys participate in a reading competition that allows them to read an array of books, discuss them, and present them in their own unique voices. The slam offers a focus for strengthening the boys' reading skills and developing their abilities to interpret, discuss, and present books. The book slam is another way the *Kicking and Reading* project directors hope to foster long-term positive attitudes towards reading and encourage a lifetime reading habit among the boys. Feedback received from past participants in the book slam clearly shows that the boys enjoy taking part in the competition.

Boys and Books

Recognizing the challenges of motivating boys to read, a German internet platform called *Boys & Books* (http://relaunch.boysandbooks.de/) offers book recommendations for male youth from primary through secondary school. The *Boys & Books* initiative is based on five key findings from the research literature on gender difference in reading: (1) girls read more frequently and for longer periods than boys, (2) girls read different books, magazines, and digital texts/media content than boys, (3) reading habits and modes of girls and boys are different, (4) reading means more to girls, and they get more gratification and pleasure from it, and (5) girls read better than boys, particularly on difficult reading tasks.

The *Boys & Books* website addresses primarily the adults (i.e., teachers, parents, librarians, social workers) involved in the mediation and promotion of literature and reading skills. The heart of this non-commercial, German language site are short book reviews grouped according to genre as well as methodological advice for supporting reading literacy of teen and preteen boys. The book reviews and reading recommendations are based on criteria from reader-oriented children and young adults' literary criticism. Thus, empirical research on children's and adolescents' reading habits and preferences undergirds the content of the site, making it unique among similar platforms and providers of reading recommendations.

The target group for *Boys & Books* is primarily inexperienced, unmotivated, and struggling male readers. In order to engage them as readers, various forms of simple reading matter, especially popular children's and young adult literature, are reviewed and featured on the site. *Boys & Books* also provides useful suggestions for increasing boys' reading motivation and skill in school, at home, and in the community. Every book reviewed is accompanied by recommendations about how to incorporate the book into classroom practice or home/community activities.

The selection and evaluation of books as well as the teaching ideas are made by a team of experts in children's and young adult literature. The team develops review templates for each popular genre and then, twice a year, evaluates the 20 top titles (five per age group 8+, 10+, 12+, and 14+). The jury is comprised of librarians, booksellers, authors, researchers, and educators. With an eye to how the book might appeal to, and be accessible to, unmotivated and low-skilled male readers, evaluation criteria ranges from the book's cover and blurbs to language and style to protagonists and plot. The book reviews are published on the website, which is maintained by reading literacy experts from the University of Cologne.

From Hobbies to Books

As a preteen, Theo still seemed to be interested in little more than playing with his toy soldiers. His parents, Jack and Peggy, had busy careers that subjected them to long days and weekends at work. When Theo's reading scores edged near the minimally acceptable cutoff on the district's standardized test, Peggy and Jack found themselves at school one afternoon, meeting with his teacher Karlene. She recommended some tutoring and agreed to provide it herself a couple of days a week after school.

Theo came to tutoring in September of the new school year. He was 11 years old and in the sixth grade. Karlene was surprised by his lackluster reading performance. She had come to discover that despite material privilege, a nuclear family, and educated parents, Theo exhibited the signs of a classic nonreader. What further surprised her was his unenthusiastic reaction to her questions about his interests. He reported no hobbies, no involvement with sports, and few regular or predictable activities that he looked forward to after school or on weekends.

Her follow-up chat with Jack and Peggy focused on helping them see the connection between having an interest in something and being motivated to read about that interest. Boys often need help discovering their interests; yet, in households where parents are extremely busy, boys are usually left to their own devices to discover what turns them on. Unfortunately, all too often, default leisure-time activities will be chosen, such as watching television and playing computer games. Karlene, therefore, urged Theo's parents to get more involved in how Theo spent his free time. This would help them find ways of engaging Theo in reading. She advised that the best way to accomplish this might be to capitalize on anything that Theo had already found enjoyable.

Theo's parents cleared their schedules for the next few weekends and dedicated themselves to spending time with Theo both outdoors and indoors. For instance, they went to the zoo for the first time in two or three years, an evening baseball game played by a local minor league squad, and the beach. Some indoor activities included putting puzzles together, playing board games, watching movies, and upon Theo's urging, setting up his arsenal of plastic soldiers and weapons on a mock battlefield. Theo was proud of his replicas of US, German, and Japanese soldiers.

Theo's response to these activities convinced Jack and Peggy that they should begin with his only genuine interest – his toy soldiers. While looking at various sets of army men in a hobby shop, Jack and Theo became inspired to build a diorama of a World War II battle. As a boy, Jack was an avid modeler, building everything from airplanes to ships to cars. His boyhood hobby was all but forgotten until he and Theo brainstormed about the diorama project. Their work would require research of World War II, as well as techniques for creating miniature though lifelike displays. Jack found Theo to be as enthusiastic about this family project as anything he had ever done and reasoned it was because they were working as a unit, father and son – a rarity of late.

They began their project by making trips to the local library and various bookstores for appropriate reference material. They checked out *Great Battles of World War II* (MacDonald, 2004) and *D-Day: The Liberation of Europe Begins* (Murray, 2007). These books are histories of various battles for junior high school students, such as the Nazi invasion of Poland, the D-Day invasion, the Battle of the Bulge in Europe, the attack on Pearl Harbor, and fighting in Guam and the Philippines. The books include plenty of black-and-white and color photos of actual battle scenes. For information on creating dioramas and miniature displays, Theo and Jack found two excellent resources at a couple of bookstores: Jerry Scutts's (2000) *World War II Dioramas* and Francois Verlinden's (2003) *Building Military Dioramas* (vol. VII). These books displayed a variety of war dioramas showing burnt buildings, weathered machines and men, and field hospitals and included detailed descriptions of the techniques for re-creating them.

Theo and Jack set aside time each evening to look through and read the books they had gathered in preparation for creating their own diorama.

Theo toiled cheerfully on every detail as the two of them spent the next two months bonding in a way that they had never done before. The project became so all-encompassing that Jack began taking less and less work home; he also limited his weekend work to a couple of hours on Sunday evenings. Activity on the diorama became a kind of curative for the workaholic funk Jack had found himself in. It also gave him and Theo time to renew the critical father–son bond, which had become frayed.

On a large piece of plywood, Jack and Theo crafted a remarkable replica of the Ardennes forest, which was the last-gasp offensive of another German invasion into France, as well as a turning point in the Battle of the Bulge. US and German soldiers were arrayed in opposition among hedgerows, trees, and burnt-out buildings, and they were also in foxholes and behind tanks. Borrowing techniques from the diorama books to create further realism, Theo and Jack had rigged a device that would emit smoke onto the mock battlefield. In addition to this achievement of visual authenticity, Theo could recount each detail of the battle, demonstrating the power of personal interest as a motivator for learning.

As for the payoff on the "literacy ledger," Jack was able to reintroduce Theo to the pleasure of reading by finding out what his interests were, then engaging him with the appropriate literature. Similar to Theo, many boys who have adequate literacy skills will often stop reading when (a) reading at home is not being modeled and (b) school reading has more to do with skills, lessons, and tests than with personal enjoyment and growth. As a result of the diorama project, Theo continued to seek and read books about World War II. Peggy even found a slim but exciting book titled *Heroes Don't Run: A Novel of the Pacific War* (Mazer, 2007) that Theo quickly finished. All of these books now leave him asking for more. According to Karlene, Theo's renewed interest in reading surely contributed to the improvement he demonstrated on the district's standardized reading test the following year.

Literacy Engagement and Boys: A Coda

Nearly 50 years ago, Illich advocated a curriculum that engendered "self-motivated learning instead of employing teachers to bribe or compel the student to find the time and the will to learn" (1970, p. 104). Today, Illich's recommendation is as viable as ever as concerns literacy engagement of boys and male youth (Atkinson, 2009; King, 2016; Wu, Anderson, Nguyen-Jahiel, & Miller, 2013). What is more, attention to boys' reading and learning engagement should be heightened given the powerful connection this "soft skill" has to other academic and career successes (Heckman & Kautz, 2012). Evidence shows that male youth become independent knowledge seekers when they perceive what they are reading and learning to be personally meaningful and relevant to their lives and futures (Enriquez, 2017; Meier, 2015). On one level, then, I am suggesting that meaningful purposes for reading can be established only when the texts and content are themselves meaningful.

Because I believe that the degree of success with any act of literacy depends on how motivated boys are, I have focused this chapter on important foundational knowledge gleaned from the literature about motivation and engagement as well as descriptions of successful practices and approaches to motivate and engage boys in reading and learning. The descriptions included here represent only a few of the potentially endless possibilities for helping boys become excited and engaged readers. All of them, however, are marked by inventive applications and adaptations of established literacy practices to entice boys to read. Boys who become engaged readers as youth stand a greater chance that the critical and mind-expanding power of literacy will follow them into adulthood and serve them throughout their lives.

CHAPTER 7

Boys and New Literacies: Evidence and Practice

> **In this chapter, I**
> - Situate male youth as active participants in the "mediasphere"
> - Explore gender differences in digital literacy achievement and behaviors
> - Make connections between boys' out-of-school interests and literacies and opportunities for engaged reading, writing, and learning in school
> - Describe successful and promising programs and practices

We live in a digital age surrounded by electronic print and media. Books, newspapers, articles, and every imaginable text form are created and formatted digitally, and virtually all print media are made available on the Internet, and delivered directly to any variety of e-readers, smartphones, and even smartwatches. Today's male youth have only experienced life as so-called digital natives (Prensky, 2009). And a growing number of their teachers, especially those new to the ranks, are steeped in digital and social media, as well (Boyd, 2014). Thus, instructional methods are reflecting these new times. Developing facility with, and thinking curricularly about, these ever-evolving digital and new literacy tools, as well as understanding their value to boys, is as important a part of the skill set of teachers as possessing expert knowledge on the topic of instruction and interpersonal competencies.

Becoming sophisticated readers and writers of print is still essential for male youth. However, we also believe being print literate is no longer sufficient in a world saturated with digitized media that have become powerful sources of information and tools for communication. While this chapter focuses on classroom applications of technology, I remind you that in virtually every chapter descriptions can be found of disciplinary teachers taking advantage of digital and media technology to increase student engagement and depth of thinking.

This chapter serves to broaden conceptions of what counts as literacy and extend visions of possible literacy practices for boys. Teaching with traditionally formatted print texts as the primary source material is no longer adequate. This is especially true for male youth whose everyday lives in the mediasphere involve constructing and re-constructing print and non-print meanings with sophisticated digital technologies (Alvermann, 2002; Leu, Kinzer, Coiro, & Cammack, 2004). Practices that fail to recognize the power of digital and new media for engaging boys, sustaining their attention, and mediating their meaningful and critical understandings of content may be leaving many behind (Kamil, 2004; Leander & Sheehy, 2004; Mistler-Jackson & Songer, 2000). Teachers who approach their craft with a thoughtful and inquiring disposition will find numerous ways to acquire and make use of technology tools for enriching learning experiences for male youth (Tapscot, 1999).

I begin this chapter by presenting evidence in support of capitalizing on the new literacies boys use in their everyday lives. This evidence lays the groundwork for practices designed to capture and sustain boys' interest in reading and writing as well as to mediate their learning in school contexts. This is followed by descriptions of teachers who employed innovative, technology-based practices that celebrate and extend the multi-literacies of male youth.

Boys and Electronic Reading: Evidence from PISA and PIRLS

One of the four major gaps identified in the EU High Level Group of Experts on Literacy Report (2012) was the digital gap. The report makes clear those students who have access to, and engage in, meaningful activities with information and communication technologies will have academic and career advantages over those who do not have these digital tools.

Analysis of the 2009 PISA database, the first cycle in which an electronic version of the reading assessment was introduced and the last cycle featuring reading literacy, reveals a great deal about the relationship between ICT use by adolescents and their overall achievement on PISA, as well as gender differences in performance relative to the traditional print and electronic versions of PISA.

Wu (2014) examined the scores of over 34 thousand 15-year-olds from the 19 countries that took part in both the printed reading assessment and electronic reading assessment. Wu was interested in the relationship between online reading activity and performance on the print and electronic versions of PISA. Specifically, he isolated the student participants' self-reported knowledge of metacognitive strategies and navigation skills and linked these to overall achievement. Wu found these skills positively predicted scores on both versions of the assessment. As reading involving navigation and metacognition activity increased, so too did achievement on either version of PISA. Considering these findings from a gender perspective, Wu documented girls' superior knowledge of metacognitive and navigation skills as well as their superior performance on the print version of the assessment, but these more advanced self-reported skills did not translate into superior performance on the electronic reading version. In other words, boys performed comparably to girls on the version of the PISA reading literacy assessment that was computer-based. This finding bolsters the contention that boys are more motivated to respond to literacy tasks that are digitally framed.

Wu also explored the connection between the presence of a computer and Internet connection in the home and PISA reading scores. Not surprisingly, there was a significant association between these variables. Students with either of these resources at home had scores half a proficiency level higher than those students without them.

This last finding by Wu is given strength by earlier analysis of PISA data from Bussiere and Gluszynski (2004), who explored links between computer use and reading achievement for Canadian youth. Using multivariate procedures, the researchers determined access to a home computer significantly correlated with PISA reading literacy scores. Among the range of computer-use variables included in the analysis, reading achievement was most highly related to students' perceptions of their ability to use computers. Canadian boys who reported higher levels of self-efficacy with computers than their female peers, had comparable reading scores to that group of girls, leading the researchers to conclude that facility with ICT tools appears to be a key moderating factor in the elimination of the gender gap.

The results for Canadian youth were echoed more recently by findings for Finnish adolescents. In Leino's (2014) study, she learned that Finnish adolescents use computers and the Internet frequently and for varied purposes. Furthermore, Leino found that students who had self-confidence in ICT tasks had higher reading literacy scores on PISA than those who lacked self-confidence in their ability with digital tools. And, like previous findings, gender differences were significant: boys were more interested in computers, were more confident about their computer skills, and had higher technical knowledge about computers than girls.

Leino offers some interesting explanations for, and claims related to, these findings. She asserts that using ICTs in various ways, and to a moderate extent, can boost reading literacy skills, particularly for boys. She goes on to argue that the text-based nature of the Internet may provide boys, who might otherwise avoid traditional print texts, supportive print experiences. What was striking is, regardless of gender, the lowest performers among Finnish 15-year-olds on PISA were those who seldom or never used computers. Like Leino, others have established an optimal use of ICT tools that positively links to reading achievement and varies according to gender. For example, Thiessen and Looker (2007) identified a curvilinear relationship between time spent with ICTs and reading, showing that little or no use and a great deal of use diminished reading performance. Interestingly, they found males' optimal use point with ICTs was higher than females.

By comparison, nine-year-old boys from the 14 countries participating in ePIRLS 2016, which assesses online reading for information, demonstrated slightly higher competence with digital reading, like older males on the digital version of PISA. In North America, boys from the United States and Canada had lower scores than girls, though the gap of 6–8 points was smaller than the gender differences on ePIRLS in most European countries. For instance, in Sweden the gap in favor of girls was 15 points; and in Norway 18 points (http://timssandpirls.bc.edu/pirls2016/international-results/epirls/student-achievement/average-achievement-by-gender/). Nevertheless, these gender differences were smaller (12 points) than those found on the print version of PIRLS (14 points) for the same 14 countries, suggesting once more that boys tend to narrow the achievement gap with girls when the reading assessment is electronically formatted.

A Multiple Literacies Perspective on Boys

My call for schools to honor the literacies and discourses of boys derives from the realization that we live in a "mediasphere" (O'Brien, 2001), "a world saturated by inescapable, ever-evolving, and competing media that both flow through us and are altered and created by us" (Brozo, 2005, p. 534). O'Brien further describes this concept and what it means to youth in these terms:

> I use the adapted term mediasphere to refer to the mediacentric world of young people. Within youth culture, we have been concerned that this massive, continual media absorption would render our young people as

passive consumers, manipulated by the bombardment. In fact, life in the mediasphere has turned our kids into keen interactors (rather than passive receptors) who understand media ... (and have) become increasingly powerful and adept at using (media) to define themselves. (p. 2)

The ubiquitous nature of new media in the lives of today's male youth was confirmed in a recent report suggesting teens in America are spending nearly nine hours a day using media such as online video and music (Common Sense Media, 2015). After undertaking multi-year case studies of adolescents and their digital media, Boyd (2014) discovered that, to teens, "these technologies – and the properties that go with them – are just an obvious part of life" (p. 42). She further maintains that adolescents "don't try to analyze how things are different because of technology; they simply try to relate to a public world in which technology is a given" (p. 41). This immersion in, and natural facility with, digital technologies appears to describe boys even more so than girls (Rowsell & Kendrick, 2013; Steinkuehler & King, 2009).

ICT tools, such as Google and other search engines and electronic databases, are also helping to transform memory processes by making them more efficient (Sparrow, Liu, & Wegner, 2011). A twenty-first century cognitive skill, then, doesn't necessarily include the capacity to memorize a vast amount of information but the ability to remember where and how to access needed information stored in digital spaces. Nostalgia may impel some of us living in the mediasphere to wish we were less dependent on our computers, tablets, and smart phones, but we have come to rely on them in essentially the same way we have relied on any source of information and knowledge. Thus, we can argue whether it is good for youth to be constantly "plugged in," but they, like all of us, must stay connected to have efficient access to the vast memory banks available in cyberspace.

An important caveat must be given here as regards computer use and online activity in school. At least for some reading tasks, like those found on PISA for both traditional and digital formatted texts, an excessive amount of computer time in school may actually depress achievement (OECD, 2015). Not too often, and for deliberately chosen activities, were found to be the optimal school uses of computers. This does not imply that browsing the Internet for assignments is harmful, except that this kind of online activity, when performed daily without appropriate teacher guidance nor commensurate with challenging and higher level reading and navigation tasks, may fail to benefit adolescent learners. At the same time, little or no school-based computer activity also appears to be associated with lower reading performance. A related concern regarding ICTs and boys comes from Harrison (2016), who wonders about the effects on weaker male readers of spending as much as nine hours a day engaged with electronic media and in online activity. Harrison makes the point that online learning from multimedia texts requires highly developed digital reading skills that boys who are struggling readers may not acquire from unstructured leisure time spent media multitasking.

A notable consequence of the spread of ICTs in the general public, reading is massively shifting from print to digital texts. For example, computers have become the second source of news for American citizens, after TV and before radio and printed newspapers and magazines (American Press Institute, 2014). Similarly, British children and teenagers prefer to read digital than printed texts (Clark, 2014), and a recent UNESCO report showed that two thirds of users of a phone-based reader across five nations indicated that their interest in reading and time spent reading increased once it was possible to read on their phones (UNESCO, 2014). This shift has important consequences for the definition of reading as a skill.

Acquiring and expanding competence with the new literacies of the Internet and other ICTs will require boys engage in practices that stretch beyond foundational literacies that may be sufficient for past forms of reading and writing (Hartman, Morsink, & Zheng, 2010; International Reading Association, 2009). Communicative competence in the twenty-first century involves negotiating and creating new forms of text found in evolving combinations of traditional offline environments with new online media within complex information networks (Dalton & Proctor, 2008; Wyatt-Smith & Elkins, 2008).

The realization that boys are the most active participants in the mediasphere, means these new forms of discourse they experience and create should be acknowledged and appreciated in school settings, since competency in these new forms of communication serve youth well in the ever-evolving global reach of the digital age (Alvermann et al., 2012; Squire, 2011). I believe the digital-discourse worlds most boys inhabit, if validated in the public sphere of schools and classrooms, could narrow achievement gaps (Leu et al., 2015) and increase engagement in literacy and content learning (Walsh, 2010). School is the setting where youths' multiple literacies – digital, graphic, aural – could find expression in the understanding, critical analysis, and reinterpretation of concepts and content (Leu et al., 2015; O'Brien & Scharber, 2008).

Boys in the Real World

"Christopher"

Christopher, a sixth-grade boy, lives with his mother in a suburb of a large metropolitan area. He has many typical outside-of-school interests for an 11-year-old boy. He plays outdoors with his friends and, when they cannot go outside, they stay in and play video games. He also "somewhat reads, but not really," admitting that his favorite activity is playing video games, such as, *Fortnite* and *World War II*.

Christopher explained that, even though reading is not his favorite subject, he still has favorite authors and series books. He was introduced to a series called *Middle School* by James Patterson. His English teacher suggested that he read some of these books for out-of-class reading and he has enjoyed them. His mother also purchases books for him, such as *The Ghost* by Jason Reynolds (2016). Mostly, though, his favorite reading material is manga, especially those books with the character Naruto.

Christopher describes himself as an "Okay reader for my grade level," but adds, "I wouldn't say I am a good reader because some words, I don't understand because the writer uses figurative language and metaphors." Although Christopher is not an enthusiastic reader, he is aware that he is reading when he reads the subtitles of his favorite anime videos, since they are in Japanese. He also expressed that he knows how important reading is but likes "video games much more than reading."

Regarding writing, Christopher reports that "for a boy, I have good handwriting." He is most proud of a fictional piece he wrote based on a picture his teacher showed to the class of a boy standing by his dying mother's hospital bed. When he read his story to the class, many of his classmates liked his story the most. Outside of school, Christopher does some writing, but likes to draw and make comics.

Christopher thinks that reading done on electronic devices instead of actual books is more interesting and fun. He also expressed that he would read more and complete his reading assignments if prizes were given for reading. He likes books that have also been made into movies, like *The Outsiders*. After the class finished reading the book, they watched the movie and he realized that the book was so much better.

Discussion and Activities

- What recommendations can you offer to teachers working with Christopher to ensure his reading and writing interests are nurtured?
- How can Christopher's interests in manga and anime be exploited for further literacy skill and vocabulary development?

> - In what ways can teachers exploit the computer games Christopher enjoys to further his reading and writing abilities?

Guidelines for Using New Literacies with Boys

A report of instructional computers and Internet access in US public schools as of 2008 (Gray, Thomas, & Lewis, 2010) documents an estimated level of 100 percent. This means that virtually all youth – regardless of whether computer technology tools are available in the home, which for over 27 percent of adolescents are not (US Census Bureau, 2014) – should be able to access ICTs in schools and classrooms. At the same time, at least 42 states in the United States require core technical competencies based on Common Core State Standards (Avila & Moore, 2012; Hutchison & Colwell, 2014). These standards serve to further institutionalize the need to weave ICTs into all areas of the school curriculum.

We know, however, that, in spite of the prevalence of ICTs in school, taking full advantage of these ever-evolving teaching and learning tools will depend on teachers' interest and willingness to become more tech savvy (Dede, 2010), as well as structural supports in schools (Hicks & Turner, 2013). I agree with Robinson and Mackey's (2006) admonition when they say:

> The classroom is full of media-literate kids who are savvy in ways far beyond their teachers' comprehension or interest. Teachers need to get used to not being the expert, because they are bound to teach students who are far more knowledgeable than they in the ways of new media. The answer lies in giving kids the chance to showcase their skills and experiences. (p. 201)

Thus, while we know boys are engaged with mediasphere technologies in their everyday lives, the full educational benefits of these skills and technologies may be going untapped (Hutchison & Reinking, 2011). Furthermore, intermedial practices for critically reading and writing across various digital and non-digital systems may not be as widespread in school as they should be (Colwell, Hunt-Barron, & Reinking, 2013). For instance, in a study of teachers' beliefs and attitudes about technology and their applications of technology in regular instruction, Ertmer and her colleagues (2012) learned that teachers' failure to use technology was due to their limited knowledge of, and lack of skills with, technology tools, as much as their attitudes and beliefs about technology. With the average age of

American teachers at about 45 years (Data USA, https://datausa.io/profile/soc/252020/), it is likely many were not provided digital and media literacy education in their university programs, so may be unfamiliar with effective instructional practices using technology tools (Hobbs, 2010). Nonetheless, the stretch from simple uses such as email to the vast and learning-rich potential of ICTs is much easier than some teachers might think (Ertmer & Ottenbreit-Leftwich, 2010).

The overriding criterion teachers of young boys and male youth should apply when considering the use of ICTs in their instructional practices is the extent to which these tools will promote engaged reading, expansive learning, and critical thinking. I believe, as others (Hicks & Turner, 2013; Walsh, 2010) do, that teachers who create learning contexts where the importance of critical reading and thinking is valued will find appropriate ways to integrate ICTs in support of boys' overall literacy development. The guidelines below should be used to help make decision about how best to link ICTs to instruction with boys in mind.

Provide Boys Opportunities for Creative Uses of ICT Tools

After at least three decades of research, what we know about the value of ICTs for teaching and learning is that achievement is more likely to rise if they are used in interesting and creative ways instead of mostly for drill in basic skills (Livingstone, 2012). In fact, using technology for drill, practice, and entertainment was found to depress achievement (Biagi & Loi, 2013; Kinzer & Leander, 2003). The idea is that it's not how much time students spend with these technologies but the quality of use, the breadth of experiences, and flexible affordances of ICTs that relate to higher achievement (Biagi & Loi, 2013). This also means teachers need to be willing to explore more flexible and creative applications of ICTs with their male students.

This guideline also emphasizes that to engage boys ICTs should be exploited for their unique instructional capabilities and not simply as media for re-presenting predictable worksheet tasks in a visual format. Interesting and creative uses of technology are more likely to enhance learning and develop higher-level thinking skills (Ananiadou & Claro, 2009; Anderson, 2008). Computers and other electronic media can help students visualize content to be learned in novel ways. For example, virtual reality programs and programs that allow students to work with geometric figures in hyperspace are made possible only through computer-based instructional technology (Dalgarno & Lee, 2009). The activities described a bit later in this chapter all emphasize the ways in which the technology can be used creatively for engendering higher-level thinking and knowledge acquisition.

Use ICT Tools in Ways That Promote Boys' Critical Thinking

With the advent of widespread access to ICT tools in homes and schools, our ideas about literacy have undergone major transformations. Literacy is no longer viewed solely as the ability to decode and encode printed words. Proponents of new and multiple literacies (Gee & Hayes, 2011; Lankshear & Knobel, 2013; Leu et al., 2015) assert that a much broader conception of what it means to be literate encompasses all forms of symbolic communication enacted by adolescents and influencing their lives and learning. This conception must include, of course, information and communications technologies.

Preparing boys for the challenges of reading, writing, and critical thinking in the mediasphere of the twenty-first century, a world where traditional print literacy is no longer enough, is incumbent upon the responsible educator. These new literacies are seen as vital tools students must have in order to navigate within and "read" our increasingly complex global society (Ananiadou & Claro, 2009; UNESCO, 2014). I agree with Brazilian scholar and activist, Paulo Freire (1987), who insisted that in order to read the word, we must also be capable of reading the world. Critically reading the world and the word should, therefore, be a vibrant feature of instruction with ICT tools for boys.

Each year, as the Internet and electronic media options grow exponentially, the need to support boys' critical reading and thinking when engaged with ICTs becomes ever more urgent. This mind-boggling expansion of digital media has created a greater need than ever before for critical consciousness and critical reading (Buckingham, 2007; Koltay, 2011). Nearly 20 years ago, Burbules and Callister (2000) offered a caution about the opportunities and problems of unrestricted self-expression on the Internet that is just as relevant today:

> Participants in this environment often need to read and evaluate so much material, from so many sources, that it becomes impossible to maintain a critical discerning attitude toward it all. The very volume and number of voices has a kind of leveling effect – everything seems to come from the same place and nothing seems much more reliable than anything else. This makes the need to evaluate the value and credibility of what one encounters on the

Internet a crucial skill if one is to be an active beneficiary of the available information and interaction (2000, p. 71).

It is because of the overwhelming proliferation of electronic media and the ease of accessibility that I urge teachers to foster in male youth a form of critical literacy of the Internet medium itself (Avila & Moore, 2012; Ladbrook & Probert, 2011; Livingstone, 2008).

Use ICT Tools in Ways That Promote Boys' Authentic Communication

Our best thinking about the most effective ways to increase literacy and learning makes it clear that students need ample time to engage in activities that have authentic purposes (Brozo, 2017). The reading and writing involved in typical computer tasks in schools can provide some much-needed time for boys to participate in authentic literacy activities (Wyatt-Smith & Elkins, 2008). Consider the literacy requirements of a ninth grader's computer research of the rocky planets in our solar system. First, he must know or learn about the most relevant search engines for his topic. Next, he must type in the best search words. Once confronted with perhaps thousands of "hits," he needs to review them to determine which ones will provide the needed information and content. All the while, he is reading, making critical judgments, and typing key words and phrases to hone his search. Although voice activation for simple search tasks is becoming increasingly available, in the foreseeable future, reading and writing skills will continue to be a necessity for school-related ICT activity.

ICT tools should also be exploited for the ways they provide an authentic sense of audience for literacy activity. Boys who participate in social media as a daily routine, like countless youth in the United States, Europe, and across the world (Boyd, 2014), may be doing so without a full awareness of the literacy skills and strategies being exercised, not unlike the attitude of "Joshua" in the *Boys in the Real World* feature in Chapter 6. Boys who communicate on the Internet may be doing so with an actual audience of one or perhaps hundreds or even thousands. These out-of-school activities that involve writing and reading in cyberspaces can be exploited by teachers to help boys develop audience sensitivity and literacy skills (Hawisher et al., 2009). For example, boys can engage in activities as simple as writing personal reactions to a current event on a blog and texts to electronic pen pals, to more complex communication tasks such as formal inquiries to experts, companies, and organizations and creating home pages and publishing e-zines (Bull et al., 2008; Coiro, 2009; Courtland & Paddington, 2008; Greenhow & Robelia, 2009).

Use ICT Tools in Ways That Increase Boys' Motivation for and Interest in Purposeful and Meaningful Learning

The strongest advocates for the use of ICTs in teaching and learning claim one of its most appealing features is that students are automatically interested in and motivated by these digital tools (Brooks-Young, 2010; Coiro et al., 2008; Nelson, 2008). Indeed, there is a growing body of research to support the motivating effects of ICTs when used with students, especially males, in school-based learning on either side of the Atlantic (Condie & Munro, 2007; DeGennaro, 2008; Eurydice, 2005; Tømte, 2008; Vekiri & Chronaki, 2008; Williams & Merten, 2008).

Bridging motivation with constructive learning for boys is, as I have been saying throughout this chapter, the artful task of the primary and secondary teacher. One of my expressed goals in this text is to help teachers develop young boys and male youth who are motivated and engaged readers, writers, and learners. If boys are more enthusiastic about learning using ICT tools, then teachers and their male students should exploit these tools to whatever extent they can mediate meaningful and critical exploration of content.

Use ICT Tools to Promote Boys' Collective Learning and Collaboration

The study of information and communication technologies is now concerned with learning in complex, interactive environments (Luppicini, 2007; Piki, 2008; So, Seah, & Toh-Heng, 2010). Because these environments are frequently inhabited by more than one person, opportunities for collective learning are ever present (Chai & Tan, 2010). Increasingly sophisticated ICTs and ever-increasing social media options are expanding possibilities for collaborative learning (García-Valcárcel, Basilotta, & López, 2014; Gutnick, Robb, Takeuchi, & Kotler, 2011). Internet tools designed to facilitate student interaction within a class, school, community, state, nation, and world are becoming easier for teachers to access. It's now possible, for example, to establish virtual relationships between students and distant experts, enabling collaboration mentoring, and community building. Teachers are taking advantage of these new communications tools by structuring technology-based activities that require frequent, critical dialog among students' immediate peers as well as others in distant virtual communities (Merchant, 2009; Parker, 2010; Sing, Wei-Ying, Hyo-Jeong, & Mun, 2011; Wang, 2008).

In the next section of this chapter, you will read descriptions of teachers exploiting the potential of new media and digital technology for increasing boys' engagement for literacy and learning. I especially like the approaches and strategies used by these teachers because, in one form or another, the guidelines presented here can be recognized in their practices, which are marked by creativity, opportunities for critical thinking, authentic communication, and engaged and collaborative learning.

Promising Programs and Practices

Alternative Texts

Adolescent boys may be the most active participants in the mediasphere, using and creating forms of discourse that could be acknowledged and appreciated in school settings. School is where youths' multiple literacies could be exploited and allowed to find expression to help them grow as readers and thinkers. To do so, teachers need to find ways of exploiting the multiple literacy competencies adolescent boys bring to school (Brozo, 2018), such as the ability to communicate through digital means and social networking (e.g., texting, Facebook, blogging, twittering); create hypertext documents; and interpret and think critically about music CDs and videos, video/computer games, and websites. Within traditional reading and language arts programs, room will need to be made for boys' out-of-school literacies in order for teachers to build on their strengths, develop academic knowledge and skills, and promote lifelong independent reading and learning (Brozo, 2013; Hinchman et al., 2003/2004).

In addition to digital media, boys are also drawn to alternatively formatted text, such as graphic novels and comic books (Brozo & Gaskins, 2009). In the United States, Hughes-Hassell and Rodge (2007) report on the leisure reading habits of 1,340 students in grades five through eight at an urban middle school in a large northeastern city. In their findings, 54 percent of male students ranked comics as the favorite leisure reading choice.

Recently, this point was brought home to a skeptical freelance writer who contacted me while researching an article about boys and reading. What are they reading? she wondered. I told her to go to her nearest bookstore on a Saturday afternoon and conduct an informal observational survey to find out. I suggested she first position herself near the young adult book section for an hour, and document the number of adolescent boys who browsed there. Then, I had her reposition herself near the graphic novel/comic book stacks and do the same thing. "Call me back and let me know what you find," I asked. But I knew what her observations would reveal before she told me how surprised she was to discover only one or two boys in the young adult section but piles of boys in the graphic novel section, sprawled on the floor, leaning against the shelves, talking excitedly with buddies about the newest discovery.

As with other youth media, comic books have traditionally been spurned by teachers and librarians. Perhaps because adults tend to hold these texts in such low regard, boys have spent a considerable amount of their outside-of-school leisure time reading nothing but comics. When in 1992, Art Spiegelman's (1986) *Maus I: A Survivor's Tale* was awarded a Pulitzer Prize, comic books and graphic novels gained newfound respect (Brozo, Moorman, & Meyer, 2014). They now come in numerous genres and are quickly becoming recognized as an engaging resource for classrooms and libraries (Boerman-Cornell, 2013; Griffith, 2010; Yang, 2008). Many teachers are now supplementing lessons on the Holocaust with graphic novels like *Maus* (Chun, 2009; Gray, 2014) and teaching about a range of other issues across the curriculum with graphic novels (Cromer & Clark, 2007). Furthermore, it has been shown that graphic novels and comic books are excellent resources for motivating reluctant readers (Cho, Choi, & Krashen, 2005; Spiegel et al., 2013). The illustrations can provide the needed contextual clues to the meaning of the written narrative, especially for struggling readers and English learners (Chun, 2009; Thompson, 2008). These features may be particularly attractive to boys, who have demonstrated higher competencies with text formatted in non-traditional ways (Bunn, 2012; Canadian Council on Learning, 2010; Gavigan, 2010).

Bridge-Building Texts

In most classrooms, a core textbook continues to be the primary source for reading and learning. Yet, unless boys are able to relate to these texts on an engaging and meaningful level, they may not take from them as much as we know they should. Thus, even if these required texts are "readable," they may turn boys off to reading. Teachers, therefore, need to recognize the value of connecting text sources from boys' everyday worlds to required course readings and topics (Brozo & Gaskins, 2009).

The goal of this bridge-building process is to take advantage of boys' relative strengths with language and literacy outside of school by transitioning them into challenging academic texts. Another goal is to motivate reluctant and disinterested male youth to read required academic texts. Bridge texts are not only more interesting to boys but also help put knowledge bases in place for academic tasks. Furthermore, alternative sources, when linked to academic texts and given legitimacy in school settings, are likely to engage boys in meaningful reading and learning that can lead to elevated achievement (Brozo, 2013).

Teachers who learn to use sources from the everyday worlds of boys as embellishment to core text sources, will find their male students reading with greater interest and enjoyment (Brozo, 2006; Fisher & Frey, 2012). Consider, for instance, the science teacher who prepared her class for a study of the laws of physics by first exploring the website Skateboard Science (www.exploratorium.edu/skateboarding/) as a bridge to reading and studying laws of physics. Boys' reading comprehension is likely to be greater with high-interest materials because interesting material maintains students' attention more effectively (McDaniel, Waddill, Finstad, & Bourg, 2000; Steinmayr & Spinath, 2009).

Teaching Shakespeare with Manga

Amanda's male students in her ninth-grade general English class could only groan when she said they would begin Shakespeare's *Romeo and Juliet* at the start of the new grading period. Their expressions of displeasure turned to curiosity, however, when she told them they would prepare for the play by first reading the manga version (Shakespeare, Appignanesi, & Leong, 2007). The art in manga graphic novels is highly stylized, originating in Japan, and the books are widely read by teens. This version of the play offers students a unique and highly readable complement to the one in their literature anthology. Set in modern-day Tokyo, the authors combine manga-style art and abridged dialogue to re-create the themes of the play. Although the richness of Shakespeare's original language may be sacrificed, the script preserves the spirit of the story, including all the major speeches. The layout and characters are well rendered in the typical gray-scale art of manga texts. By situating the play in modern Tokyo among rival yakuza, or organized-crime families, the authors present adolescent boys with a world they will recognize. And these features, along with the engaging illustrations, help boys comprehend the original story, and prepares them for reading the actual Shakespeare play.

Amanda employed a kind of impromptu Readers Theater to read the manga text. Groups of students went to the front of the room with their books and read parts. A new group took over after five to ten pages. Students were expected to use simple gestures and actions to accompany their readings. In between groups, Amanda engaged the class in discussion about the plot, characters, and theme, and then helped her class make connections between the twenty-first-century storyline from Japan and its original setting in Renaissance Italy. The boys were especially enthusiastic about this approach, because the illustrations and modern context made the story much more accessible than if they had launched the unit with Shakespeare's original heartbreaking tragedy. With the manga version, the boys were able to understand and follow the storyline, making it easier to appreciate the teenage heroes, the scheming and villainous adults, and the overarching theme of star-crossed lovers.

When the time came to break open the literature anthology and begin reading *Romeo and Juliet*, Amanda's entire class, especially the male contingent, was much more enthusiastic about taking on the Bard. Her students now had an appreciation for the drama and excitement of the play. They took full advantage of the compelling illustrations in the manga version to envision scenes of teenage romance; family feuding; fights over honor between Tybalt, Benvolio, Mercutio, and Romeo; and even suicide. With each scene, students were asked to compare the Shakespeare text, events, and characters with the manga version. Amanda had students rewrite scenes using everyday language, create their own cartoon panels, and perform impromptu dramatic interpretations, which they did with greater competence and accuracy as a result of the bridging experiences with manga.

Teaching Word Families with Rap Music

As demonstrated by the work of Amanda, creative teachers find ways to honor youths' outside-of-school media while bridging them to the concepts and information in the classroom. An obvious source for enlivening school-based learning for boys is popular media and music (Brozo, 2013). Because today's male youth live in the mediasphere, it makes good sense to find as many linkages as possible between the images and music with which they are familiar and topics under study in the classroom.

Music, as a medium of identity construction for boys, is a viable alternative text form that is underused by most teachers. Scaffolding for new understandings means working with what boys bring to the classroom, including their interest in and knowledge of popular music (Morrell & Duncan-Andrade, 2002).

Derrick, an eighth-grade special education teacher with mostly boys in his self-contained English class, had been frustrated by his students' lack of engagement in the lessons and readings, until he began tapping into their media and music for teaching aspects of language and composition.

For instance, when preparing his class for a study of word families, he first found out what his male students had programmed on their phones. He then tracked down the lyrics from some of these songs and raps and found they possess a variety of words that could be studied as families and then could be used as models for other similar words in school texts and in their own writing. With his students' own music as the text for learning word families, Derrick noted the boys in class were eager to participate in the lessons, remembered more content, and gave more thoughtful responses.

When studying the /ch/ and /ck/ digraphs, Derrick invited students to bring in lyrics with these elements. As long as the song or rap lyrics met acceptable school standards (no profanity, excessive violence, or degrading messages about women and girls), students were allowed to work with them in their analysis. With a partner, first students were to create a t-chart listing all the words that had either the /ch/ or /ck/ element.

One pair of African American boys brought in and analyzed the rap lyric "I Love to Give You Light" by Snoop Dogg. The boys found many words with the word family elements. Derrick then directed the students to generate new words with the /ch/ and /ck/ sounds and add these to their t-chart. The pair with Snoop Dogg's rap lyrics added *catch, match, reach,* and *bunch* to the left column and *socks, locker, backpack,* and *stick* to the right column words. Each pair of students completed activities with the song lyrics they had brought to class to analyze.

With their new words, students were then asked to write lyrics based on the genre of music they analyzed. The lyrics had to contain the new words they generated to match the /ch/ and /ck/ sounds. Thus, the boys working with the Snoop Dogg rap wrote their own. While one kept rhythm on his desk top, the other one read the rap:

> I put my socks in my backpack
> when I go to school.
> I put my backpack in my locker
> or I look like a fool.
> I get my socks from my backpack
> when I go to gym.

Where I catch the ball
then stick it in the rim.

Derrick witnessed a new level of enthusiasm for learning among his students, especially the boys, doing word study work with their own song lyrics. The best result, however, was that his students' enthusiasm translated into genuine learning. Derrick noticed their ability to recognize many of the same words and those with the same word family elements in their own and their classmates' compositions, and as they read stories and other texts. This level of application and transfer occurred because Derrick eliminated barriers between outside-of-school interests and literacies of his students and classroom practices. And his male students were the special beneficiaries, as their engagement in reading and learning as well as their language competencies increased.

Words from "I Love to Give You Light" with /ch/ and /ck/ Sounds

Ch	Ck
such	background
preach	jackers
church	glock
teachin'	block
watchin'	locked
each	black
preachin'	
beach	
reach	
child	

Teaching Allusion with Digital Media

Alejandro decided to administer a questionnaire to his tenth graders at the beginning of the school year to try to gain insights into ways of structuring learning that would be more appealing to them. One of the strongest suggestions came from most of his male students who were univocal in asking for more choices and options, particularly in the ways they are assessed. Another recommendation that came mostly from the boys in his class was being able to use the computer and Internet for class assignments. Using this information as a guide, Alejandro created a range of different ways students could demonstrate understanding of newly learned content with digital media.

One striking example of how Alejandro took advantage of his male students' input was the approach he used to teach about allusion in literature. Allusion is a difficult literary device for students to appreciate, because it's a reference in a literary work to a person, place, or thing in history or another work of literature. Allusions are often indirect or brief references to characters or events, but if readers don't know the events and characters to which an author alludes, then the allusion loses its impact.

To help sensitize his students to this literary device and bring them to appreciate its significance, Alejandro gave the class its initial exposure to allusion through a YouTube video clip from *Shrek 2*, a popular animated film for youth. The three minute clip includes several visual allusions to other films and film characters, both real and animated, with the song "My Boy Lollypop" as the soundtrack. As the clip played, Alejandro asked students to note any images that referenced other movies or movie characters, and then held a discussion afterward.

This visual approach, using media from his students' everyday lives, proved quite successful, as they were able to identify several allusions in the video. Alejandro was especially pleased with the involvement and participation of his male students in this activity.

Next, Alejandro guided his students through a class blog he had established. He indicated where they were to make entries and respond to their classmates. His assignment to them was to find examples of allusion in their own media – books, films, games, music, etc. – and post it on the blog with an explanation of the allusion. Each student was required to post two examples on the blog and write two entries in response to their classmates.

Alejandro was overjoyed to find the range and depth of student responses to his assignment when he checked the site a couple of days later. What pleased him the most were the contributions from his boys. They were at a level of sophistication and reflected a level of involvement he was sure he wouldn't have seen if the assignment had been framed in a more traditional way, as these examples attest.

> **"Evan"**
> The avant garde music group Mr. Bungle modified the Warner Brothers' logo into their own creation. By simply flipping and turning their record's label (Warner Brothers), they made an already existing logo into something

brand spanking new. This is an allusion to the band's label, so it is kind of like a self-promoting allusion.

"Jung-Hee"
My allusion is from the anime *Lucky Star* (which no one has probably heard of, but is the only one I can think of at the moment). In one of the episodes, the main character, Konata, cosplays (dresses up) as a character from another anime, Haruhi from *The Melancholy of Haruhi Suzumiya* at a cosplay café. The function of this allusion, in a way, is self-promotion because the writers of *Lucky Star* also wrote *The Melancholy of Haruhi Suzumiya*.

"Fareed"
In a *Jimmy Neutron–Boy Genius* episode, Jimmy goes to find out why the Bermuda triangle has so many problems. On his way into the ocean to search for an underwater entrance, the viewers see a small pineapple. As all Nickelodeon viewers know, Spongebob Squarepants lives in that pineapple. This was the producers' way of saying "Hi" to the cast of *Spongebob*.

"Carlos"
I found one from *Family Guy*. This is an allusion to *The Ring*, like how when you watch the cursed video in the movie *The Ring*, you'll die. In *Family Guy*, the cursed video is *The Simpsons*, which is their rival. And if you watch it, they're basically [saying] *The Simpsons* is bad for you.

From here, Alejandro transitioned his class into looking for and uncovering allusions in traditional print texts, which they did with far greater success than his students had in previous years. With this assignment, Alejandro was able to take advantage of his students' competencies with media and literacies outside of school to achieve his goal of motivating reluctant and disinterested male youth to read and respond on a more thoughtful level to required texts in his classroom. Of course, the most pervasive popular medium in youth's lives is the computer, so it's a natural entry point.

Teaching Science Vocabulary with Video Games

One of Bianca's fifth-grade science students, Ubikway, was a daydreamer. She would catch him during class staring out the window, blissfully disengaged from the flow of instruction. When confronted, he would apologize and refocus, only to fall back into his private reverie at the next available moment. Although the school year was new, Bianca sensed that Ubikway was a bright young man, capable of accurate and thoughtful work, but wondered what it was that distracted him during her lessons.

Bianca decided to talk with Ubikway after class. She asked for an honest response when she questioned him about how she could make her science class more interesting to him. Without hesitation, Ubikway said he was thinking about his new Star Wars video game, and if he could use video games like that or others, he would pay much closer attention in class. To Ubikway's delight, Bianca asked him to bring the video game to school to show her how it's played.

Bianca discovered as Ubikway helped her move through the game, talking strategy and using terminology animatedly, that science concepts and vocabulary were plentiful. After a more thorough review of the game, Bianca decided to incorporate it into an approaching unit on space exploration. She knew this approach would be enthusiastically received by Ubikway and the other boys in his class.

Bianca gave each student a chart with keywords to be studied during the unit. She directed students to fill in definitions of the vocabulary terms based on their contextualized definitions within the Star Wars video game. She then projected the game on the screen and allowed different students to come up and play it while the class looked on. Bianca would pause periodically when the game narrator, intoning like Darth Vader, uttered a term from their chart. Using the visual information, students were to write what they thought the word meant. This process was repeated for each of the terms from their charts.

Afterward, Bianca discussed the same terms as they appeared in the class textbook, helping students use context and the glossary to determine word meanings. She then asked students to fill in the third and final column of the chart.

To reinforce the acquisition of the new science vocabulary, Bianca next had students work with a partner to write their own Star Wars story using the words in context. One pair of her male students wrote:

> Luke Skywalker sat in a ***space station***. It was in our ***galaxy***. He was going to set off the ***booster rockets*** so he could travel to a ***planet***. The planet was going to be hit by a ***meteor*** and Luke had to save it.

Throughout the unit, when students earned free time, Bianca allowed groups of two to three to play the Stars Wars game she had set up in a computer carrel in the classroom. Thanks to Ubikway and his video game, Bianca's class remained actively involved in learning the content and vocabulary of the unit on space exploration and demonstrated their heightened understanding on the unit test. This positive outcome for learning and memory as a result of playing video games requiring strategic thinking has been confirmed in recent research (Oei & Patterson, 2013). Noticing that her boys were especially engaged by this approach to learning, Bianca has continued to find ways of incorporating their interests in alternative texts and media into her science lessons.

New Literacies and Boys: A Coda

Understanding boys in today's society requires knowing and learning to value their literate practices beyond the school walls. These practices pose new challenges for teachers, especially those who hold to traditional notions about reading and writing. What it means to be literate is undergoing perpetual revision in this age of ever-evolving ICTs. And boys are inveterate purveyors of these new literacies. In addition to digital media, boys are also drawn to alternatively formatted text, such as graphic novels and comic books. Teachers who recognize and understand these new literate practices are more likely to craft successful language and literacy curriculum for male youth.

I have shown in the Promising Programs and Practices section of this chapter that school is where boys' multiple literacies could be exploited and allowed to find expression to help them grow as readers and thinkers. To do so, teachers need to find ways of exploiting the multiple literacy competencies and interests boys bring to school in order to build on their strengths, develop academic knowledge and skills, and promote lifelong independent reading and learning. Furthermore, as teachers increase their knowledge of classroom applications of ICTs, it is my hope that they will help boys become wise and purposeful consumers and generators of new media.

CHAPTER 8

Boys and Writing: Evidence and Practice

> **In this chapter, I,**
> - Analyze relevant NAEP writing and SAT writing findings demonstrating boys' challenges with writing achievement
> - Present research evidence on gender and writing performance from Europe
> - Describe successful and promising programs and practices

Writing, for most youth, girls and boys alike, is an everyday occurrence, though they may not always recognize it as writing (Lenhart, Arafeh, Smith, & Macgill, 2008). Their thumbs and fingers are pressing out missives, notes, abbreviated responses to friends, family, and even strangers in virtual social spaces all day, every day, so reflexively as not to be noticed (Boyd, 2014). Yet, according to Lenhart and her colleagues, even though a large majority of adolescents believe writing well is more important today than it was for previous generations and that skilled writing is essential for a successful life, they do not see a connection between their personal digital writing and school-based writing.

This finding is especially concerning for boys, since it is well established that the gender achievement gap in writing is even wider than it is in reading (Disenhaus, 2015; National Center for Education Statistics [NCES], 2011; Peterson & Parr, 2012). Thus, in addition to boys' personal writing, they also need to expand their capacities for writing in academic contexts (Kohnen, 2013; Riley & Reedy, 2000). Developing writing skills and abilities can position boys for an efficacious life beyond the school walls. Thus, the admonishment that every teacher should not only assign but teach writing in order to prepare male youth for college, careers, and life is made all the more compelling by the eloquent rationale from the National Writing Project (www.nwp.org/cs/public/print/doc/about.csp):

> Writing is essential to communication, learning, and citizenship. It is the currency of the new workplace and global economy. Writing helps us convey ideas, solve problems, and understand our changing world. Writing is a bridge to the future . . .
> [We envision] a future where every person is an accomplished writer, engaged learner, and active participant in a digital, interconnected world. (n.p.)

When writing guided by this perspective is integrated into primary and secondary classrooms, it is especially advantageous to struggling students (Gillespie, Graham, Kiuhara, & Hebert, 2014), who are more often than not boys (Collie, Martin, & Curwood, 2016; DeFauw, 2016; Scanlan, 2012; Senn, 2012). Writing has been shown not only to facilitate the learning of content but also engage students in higher-level thinking and reasoning (Klein, Arcon, & Baker, 2016). Furthermore, teachers once brought to see the benefits that result when their students engage in writing to learn activities, have embraced practices that integrate writing into daily instruction (Adu-Gyamfi, Bosse, & Faulconer, 2010; McNaught, 2010).

Writing in the Twenty-First Century

Consider for a moment all of the writing boys do in the course of their daily routines. They start with rolling over in bed and finding their iPhone to check emails and texts. After these have been screened, they might respond to one or two quickly, saving the more important ones for longer considered responses using a larger keyboard device. From there they might find themselves sitting at the breakfast table with their iPad reviewing homework texts and assignments. On the commute to school, they might text friends to make plans to meet when they arrive or continue a game started the evening before. At school, in classrooms and media centers, they complete assignments on laptops, conduct Internet searches, and compose papers and reports. During breaks at school, they screen, read, and respond to the constant flow of incoming messages and voicemail. After school, these often staccato-like reading and writing activities with personal digital devices continue unabated into the evening, right up to the moment they fall asleep.

Reflecting on this description should help us appreciate that, like millions of others in the United States, Europe, and around the world, in the twenty-first century, youth routinely spend a large portion of their day with their hands on keyboards and their minds on audiences. This suggests that writing has ascended as the main basis of many people's daily literacy experiences and the main platform for their literacy development (Brandt, 2015). This has profound implications for the way students learn literacy in school and how their literacy learning is situated. Furthermore, greater emphasis on developing students' writing abilities will better prepare them for the literate challenges of this evolving century.

If writing truly is the neglected literacy skill, as Brandt and others have characterized it, then data from the NAEP (NCES, 2011) would seem to confirm this perception in the US context. Results show that for both eighth-and twelfth-graders, as many as 20 percent scored at the Below Basic level and another 53 percent at the Basic level, while only 27 percent had scores in the proficient range and a mere 3 percent reached the highest achievement category of Advanced.

When the results are explored along gender lines, we find that girls outperform boys at both age groups to a significant degree, and have been doing so for some time. For instance, the 2008 NAEP writing results showed boys continuing to fall far short of the performance of girls, by 20 points among eighth graders and 18 points among twelfth graders. Similarly, on the 2011 assessment, female students again outscored male students in writing at both grades. The performance gap was 19 points at grade eight and 14 points at grade twelve. The gender gap in writing has been far wider than in other subjects assessed on NAEP (e.g., reading, math, science). Beyond the point-score differences between boys and girls, on the 2011 assessment, some 40 percent of eighth grade girls were proficient on the test, more than double the proportion of boys who scored at the proficient level.

Furthermore, black and Hispanic students and students from city schools had the lowest achievement levels of all groups. Low-income students were also among the weakest performers. Finally, for English learners, a full 79 percent were at the Below Basic level, with another 20 percent at the Basic level and a mere 1 percent at the Proficient level (www.nationsreportcard.gov/writing_2011/writing_tools.aspx). Although not identified specifically in the NAEP data, one can imagine the neediest of writers as boys of color from high poverty communities, and whose heritage language is not English.

These NAEP findings surely point to the need for schools to prioritize high-quality writing instruction for all youth, and particularly for boys who are struggling (Coleman, 2011), as well as multi-ethnic, multi-linguistic and multi-cultural male youth (Diaz-Rico, 2018; Perry, 2018).

In Canada, although the last pan-provincial/territorial assessment of writing (Student Achievement Indicators Program) was administered in 2002, the results indicate a significant percentage of adolescents at age 13 and 16 failing to reach the benchmark of competency for their respective grade levels. At that time, 60 percent of 13-year-olds and 40 percent of 16-year-olds fell short of the expected benchmark in writing (Peterson & McClay, 2014). Other broad-level indicators of writing achievement based on provincial assessments show that boys in grades four and six perform significantly less well than girls (Expert Panel on Literacy in Grades 4 to 6 in Ontario, 2004). This pattern has been verified by writing assessment results at the secondary school level in Canada, as well (Canadian Council on Learning, 2008).

It is more difficult to capture the state of affairs regarding writing achievement and gender in the European context due to a lack of cross-national assessments in this area. Unlike PISA and PIRLS, there are no similar tests of writing ability for children and youth taken across nations on that continent. At best, we can deduce conditions with gender-based writing achievement from individual studies conducted in separate European countries, as well as from broad-level reports summarizing literacy achievement in general.

Daly's (2002) review of the literature on improving boys' writing sponsored by the United Kingdom's Office of Standards in Education was prompted by the perceived lack of attention this aspect of literacy had been receiving by policy makers and researchers alike. According to Daly, the emphasis on reading literacy by the OECD and its "investment in reading as a prime measure of literacy for the global economy ... [has] overshadowed a focus on writing" (p. 3). Exploring findings from studies conducted primarily in the United Kingdom and Europe, one of Daly's key overall findings was a growing research base in support of teachers' perceptions of boys' underachievement in writing and the importance teachers place on this issue.

Further evidence from the United Kingdom's national assessments indicate that the gender gap in favor of girls is more pronounced on the writing scale than on any of the other achievement scales (e.g., reading, language, mathematics). Starting at age five, nearly 20 percentage points separate girls from boys, and this trend holds throughout the eleven years of compulsory education up through age 16 (Bourke & Adams, 2011). Investigating the causes of this achievement disparity, Bourke and Adams found that, in addition to gender, general language ability, such as vocabulary knowledge and expressive language, accounted for the largest proportion of variance. Girls included more words and a wider range of vocabulary in their writing as compared to boys, demonstrating a clearly identifiable and quantifiable mastery of written expression.

Beard and Burrell (2010) documented a similar gender-based pattern of writing achievement in British nine- and ten-year-olds. In their study, writing on a standardized measure was evaluated using test-specific criteria and research-based genre-specific rubrics. The overall results reinforced the pattern of boys' underachievement in writing relative to girls. Boys scored significantly lower than girls in all elements of the evaluation criteria for their written texts. Furthermore, a larger percentage of girls scored in the highest levels of competence on the writing text.

Pape and her associates (2011) in Norway confirmed that adolescents with reading and writing difficulties also were far more likely to need extensive social and medical services in later life. Boys had lower writing achievement levels than their female counterparts and male youth with low writing achievement levels were at the highest risk of welfare dependence in adulthood.

Another look at boys and writing in the European context is Merisuo-Storm's (2004) study of the writing attitudes and achievement of upper-primary-level boys in Finland. The researcher found that boys' attitudes toward writing were significantly more negative than those of the girls and even more negative than their attitudes toward reading. Not surprising was the finding that boys were significantly more reluctant writers than the girls, as well. The Finnish boys in the Merisuo-Storm study demonstrated heightened interest in writing when tasks had a meaningful purpose or a communicative function, such as receiving and writing letters.

It is clear that limited writing competence of boys and male youth represents a serious literacy concern for educators, as well as an economic challenge for policy makers and employers in North America (Alliance for Excellent Education, 2007; Fletcher, 2006; OISE Research Team, 2009). And, though in the European context, pan-national assessment data on writing are not available like those in the United States and Canada, other indicators point to the importance many European countries place on ensuring boys possess skillful writing ability (EURIDYCE, 2010).

Despite the recognition of the importance of children and youth possessing highly developed writing skills, writing, according to the National Commission on Writing (2003), has not been placed "squarely in the center of the school agenda" (p. 3). Applebee and Langer (2011), among others (Gilbert & Graham, 2010; Harris & Graham, 2013; Peterson & McClay, 2014), have documented the small amount of time devoted to teaching writing in most American and Canadian schools. Moreover, teachers report they are inadequately prepared to teach writing (Brindle, 2012). These patterns may be explained, in part, because reading literacy is the targeted skill assessed throughout North America and Europe, whereas writing literacy tends to receive less attention. Consequently, teachers on both continents are far more familiar with university-based training and in-service professional development in reading than they are in writing.

In the next section, I describe the links between writing and reading. These links remind teachers of the many ways writing can be braided with reading activities resulting in skill growth in both aspects of literacy.

Writing and Reading

For the past few decades, literacy researchers have attempted to demonstrate how reading and writing represent similar thinking processes. For instance, in the 1990s it was common to hear and read about the so-called "reading and writing connection." Reading and writing were thought to be overlapping processes that offer students alternative ways of constructing meaning (Tierney & Shanahan, 1991; Shanahan, 1997). According to Shanahan (2006) "reading and writing are dependent upon common cognitive substrata of abilities (e.g., visual, phonological, and semantic systems or short-and long-term memory), and anything that improves these abilities may have implications for both reading and writing development" (p. 174). Today, it is generally understood that reading and writing are interrelated processes and that purposeful instruction designed to develop these processes in tandem will benefit both (Gogan, 2013; Lockhart & Soliday, 2016).

According to a variety of authorities (Bazerman & Prior, 2008; Graham & Perin, 2007; MacArthur, Graham, & Fitzgerald, 2008), the writing process, like the reading process, has these overlapping and recursive elements:

1. ***Planning.*** Just as active learners use what they already know and set purposes before they begin to read, they also spend extended periods of time before actual writing to plan, to discover ways of approaching the compositional task, to self-question, and to identify purposes or problems. This phase of the writing process is often ignored because of an inordinate concern for generating a finished product to be

evaluated. If students could be provided more time to brainstorm ideas and discuss writing plans with peers and their teachers, the quality of their writing would significantly increase (Applebee & Langer, 2011; Kellogg & Whiteford, 2009).

2. ***Drafting.*** The second phase of the writing process focuses on the initial draft. At this point, the writer is attempting to get words onto screen or paper, into sentences, paragraphs, and sections. Similar to the challenge for readers, writers work to make things cohere and fit between the whole and parts and among the parts. Most writers, however, do not follow an orderly process in this initial drafting. Often students are not allowed enough in-class time for this initial drafting. Instead, writing may occur mostly out of class where peers and the teacher are not available for support and coaching.

3. ***Revising.*** The third phase of the writing process involves students in revising and reformulating. Just as active readers pause to reflect and monitor and then reread to verify and evaluate, effective writers take the time to read, reflect, and evaluate writing as another individual would. By taking the role of reader during this phase, students begin to see their "writing" as a piece of "reading."

    When students are involved in the revising process, they think about their main assertions, modifying them when they are not clear for their anticipated readers. They may also reorganize their papers, adding support and deleting information elsewhere, especially if they have not made their case for their audience. Hence, the recursive nature of the revising process often leads writers back to previous phases and processes (e.g., planning).

4. ***Editing and polishing.*** At this phase writers move from macro- to micro-level text concerns. They do so by examining their sentence structure, search for correct word choices, and proofread for basic errors in spelling, punctuation, or grammar.

5. ***Post-writing and sharing.*** Just as readers use and share the information they have read in some meaningful way, so should writers by sharing and making public their texts. In most situations, this sharing typically occurs in a private and limited way because teachers are the sole readers of students' compositions. Ideally, the audience for students' writing should be more public, whether that means other students, administrators, parents, community members, or individuals outside the community (e.g., politicians, business leaders, a virtual public).

The intensity and willingness male students devote to any of these phases depends on the two conditions that are within the control of teachers. When teachers share with them the processes of their own writing tasks, they are often surprised to discover that professional and competent writers must evaluate and revise extensively before they concern themselves with the surface features of spelling and grammar, aspects novice and challenged male writers tend to focus on. Furthermore, boys who have never written for anyone but the teacher often feel their ideas are not worthy of extended writing and revision or that the teacher already understands the ideas, so there is no need to be explicit and clear. They may also have difficulty believing in a real audience because the writing task to them is no more than an occasion for a grade. This misconception can be changed by providing boys with real and intriguing audiences for their writing, so the urgency of communicating ideas becomes a passion and a drive (Coleman, 2011). Evidence shows that male students who are motivated to write have greater self-efficacy (Villalón, Mateos, & Cuevas, 2015), are more likely to complete composition assignments (Pajares & Valiante, 2001), and are more willing to revise and edit their writing (Hawkins & Certo, 2014).

In sum, teachers can help their male students understand these recursive and overlapping stages by reserving time in class for brainstorming, planning, drafting, revising, editing/polishing, and sharing. However, it is important to bear in mind that not all students' school-based writing requires revision, editing, and publishing. For example, boys in biology maintaining a journal to document experiments, pose questions, and add comments that connect the learning that occurs in biology with their own lives and aspirations will likely only need to keep their journal entries in draft form, since this repository of questions, ideas, and descriptions is intended as a reflective tool and study aid.

Enhancing Reading through Writing

A common concern from teachers is that students read at a superficial level, resulting, at best, in memorized bits and pieces, but without depth of understanding or an appreciation of overall patterns and big ideas. This approach to reading may be particularly prevalent among boys, many of whom, as we have been shown, experience more challenges with complex text than their more able peers (EURIDYCE, 2010; Loveless, 2011).

The following example demonstrates the proclivity for shallow reading by struggling male readers and its fall-out.

> Mr. Gonzalez assigns his tenth grade history class the 1934 presidential inaugural speech of Franklin Roosevelt, which describes his vision for moving the United States out of its deep economic depression. He requests his students read the speech closely and come to class prepared to discuss its meaning and significance. To hold his students further accountable for the reading, he also suggests there might be a quiz over the content.
>
> Aziz, who with his father recently emigrated from Eritrea, is a diligent student, but lacks strategies for processing academic text in ways that lead to meaningful and critical understandings. Furthermore, while his English language skills are fairly well developed, idiomatic English poses special challenges for him. Thus, in preparation for class discussion, Aziz attempts to memorize the speech word-for-word by repeating each sentence several times.
>
> Mr. Gonzalez begins the next class with a quiz that asks students to identify three big ideas in the Roosevelt inaugural address and to explain the meaning of certain phrases, such as the lines, "The only thing we have to fear is fear itself" and "The unemployed face a problem of existence."
>
> Aziz fails the quiz because his surface-level approach to reading did not prepare him for Mr. Gonzalez's expectation that he and his classmates read more deeply and critically.

Although Mr. Gonzalez was justified in not accepting rote memorization by his students, he could have better prepared students like Aziz for his quiz and class discussion by integrating processes of reading and writing into his instruction. The combined use of reading and writing in this class would have provided Aziz with several advantages. A synthesis of the literature is clear when students write:

1. At the most simple level they are paraphrasing, summarizing, organizing, and linking new understandings with familiar ones (Chuy, Scardamalia, & Bereiter, 2012; Monte-Sano & De La Paz, 2012).
2. They are monitoring their comprehension, making it easier for them to identify what they know and what is confusing to them (Hebert, Gillespie, & Graham, 2013).
3. They are provided affordances in higher-level thinking, such as elaborating, synthesizing information across texts, and expressing critical perspectives and interpretations (Schwartz, 2015).
4. Teachers have an additional tool to motivate students and engage them in learning activities (Bernacki, Nokes-Malach, Richey, & Belenky, 2016).

5. Teachers can readily identify students' lack of conceptual understandings (Manzo & Manzo, 2013).

In connection to each of these advantages, Mr. Gonzalez could have capitalized on writing if he had assigned his students to read the Roosevelt inaugural speech and then summarize the key ideas, using their own words. In giving the assignment, Mr. Gonzalez could have modeled how he summarizes and explained how he uses brief summary notes and annotations to monitor his comprehension. After creating their summaries, students could have worked together to compare them while Mr. Gonzalez circulated around the room to eavesdrop on conversations. By doing this, he could have gained valuable insights into the students' depth of knowledge and the problems they were having with the text. Moreover, he could have used this input as a way to open a whole-class question-and-answer session. This approach to scaffolding the summary writing process could have been particularly helpful to students like Aziz.

Alternatively, Mr. Gonzalez could have capitalized on the power of writing by frontloading the assignment he gave his students. That is, he could have introduced the chapter and unit by asking the students to take five minutes to describe in their journals their opinion about a controversial policy or law. After several students had shared their journal entries, he could have asked them to brainstorm reasons why there were so many differences of opinion across the classroom. Mr. Gonzalez's students would have been better prepared and more motivated to read about the Roosevelt address, having brainstormed many of the important ideas in advance.

Finally, Mr. Gonzalez could have used writing as a way to encourage his student to think critically and creatively. For example, if Mr. Gonzalez wanted his students to apply the concepts in the address to situations in the community, he could have asked his students to work in small groups and poll a representative sample of 25 individuals about a variety of important issues related to the economic health of the community (e.g., employment opportunities for youth and addressing problems of homelessness). Once they completed their interviews, the groups could have then prepared a written report that summarized their findings and explained the results in light of the conditions of the country in the mid-1930s and Roosevelt's admonishments presented in the speech. Mr. Gonzalez could have also encouraged the students to formulate additional ideas for addressing economic injustice or challenging the FDR's assertions about these conditions and their solutions.

The writing options for Mr. Gonzalez and Aziz and his classmates were many and varied, as they are for all teachers. Regardless of the option, Aziz's reading cannot remain superficial if he is asked to write out his ideas about what he reads. Writing related to reading demands active participation and mental engagement. More important, when students share their writing, teachers can quickly discover which boys understand and which ones struggle with understanding so that additional instructional supports can be provided.

Guidelines for Writing Instruction

In this section, four overarching guidelines are described for making writing engaging to disinterested and struggling male writers. These guidelines are also meant to lead to practices that make writing integral to learning any content and for ensuring boys in particular come to see writing as a natural way to explore and extend understandings.

Integrate Low-Stakes Writing into Daily Lessons

Boys are more likely to recognize the potential value of writing if every written product they produce is not necessarily handed in for a grade. Of course, there are occasions when students should produce a final written product to be evaluated, such as responses to essay questions in history or a summary of findings in a lab report for chemistry. These are "high-stakes" assignments that may be evaluated formally and thoroughly. However, a considerable amount of writing should be informal or "low stakes" (Bean, 2011). The benefits of low-stakes writing, particularly for boys, are many, including the following:

- Low-stakes writing promotes active engagement in the ideas and content, as compared with listening to lectures or even class discussion.
- Low-stakes writing helps boys find and develop their own language for the issues and content. To really know the content, boys need to be able to write and talk about the concepts in their own words. Parroting an author's language can mask a lack of understanding.
- Frequent low-stakes writing improves high-stakes writing. Boys will already be warmed up and fluent before they write something in a more formal way.
- Low-stakes writing helps teachers understand how their male students are thinking and feeling about the content.

- Low-stakes writing can promote metacognition, when boys are asked to document their thinking about a topic or text and explain their interpretations and ideas. This can be achieved with reflective logs boys maintain with regular and frequent entries.
- Regular low-stakes writing assignments will help boys keep up with the assigned reading. This means they are likely to contribute more and get more from discussions and other class activities.

Low-stakes writing can take a multitude of forms depending on the content, the level of engagement of students, and the creative imagination of teachers. When learning is deconstructed, it quickly becomes apparent how readily writing of an informal nature can be infused into daily lessons. As the benefits just enumerated make clear, since this type of writing does not require formal grading or even comment, it can occur in planned or spontaneous ways.

Mr. Summers exploited an opportunity for low-stakes writing after his class of computer programming students read an online article about counter computer-hacking measures being taken by political parties in Europe and the United States. His students, mostly boys, were eager to discuss the article, but before doing so, Mr. Summers spontaneously thought of asking them to write for just a few minutes their attitudes, opinions, and ideas in response to the issues raised in the article. Afterward, he arranged the class into two rows of ten standing students facing one another at a normal conversational distance. He set his computer timer for one minute, then asked students to exchange their points of view based on their written assertions. When the alarm sounded, he had them shift like an elongated rubber band, so that students faced someone new and commenced their dialog again. This process continued for about 10–12 minutes. Afterward, Mr. Summers asked his students to return to what they had initially written and add any new insights gleaned from the conversations with various classmates.

Foster Writing to Learn

Writing-to-learn strategies offer boys creative and engaging options for exploring topics, whether in science, history, language, or mathematics. These strategies can take on a number of forms, either specific to the content under study or general enough to be applied across topics and courses. Regardless of the format and structure, writing to learn is intended to increase interaction with topics and texts, explore content in deep and

Letter to the Editor in Civics	Essay about a Poem for English	Essay for Science
Personal opinion or experience; may include argumentation; clear stance; language used to indicate personal opinion	Personal opinion or experiences AND logical reasoning or illustrative imagery; language used to argue a point or to convey images and experiences	Distanced stance, evidence to support stance, logical reasoning to tie evidence to claim; language used to convey distance and objectivity

Figure 8.1 Differences in Features of Persuasive Essay across Content Areas

meaningful ways, and use writing as a reflection of knowledge and record of learning (Bangert-Drowns, Hurley, & Wilkinson, 2004; Graham & Hebert, 2010; Graham & Perin, 2007; Murray, 2004). This type of writing will also involve boys in the kind of thinking, problem solving, and communicating needed for academic success in primary and secondary school.

Regardless of the subject or course, boys need to develop the ability to form and defend arguments in writing (Wissinger & De La Paz, 2015). This may look different in a history class exploring the causes of the First World War than in a class studying the process of extracting usable DNA from ancient carcasses and bones. In the United States, the Common Core State Standards (2010) stipulate that writing be integral to the curriculum of the four major content domains – science, social studies, mathematics, and English/language arts – as well as in technical subjects. This means students in these various subjects should be taught to compose arguments linked to major claims and supported by valid reasoning and pertinent evidence.

Consider how a persuasive essay, which might typically be taught to students as a single form applicable across subject and disciplines, actually takes on unique features and purposes depending on the content area (Moje, 2010). Notice in Figure 8.1 that a persuasive essay in the form of a letter to the editor in social studies differs in significant ways to one students might write in English class or science.

Promote Real Writing with Real Audiences

The writing we ask boys to do in school should help them learn to write to a variety of specific genuine audiences, instead for insular academic purposes only. A writing task only the teacher will read and evaluate does little to foster the perception among male youth that writing can be used for authentic and meaningful communication (Sarroub & Pernicek, 2016). As was already noted, many boys do not think of magazine, comic book, or graphic novel reading as "real" reading. Nor do they consider texting, emailing, tweeting, or writing comics as "real" writing. This perception is due in large measure to how school defines reading and writing for youth as exclusively academic based (Newkirk, 2006). From this perspective, academic writing and reading are meant to prepare students for more academic reading and writing. In light of this curriculum-entrenched view, consider Yancey's (2009) assertions that

> 21st century writing marks the beginning of a new era in literacy, a period we might call the Age of Composition, a period where composers become composers not through direct and formal instruction alone (if at all), but rather through what we might call an extracurricular social co-apprenticeship (p. 5).

Clearly, we must do a better job of preparing male youth for writing in the real world. One way to do this is to target student writing to public audiences (Coleman, 2011; Yancey, 2009).

Use Evidence-Based Principles to Guide Writing Activities

In compiling the major report *Writing Next*, Graham and Perin (2007) scoured the research literature on writing for adolescents and found substantial evidence to support eleven elements (see Figure 8.2). The researchers make clear that these elements are broad enough to account for a variety of specific instructional practices. For example, the different studies that were found to have significant positive effects related to the eleventh element, *writing for content learning*, approached writing to learn in the content areas in several different ways. Teachers concerned about the writing development of boys should be ever mindful of how their writing practices and strategies represent expressions of one or more of the eleven evidence-based elements in this important report.

Promising Programs and Practices

Boys Writing from Experience

One of my guidelines of effective writing instruction for boys is to give them authentic purposes and real audiences. Authentic purposes grow out

1. **Writing Strategies** – teaching students strategies for planning, revising, and editing their compositions
2. **Summarization** – explicitly and systematically teaching students how to summarize texts
3. **Collaborative Writing** – using instructional arrangements in which adolescents work together to plan, draft, revise, and edit their compositions
4. **Specific Product Goals** – assigning students specific, reachable goals for the writing they are to complete
5. **Word Processing** – using computers and word processors as instructional supports for writing assignments
6. **Sentence Combining** – teaching students to construct more complex, sophisticated sentences
7. **Prewriting** – engaging students in activities designed to help them generate or organize ideas for their composition
8. **Inquiry Activities** – engaging students in analyzing immediate, concrete data to help them develop ideas and content for a particular writing task
9. **Process Writing Approach** – interweaving a number of writing instructional activities in a workshop environment that stresses extended writing opportunities, writing for authentic audiences, personalized instruction, and cycles of writing
10. **Study of Models** – providing students with opportunities to read, analyze, and emulate models of good writing
11. **Writing for Content Learning** – using writing as a tool for learning content material

Figure 8.2 11 Elements of Effective Writing Instruction

of a need or desire to communicate about an experience or interest. This kind of writing is motivating for boys who want to tell others about what they have seen or done that was fun, exciting, and real. For example, a boy who is a skateboarding fanatic is more likely to write about and share with others what he knows about his hobby, and through this engagement writing skills, such as editing and polishing, can be taught and reinforced.

This was the case with sixth-grade boys who were reluctant and low skilled writers living in a coastal town in far southwest Britain (Coleman, 2011). The town was experiencing a decline in fishing, a once thriving industry, and school leaders and others designed a project to allow the boys to explore issues surrounding the loss of jobs once held by their family members, relatives, and neighbors.

The curriculum used with the boys to improve their writing was based on place-based learning, which situates the learner in their communities to explore issues such as heritage, culture, and the environment through which school subjects can be studied (Smith, 2002). The project capitalized on older community members' involvement with the boys and had as its goals empowering the boys through a sense of achievement and pride in their work, as well as helping them develop global consciousness so as to recognize how small actions taken in their community might have consequences for people and communities around the world.

Based on the boys' writing assessment scores, which were below grade-level expectations, there was a clear need to improve specific skills such as spelling, sentence variety, clarity, and organization and structure. The program consisted of 12 ninety-minute sessions once per week targeting six boys with the lowest writing scores.

The sessions were organized into three phases focusing on newspaper reporting and using journalistic techniques, tele-journalism, and documentary filmmaking. In phase one, the boys worked with a freelance reporter to learn what newspaper journalists do. They established criteria for successful reporting and engaged in role plays. The boys, with the assistance of their journalist teacher, explored copies of the local newspaper from years past and deconstructed the essential elements of good journalistic writing, such as providing answers to the 5-Ws (Who? What? Where? When? Why?) as well as descriptive vocabulary, use of connectives, sentence variation, establishing a clear purpose, and structuring information in an organized way. In the second phase, a filmmaker was invited to teach the basics of tele-journalistic techniques. The boys participated in research on the local fishing industry and filmed themselves in mock interviewer/interviewee contexts focusing on issues related to fishing. In the third and final phase, the boys generated interview questions and, with the filmmaker's assistance, went to their town's harbor to talk with community members, capturing the conversations on video. Back in school, the interviews were edited and the issues raised in the interviews were mapped and labeled. These labels were then fleshed out into notes and finally scripts for a documentary film and a written newspaper report. Boys worked in pairs to develop sections of the report, making sure the essential 5-W questions were answered and the writing contained the other features of good journalistic stories. At the conclusion of the program, each boy was responsible for writing a story based on the information gleaned from the research on local fishing and the interviews.

The film was shown to parents and community members at the school and the boys' articles were published in the local paper.

All six boys expressed their satisfaction with the program and recognized improvements in their writing. They particularly enjoyed the "hands-on" nature of the project that took them out of their school and into the community. Their research brought them to a new level of appreciation for the challenges of, and opportunities for, local fisherman, as well as how issues such as overfishing in one small area of the ocean can impact the livelihoods of individual fishermen, the industry worldwide, and marine ecosystems.

Another hoped-for outcome of the program was realized, as all the boys raised their scores and demonstrated significant improvement, and three of the six boys met their grade-level performance benchmark in writing on the national assessment. One of the overarching goals of the program was to bring about school-based academic gains through place-based learning experiences. The improvement of the boys' writing self-concepts, and the increase in their writing literacy scores, strongly suggest the project's main goal was reached.

This program reminds us that even for boys who are reluctant and weak writers, engagement can be heightened and improvements made when literacy skill development is situated within authentic learning contexts. Before the project began, the boys made clear to their teachers they wanted nothing to do with writing. By the end of the project they were eager to recount their experiences researching the local fishing trade by generating newspaper articles and making documentary films. They also began to pay closer attention to the craft of writing by becoming more involved in editing and revising their compositions.

Boys in the Real World

"Adam"

Adam is a 15-year-old in the tenth grade. He is Caucasian and a monolingual English speaker. Adam loves to play sports explore the woods and hang out with friends. He specifically likes running, riding on his long board, and playing lacrosse. Unlike many boys his age, and in contrast to stereotypes about adolescent males, Adam is not interested in playing video games.

Adam does not describe himself as a good student and attributes his struggles in school to his poor reading skills. As an adolescent, Adam does not read books on his own for pleasure. He is very uncomfortable with the idea of sitting for the long periods it takes to read and finish a book. Since reading is not fun for him, Adam prefers short stories and articles that are entertaining. The only reading he does outside of school is online, especially articles about new science and technology breakthroughs. He also reads the newspaper, both the electronic and paper version, to keep current with his favorite sports teams and players. When he reads, he wants to read about things that can happen in real life or about the details of how something works. Thus, he reads manuals for building things, paying close attention to the pictures and graphics. He explained that when he bought an electric long board, he had to read through the entire manual to figure out the charging system and how far the board could be ridden.

The only books Adam has read as a teenager are from *The Lord of the Rings* series. He described his fascination with the author's attention to detail in these books. He was also fascinated by how the author made up an imaginary world. Otherwise, Adam said he did not have the time to read fiction. He also suggested that reading was not necessary today because of the Internet and video.

Regarding writing, Adam said, "I'm not the best writer. I'd be a better writer if I read more." But then he added, "But I don't read so I don't write either." He said he does write email, primarily to teachers, and recognizes when he does this that he has to change his vocabulary and use more formal words. He also said he texts friends but he does not recognize this informal messaging as real writing. He went on to say that writing was not very important to him because he often uses a voice-to-text app. He said it was faster to speak a message than to write it. Adam is very disinterested in, and struggles with, required school writing, such as a research paper. His only mention of an enjoyable writing assignment was a one-and-a-half-page paper he recently wrote for his English class. It was a story about a make-believe land with people from opposing villages that engage in a battle. Adam found it particularly fun to make up the details for the battle.

Discussion and Activities
- What recommendations can you offer to teachers working with Adam to nurture enthusiasm for reading and writing?
- How can Adam's interests in sports be exploited for further literacy skill and vocabulary development?
- In what ways can teachers take advantage of the kinds of topics Adam enjoys to further his reading and writing abilities?

Boys Writing Poetry

Boys writing poetry? It's not the genre that immediately springs to mind when one thinks of what boys might prefer to write in school. And yet, even though boys are often thought to be resistant to poetry instruction, approaches that are sensitive to their "discourses of desire," which are, according to Simon (1987), the issues and needs that impel adolescent males' to communicate and engage in literacy processes, can transform negative attitudes. Poetry offers boys a medium of expression for their desires, dreams, and experiences (Hawkins & Certo, 2014), while poetry instruction offers teachers the language context for developing literacy skills and the craft of writing (Wilfong, 2008). Furthermore, poetry instruction targeted to boys can help them expand their vision of what poetry is and work against perceptions that writing poetry is not something guys do (Fisher, 2007; Greig & Hughes, 2009). Through exposure to poems that capture boys' imaginations and explore issues of social justice, it is possible to disabuse them of the perception that poetry is "for girls" and bring them to a new appreciation of poetry as a medium for thinking and feeling about issues that matter to them (Damico and Carpenter, 2005).

Poetry Writing in School
In a four-week poetry genre study unit in a low-income urban school, fifth-grade students were provided instruction by a poet teacher and several guest poets three times weekly for one hour each session. Focusing on 20 male students in the fifth-grade class, each session began with a guest poet sharing poetry by delivering repeated oral readings of poems. The boys had not experienced poetry read aloud to them very often before this unit, so hearing the words and rhythm of the language helped them appreciate how a poem sounds. After hearing a poem, the boys were encouraged to respond and discuss what they noticed and what stood out for them. In this way, the boys were offering input on the content of a poem as well as its structure and linguistic features. This work brought to the boys' attention the words, phrases, and aesthetic devices employed by poets to express their feelings and ideas. The advantage of having actual poets share their work was that these discussions allowed them to describe in detail for the boys their motivations, word choices, and other important insights into the practices of constructing a poem.

As a follow-up to discussing and deconstructing a particular poem or set of poems and the poetry writing process, the boys were given sustained individual or collaborative time to attempt to compose their own original poetic texts. Short, focused lessons on generating ideas and revising poems were interspersed, and individual sharing and feedback offered by a peer, the teacher poet, or guest poet. Each session also included group sharing time for any of the boys who wanted to read aloud their completed or draft version poems to the class.

At the conclusion of the poetry unit, each of the male students had compiled a portfolio of their original poems, drafts, and revisions. From these collections, each boy was asked to select a poem to revise and publish in a class poetry anthology. In addition, each of the boys was provided guided practice in reading an original poem for a school poetry event. The rehearsals were conducted with peers, the poet teacher, and guest poets. An individually tailored revision checklist was provided to guide the boys as they practiced their performance of the poem.

The results of the poetry genre unit clearly show that, contrary to the widespread perception that boys are inherently averse to writing poetry, an approach that invites them to translate experiences and attitudes into lines of verse with thoughtful guidance and personal support from enthusiastic role models can be successful.

Poetry Writing Outside of School: Rap Lyrics as Poetry
Teachers should support students' literacy practices in and out of school (Hinchman et al., 2003/2004). Ideally, boys take what they learn about writing in school and use it on their own, in their daily lives. As regards poetry, a fruitful focus of instruction, particularly for urban males, to promote literacy learning in and out of school has been teaching that genre through rap music and hip-hop culture (Christianakis, 2011; Low, 2010; Morrell & Duncan-Andrade, 2002).

Boys in an English class in a large metropolitan area of the American Northeast were taught to critically analyze lyrics from some of their favorite raps. Linguistic features, such as rhyme, repetition, and onomatopoeia, were deconstructed for the effect it had on them as listeners. In addition to deconstructing stylistic elements, the boys explored the meaning of the raps, paying attention to issues such as identity and social commentary, as well as lyrics that spoke of hyper-masculinity, violence, misogyny, poverty, and other topics that populate urban hip-hop and rap songs.

The students were also encouraged to craft their own rap lyrics and raps in class or bring to class raps they had already created on their own. Some of the boys were aspiring rap artists and took advantage of the assignment to compose and record songs using available hand-held and Internet technology. For example, three African American boys in the class brought in a recorded rap for the poetry assignment with the printed lyrics for their classmates to follow. They described how they downloaded beats from a popular website and used a cheap Casio keyboard to generate a repeating pattern of chords to accompany the beat. They also explained that they arranged a makeshift recording studio in one of the boys' bedroom. The trio called themselves King Negus after an ancient Ethiopian ruler, since two of the members had parents from Ethiopia. Their teacher invited the class to listen and follow along, paying attention to poetic elements. The teacher paused the rap after the opening section:

> *One plus two plus three ways to be*
> *It don' matter to me 'cause I'm divisible by three*
> *Other brothas wanna be one thing, one thing only*
> *But there's a whole lotta lonely in acting one way*
> *Thinking one way like this is yo last day to live*
> *Give, unable to deliver when somethin' new*
> *Comes yo way*
> *When I was a kid I got this mask from my dad*
> *One side had a smile one was sad*
> *Like my face when my rap goes down*
> *Or goes down in flames . . .*

The students were then invited to comment first on the structure of the lyrics, prompting statements about the unique rhyming pattern, the repetition of words and phrases ("one plus two plus," "one thing," "one way,") and other features. The boys were also asked to consider the meaning of the lyrics and the imagery employed, such as the allusion to a Janus mask. The King Negus rappers were invited to talk about what motivated the lyrics and the message they hoped would be conveyed through them. With pride the trio explained the intended message of the rap, that being multidimensional was important and that they did not want to be stereotyped just because they were black and rappers.

As I have asserted throughout this book and elsewhere (Brozo, 2010; Brozo & Gaskins, 2009), schools need to come to know and learn to value struggling adolescent boys' interests and literate practices beyond the school walls. Low-achieving male writers are likely to become more engaged writers, and improve their self-efficacy and skills when room is made in school for their out-of-school interests and literacies (Matthews, Kizzie, Rowley, & Cortina, 2010). Urban male youth who have antipathy toward traditional poetry may be transformed into "poets" when their experience and discourses are valued and given a forum for expression within the classroom walls (Morrell & Duncan-Andrade, 2002).

Boys Writing in Response to Young Adult Literature

Another teacher who strives to keep her struggling male readers engaged in the texts they read and write does so by offering them opportunities to connect these texts to issues and events relevant to adolescents. For example, while reading Walter Dean Meyer's (2004) *Monster*, she prompted boys to research why young people turn to delinquency, and she structured a WebQuest (Halat, 2008; Salsovic, 2009) as a guide to online sites, reports, and articles on the topic. These served as a valuable resource for current facts, trends, analysis of causes, and successful prevention and treatment programs. When a question came up in their conversation or reading that seemed to require an immediate answer, they consulted sites and links in the web quest. Through this process, for instance, they discovered youth crime in the United States has actually been on the decline since the mid 1990s, in contrast to a widespread public perception that it is ever increasing. They also found statistical documentation that youth of color are processed in the juvenile justice system in numbers far out of proportion relative to their white peers. This issue came up when they were reading a newspaper article about a 14-year-old African American boy convicted of murdering his teacher in Florida.

Shortly into *Monster*, the teacher and her students realized that virtually all the issues of juvenile crime and justice were embodied in the experiences of the main character and narrator, Steve Harmon. Steve, a teenager and aspiring scriptwriter who is accused of complicity in a murder, tells the story of his experience from arrest through trial verdict in the form of a film script. This unique perspective drew the boys into the details of Steve's life in a way that evoked empathy, disgust, suspicion, and finally vindication.

As they read *Monster* together, the teacher and her class kept an e-journal of their reactions to critical questions that arose during conversation and discussion. For example, she asked them to compare and contrast how the American legal system is portrayed in the novel with what they were learning about it from the web quest sources. To do this, she taught her students how to employ a split-page approach, putting direct quotes and brief descriptions in one column and what they learned about youths' treatment in juvenile court and detention in the other. At one point in the book, Steve says, "The best time to cry is at night, when the lights are out and someone is being beaten up and screaming for help." The students put this in their journal, then recorded a description from one of their web quest readings of a juvenile offender remembering his own crying at night once he realized for the first time he was behind bars and would be for the next two years.

Another interesting writing activity the teacher employed with her boys while reading *Monster* was to have them assume the identities of different figures in the courtroom and compose arguments based on the scenes of the trial and details of the case from those points of view. One group of students chose to look at the events in one chapter from the perspective of

Mr. Petrocelli, a witness for the prosecution, while another group pretended to represent O'Brien, Steve's attorney. They presented their written arguments orally asserting that most of the jurors saw a teenage black kid and assumed he was guilty, even if they didn't tell the lawyers that upfront. One of the students in the group, responding as if he were Petrocelli, said all the kids involved in the fatal shooting were equally guilty; that included the one who took the cigarettes, the one who wrestled the gun from the convenience-store owner, and Steve, the one who made sure the coast was clear.

At the conclusion of *Monster* and related readings on juvenile crime, the teacher capitalized on the boys' strong feelings about what they believed was the unfair treatment of minors in the criminal justice system by urging them to express their attitudes in some way that might influence lawmakers. This led to further research, taking them online to find information on their district's state representatives' policy positions related to youth crime. Their search uncovered some interesting facts. While both representatives had co-sponsored a youth advocacy task force, they also voted in favor of trying minors as adults and one even supported legislation to make the death penalty an option for minors found guilty of capital murder. The teacher formed several small teams of writers to compose an email letter to make their case to these legislators. The composition process itself necessitated discussion and work on form, punctuation, and grammar, as well as finding statistics and quotes from the various articles and books they had accumulated during their exploration of the topic. The teacher observed a level of enthusiasm for this effort unlike any she had seen from the boys before. Even though their sense of empowerment was diluted once the students received a perfunctory reply from their state representatives, stating that they appreciated their input and asking them to continue to remain engaged in the political process, the boys remained proud of themselves for doing it.

Boys Writing in Mathematics Class

According to the 2000 Principles and Standards from the National Council of Teachers of Mathematics' (NCTM, 2000) in the United States, wrestling with complex problems, reflecting on thinking, and communicating that mathematical thinking to others is an integral part of learning and studying mathematics. Indeed, the NCTM's communication standards stress the need to develop students' abilities to (a) organize and consolidate mathematical thinking through communication, (b) communicate mathematical thinking coherently and clearly to peers, teachers, and others, (c) analyze and evaluate the mathematical thinking and strategies of others, and (d) use the language of mathematics to express mathematical ideas precisely.

In STEM-related fields, words, equations, and visuals have always gone hand-in hand, leading some to advocate full integration of the arts into science, math, engineering, and other technology curricula (Land, 2013). Mathematical properties and concepts are often best understood with diagrams and pictures (Dabell, Keogh, & Naylor, 2008), including cartoons and comics (Cho, 2012). Recent studies have shown the value of comics and graphic texts in mathematics. Either provided as alternative learning resources or generated by students, they have been useful in (a) expanding knowledge of mathematics concepts (Kessler, 2009; Pelton & Pelton, 2009), (b) diminishing math anxiety (Sengul & Dereli, 2010), (c) encouraging active participation in math learning among struggling students (Halimun, 2011), and (d) improving understanding of math vocabulary (Gilles, 2012).

A math teacher in a culturally diverse low-income school gives his basic math students, most of whom are struggling males and English learners, writing tasks that are tied directly to the content under study. In addition, he emphasizes how writing can relate directly to math-related issues in the real world. For the teacher, whose inner-city male students need, above all, to see the relevance of their learning in order to remain engaged, mathematical thinking is not solely a cognitive activity, but also an important life skill. He helps his boys come to appreciate this by constantly making connection between mathematical concepts and processes and solving genuine everyday problems with those particular concepts and processing tools. The following is a typical type of math writing prompt the teacher gives his students.

Graphic novels from the collection of the Manga Guide series have been highly effective in motivating his low-performing reluctant male students as well as increasing their achievement. These manga-formatted books cover such topics as regression analysis, calculus, linear algebra, and databases. Woven into a story involving characters typical of this illustrated Japanese genre are numerous tables, graphs, and figures designed and explained using the relevant technical math terms alongside accessible teen-friendly prose.

During the study of statistics, the math teacher introduces his students to Takahashi's (2009) *The Manga Guide to Statistics*. With the assistance of the school librarian, he is able to acquire multiple copies of the book to use with small groups of students, one copy per group. The plot centers on Rui, who, after meeting her father's new handsome assistant and developing a teenage crush for him, begs for a math tutor. Assuming her heartthrob will become her tutor, Rui is crushed when her father brings home another of his employees, Mr. Yamamoto. Over time, though Rui comes to appreciate the help and patience of her tutor, who guides her and readers of the book through the world of statistics.

In this basic math class, the teacher is given flexibility with respect to the texts and instructional approaches he could use. His principle goal is to elevate the male students' motivation and achievement, enabling them to succeed in the regular high school math curriculum. Thus, he takes care to select topics from the more challenging math textbook that could be supported by the more accessible graphic novels. In the unit on statistics, the teacher provides extensive scaffolded instruction for content from the textbook and then creates opportunities for independent group reading and problem solving with the manga text.

A typical prompt for group problem solving focuses on a real-life situation requiring application of statistical knowledge and processes gleaned from teacher-directed lessons with the textbook and from students' guided reading through the graphic novel. For example, in connection with an investigation of numerical data presented in the textbook and the teacher's lectures, students in their groups are also directed to chapter 2 of *The Manga Guide to Statistics* to read and use the information and processes described to solve the following problem:

> Rui's father installs new insulation to save money on heating costs, but then learns that his bills have not declined by much from the previous year. His contractor points out that heating costs have risen and weather has been colder. Rui's father wants to find out how much he has actually saved due to the insulation he installed.

To help his male students better understand this situation, the teacher also provides them details about Rui's father's heating bills (rates, units of heat used), temperature changes, and directs them to an internet site for information about "heating degree days," such as the National Weather Service Climate Prediction Center (www.cpc.ncep.noaa.gov/products/ana lysis_monitoring/cdus/degree_days/ddayexp.shtml) and Physics4Kids .com. The teacher forms pairs of male students and then gives them two tasks, including an important writing assignment:

Help Rui's Father Save Money on His Gas Bill

(1) Assess the cost-effectiveness of Rui's father's new insulation and window sealing. In their assessment, they must do the following:
- Compare his gas bills from January 2016 and January 2017
- Explain any savings after the insulation and sealing
- Decide if the insulation and sealing work on Rui's house was cost-effective and provide evidence for this decision

(2) Create a short series of graphic panels for gas company customers to guide them in making decisions about increasing the energy efficiency of their homes. The graphic panels must do the following:
- Using descriptive statistics, list the quantities that customers need to consider in assessing the cost-effectiveness of energy efficiency measures.
- Using statistics for relating two variables, explain to gas customers how energy efficiency relates to savings on their gas bills.

The students are allowed to access all available resources to complete the two tasks. This includes the numerous math texts in the classroom library, *The Manga Guide to Statistics*, and any relevant websites. Once student pairs have acquired the requested information, those who wish to create graphic panels for gas company customers with a web-based comic generator work with the teacher who shows them how to use Pixton (www.pixton.com), a drag-and-drop comic making tool. Other pairs of boys gather clipart figures and insert dialogue and tables available in MS Word. The panels and clipart are then printed and placed on poster paper attached to the classroom walls. Still other boys, more confident in their drawing ability, produce graphic panels using colored pencils and markers directly on poster paper. The teacher then directs his class to go on a gallery walk to observe the panels, check for accurate application of the required statistics, and make comments and ask questions about them to their owners. The teacher takes advantage of the discussion that ensues to reinforce how statistics can be applied in their everyday lives, such as, in this case, to inform gas company consumers about how to assess their energy efficiency behaviors and how these correlate with their home heating expenses.

Boys Writing in Science Class

A biology teacher decided to employ several writing activities specifically to spark his low-performing male students' interest in a unit on the environment he was starting. He began the unit with an activity designed to assess his students' present attitudes toward the environment. The students were expecting another lecture and textbook assignment when they entered class on the second day of the unit. Instead, they were greeted with rapper, Prince Ea's YouTube video "Man vs Earth," with its powerful message about environmental degradation, climate change, and animal extinctions. When the video concluded, the teacher projected the following on the white board:

> Respond as completely as possible. There are no right or wrong answers, so Express yourself freely.
> 1. How did the video make you feel?
> 2. What message did you take away from the video?
> 3. Is there a place outdoors that you especially like to go? Where? Why?
> 4. Have you ever thought or read or heard about the ideas in the video? If so, explain.

The teacher read his students' responses and during class the next day initiated a discussion before he revealed the overall objective of the unit. That is, he wanted his students to localize and personalize the issue of the environment and to appreciate the personal impact they can have on reversing environmental degradation. To do so, he first engaged the class in brainstorming what they could do to help improve problems with environmental pollution, global warming, and endangered species. Among the many interesting suggestions was to write letters to legislators. This idea quickly took hold, and the teacher helped students write a letter to one of their senators or representatives.

He allowed the boys to work with a partner for this activity, which involved Internet research of legislators' email addresses, as well as any positions or legislation associated with them on local environmental issues. Writing teams were given time in class to compose rough drafts and were asked to post these on the class Blackboard site. Students were encouraged to read and respond to each other's drafts. This input, along with providing his own revisionary assistance to each writing pair, improved all of the letters. The teacher attached his student letters to his own emails to either a senator or representative, explaining the intent of the assignment and urging replies to the specific issues raised in the letters. Within a week, responses arrived, which the teacher posted to the Blackboard site. Many students were unsatisfied with the lack of specifics in the emails from the legislators, so continued to research each of their particular positions and voting records on environmental issues. This led to follow-up letters with questions, which eventually resulted in more detailed responses from the legislators' offices.

Boys and Writing: A Coda

In this chapter, I made the case that the writing process can be a powerful tool for boys. Writing, like reading, is a constructive process that can stimulate passive male learners to become active learners as they negotiate meanings and reflect on burgeoning understandings.

I also highlighted the documented challenges boys experience with writing and emphasized known benefits of writing as a process of literacy growth and knowledge development. I demonstrated that writing helps boys (1) explore topics and issues of concern and interest, (2) communicate ideas and feelings, (3) express themselves creatively, and (4) summarize and organize information and concepts and monitor comprehension. Based on these important evidence-based outcomes, I described and exemplified a variety of writing strategies and practices that promote the writing to learn habit, create contexts for meaningful communication with authentic audiences, and capitalize on aspects of writing inherent in the digital media boys today navigate and contribute to daily.

References

Abdorahimzadeh, S. (2014). Gender differences and EFL reading comprehension: Revisiting topic interest and test performance. *System, 42*, 70–80.

Aboudan, R. (2011). Engage them, don't enrage them: Student voices and what it takes to participate. *English Language Teaching, 4*(1), 128–134.

Abraham, J. (2008). Back to the future on gender and anti-school boys: A response to Jeffrey Smith. *Gender and Education, 20*(1), 89–94.

Adu-Gyamfi, K., Bosse, M., & Faulconer, J. (2010). Assessing understanding through reading and writing in mathematics. *International Journal for Mathematics Teaching and Learning, 11*(5), 1–22.

Agee, J., & Altarriba, J. (2009). Changing conceptions and uses of computer technologies in the everyday literacy practices of sixth and seventh graders. *Research in the Teaching of English, 43*(4), 363–396.

Aikens, N.L., & Barbarin, O. (2008). Socioeconomic differences in reading trajectories: The contribution of family, neighborhood, and school contexts. *Journal of Educational Psychology, 100*(2), 235–251.

Akey, K. (2008). *The adolescent's sense of being literate: Reshaping through classroom transitions.* Dissertation Abstracts International Section A: Humanities and Social Sciences, 68(11-A), 4647.

Alexander, K. (2014). *The crossover.* New York: Houghton Mifflin Harcourt.

Alfaro, E.C., Umana-Taylor, A.J., Gonzales-Backen, M.A., Bamaca, M.Y., & Zeiders, K.H. (2009). Latino adolescents' academic success: The role of discrimination, academic motivation, and gender. *Journal of Adolescence, 32*, 941–962.

Alliance for Excellent Education. (2007). *Making writing instruction a priority in America's middle and high schools.* Washington, DC: Author.

Alvermann, D.E. (2002). *Adolescents and literacies in a digital world.* New York: Peter Lang.

Alvermann, D.E. (2009). Reaching/teaching adolescents: Literacies with a history. In Y. Goodman & J. Hoffman (Eds.), *Changing literacies for changing times: An historical perspective on the future of reading research, public policy, and classroom practices* (pp. 98–107). New York: Routledge.

Alvermann, D.E. (2010). Sociocultural constructions of adolescence and young people's literacies. In L. Christenbury, R. Bomer, & P. Smagorinsky (Eds.), *Handbook of adolescent literacy research* (pp. 14–28). New York: Guilford.

Alvermann, D.E. (2011). Popular culture and literacy practices. In M.L. Kamil, P.D. Pearson, E.B. Moje, & P.P. Afflerbach (Eds.), *Handbook of reading research* (vol. IV, pp. 541–560). New York: Routledge/Taylor & Francis Group.

Alvermann, D., & Eakle, A.J. (2007). Dissolving learning boundaries: The doing, redoing, and undoing of school. In A. Cook-Sather & D. Thiessen (Eds.), *International handbook of student experience in elementary and secondary school* (pp. 143–166). The Netherlands: Springer.

Alvermann, D.E., Marshall, J.D., McLean, C.A., Huddleston, A.P., Joaquin, J., & Bishop, J. (2012). Adolescents' web-based literacies, identity construction, and skill development. *Literacy Research and Instruction, 51*(3), 179–195.

American Press Institute. (2014). *How Americans get their news*. Retrieved from www.americanpressinstitute.org/publications/reports/survey-research/how-americans-get-news/.

American Psychological Association, Presidential Task Force on Educational Disparities. (2012). *Ethnic and racial disparities in education: Psychology's contributions to understanding and reducing disparities*. Retrieved from www.apa.org/ed/resources/racial-disparities.aspx.

Ananiadou, K., & Claro, M. (2009). *21st century skills and competences for new millennium learners in OECD countries* [OECD Education Working Papers, No. 41]. Paris: OECD Publishing. http://dx.doi.org/10.1787/218525261154.

Andermann, E., Andrezejewski, C., & Allen J. (2011). How do teachers support students' motivation and learning in their classrooms? *Teachers College Record, 113*(5), 969–1003.

Anderson, K.A., Howard, K.E., & Graham, A. (2007). Reading achievement, suspensions, and African American males in middle school. *Middle Grades Research Journal, 2*(2), 43–63.

Anderson, R.E. (2008). Implications of the information and knowledge society. In J. Voogt & G. Knezek (Eds.), *International handbook of information technology in primary and secondary education* (pp. 5–22). New York: Springer.

Andon, A. (2012). *What is the immigrant achievement gap?: A conceptualization and examination of immigrant student achievement globally*. Tallahassee, FL: Florida State University.

Applebee, A., & Langer, J. (2011). *The National Study of Writing Instruction: Methods and procedures*. Albany, NY: Center on English Learning & Achievement. Retrieved from www.albany.edu/cela/reports/NSWI_2011_ methods_procedures.pdf.

Appleman, D. (2006). *Reading for themselves: How to transform adolescents into lifelong readers through out-of-class book clubs*. Portsmouth, NH: Heinemann.

Archer, L., Pratt, S.D., & Phillips, D. (2001). Working-class men's constructions of masculinity and negotiations of (non) participation in higher education. *Gender and Education, 13*(4), 431–449.

Ardila, A., Rosselli, M., Matute, E., & Inozemtseva, O. (2011). Gender differences in cognitive development. *Developmental Psychology, 47*(4), 984–990.

Arellano, M.D.C. (2013). Gender differences in reading comprehension achievement in English as a foreign language in compulsory secondary education. *Tejuelo, 17*, 67–84.

Atkinson, C. (2009). Promoting high school boys' reading engagement and motivation: The role of the school psychologist in real world research. *School Psychology International, 30*(3), 237–254.

Aud, S., Fox, M.A., & KewalRamani, A. (2010). *Status and trends in the education of racial and ethnic groups*. Washington, DC: National Center for Education Statistics. Retrieved from https://nces.ed.gov/pubs2010/2010015.pdf.

August, D., & Shanahan, T. (2006). *Developing literacy in second-language learners: Report of the National Literacy Panel on Language Minority Children and Youth*. Mahwah, NJ: Lawrence Erlbaum Associates.

Avila, J., & Moore, M. (2012). Critical literacy, digital literacies, and Common Core State Standards: A workable union? *Theory Into Practice, 51*(1), 27–33.

Babayiğit, S. (2015). The dimensions of written expression: Language group and gender differences. *Learning and Instruction, 35*, 33–41.

Bacallao, M.L., & Smokowski, P.R. (2005). "Entre dos mundos" (Between two worlds): Bicultural skills training with Latino immigrant families. *Journal of Primary Prevention, 26*(6), 485–509.

Baines, L., & Fisher, J. (2013). *Teaching challenging texts: Fiction, non-fiction, and multimedia*. New York: Rowman & Littlefield.

Baker, C., & Wright, W.E. (2017). *Foundations of bilingual education and bilingualism* (6th ed.). Bristol, UK: Multilingual Matters.

Baker, C.E., Cameron, C.E., Rimm-Kaufman, S.E., & Grissmer, D. (2012). Family and sociodemographic predictors of school readiness among African American boys in kindergarten. *Early Education and Development, 23*(6), 833–854.

Bangert-Drowns, R.L., Hurley, M.M., & Wilkinson, B. (2004). The effects of school-based Writing-to-Learn interventions on academic achievement: A meta-analysis. *Review of Educational Research, 74*, 29–58.

Batista, D., & Roberts, J. (2007). *Batista unleashed*. New York: Pocket Books.

Baxter, K.A., & Kochel, M.A. (2010). *Gotcha again for guys! More nonfiction books to get boys excited about reading*. Santa Barbara, CA: Libraries Unlimited.

Bazerman, C., & Prior, P. (2008). *What writing does and how it does it: An introduction to analyzing texts and textual practices*. Mahwah, NJ: Lawrence Erlbaum Associates.

Bean, J. (2011). *Engaging ideas: The professor's guide to integrating writing, critical thinking, and active learning in the classroom* (2nd ed.). San Francisco: Jossey-Bass.

Bean, T.W., & Harper, H. (2007). Reading men differently: Alternative portrayals of masculinity in contemporary young adult fiction. *Reading Psychology, 28*(1), 11–30.

Beard, R., & Burrell, A. (2010). Writing attainment in 9- to 11-year-olds: Some differences between girls and boys in two genres. *Language & Education: An International Journal, 24*(6), 495–515.

Beckett, C., & Taylor, H. (2016). *Human growth and development*. London: Sage.
Benson, J., & Borman, G. (2010). Family, neighborhood, and school settings across seasons: When do socioeconomic context and racial composition matter for the reading achievement growth of young children? *Teachers College Record*, 112(5), 1338–1390.
Berliner, D.C. (2009). *Poverty and potential: Out-of-school factors and school success*. Boulder and Tempe: Education and the Public Interest Center & Education Policy Research Unit. Retrieved from http://epicpolicy.org/publication/poverty-and-potential.
Bernacki, M., Nokes-Malach, T., Richey, J.E., & Belenky, D.M. (2016). Science diaries: A brief writing intervention to improve motivation to learn science. *Educational Psychology*, 36(1), 26–46.
Bertolote, J.M., & Fleischmann, A. (2002). A global perspective in the epidemiology of suicide. *Suicidologi*, 7(2), 6–8.
Bertschy, K., Cattaneo M.A., & Wolter, S. (2009). PISA and the transition into the labour market. *Labour*, 23(1), 111–137.
Biagi, F., & Loi, M. (2013). Measuring ICT used and learning outcomes: Evidence from recent econometric studies. *European Journal of Education Research, Development and Policy*, 48(1), 28–42.
Bigler, R., Hayes, A.R., & Hamilton, V. (2013). The role of schools in the early socialization of gender differences. In R.E. Tremblay, M. Boivin, & R. De V. Peters (Eds.), *Encyclopedia on early childhood development* (pp. 1–5). Montreal, QC: Centre of Excellence for Early Childhood Development and Strategic Knowledge Cluster on Early Child Development.
Binkley, M., Erstad, O., Herman, J., Raizen, S., Ripley. M., & Rumble, M. (2010). *Draft white paper 1: Defining 21st century skills*. Melbourne: The University of Melbourne: Assessment and Teaching of 21st Century Skills.
Birkerts, S. (2006). *The Gutenberg elegies: The fate of reading in an electronic age*. New York: Farrar, Straus and Giroux.
Blair, H., & Sanford, K. (2004). Morphing literacy: Boys re-shaping their school-based literacy practices. *Language Arts*, 81, 452–460.
Boerman-Cornell, B. (2013). More than comic books. *Educational Leadership*, [online] 70(6), 73–77. Retrieved from www.ascd.org/publications/educational-leadership/mar13/vol70/num06/More-Than-Comic-Books.aspx.
Boltz, R.H. (2007). What we want: Boys and girls talk about reading. *School Library Media Research*, 10, 1–19.
Bond, T.F. (2001). Giving them free rein: Connections in student-led book groups. *The Reading Teacher*, 54(6), 574–584.
Bourke, L., & Adams, A. (2011). Is it difference in language skills and working memory that account for girls being better at writing than boys? *Journal of Writing Research*, 3(3), 249–277.
Boyd, D. (2014). *It's complicated: The social lives of networked teens*. New Haven, CT: Yale University Press.
Bozack, A. (2011). Reading between the lines: Motives, beliefs, and achievement in adolescent boys. *The High School Journal*, 94(2), 58–76.

Bracey, G. (2011). *Parents, poverty and achieving in school.* Retrieved from www.huffingtonpost.com/gerald-bracey/parents-poverty-and-achie_b_61105.html.
Brandt, D. (2015). *The rise of writing: Redefining mass literacy.* Cambridge: Cambridge University Press.
Brantmeier, C. (2003). Does gender make a difference? Passage content and comprehension in second language reading. *Reading in a Foreign Language, 15*(1), 1–24.
Brantmeier, C., Schueller, J., Wilde, J., Kinginger, C. (2010). Gender equity in foreign and second language learning. In S. Klein et al. (Eds.), *Handbook for achieving gender equity through education* (2nd ed., pp. 305–333). New York: Routledge.
Brindle, M. (2012). *Examining relationships among teachers' preparation, efficacy, and writing practices* (Unpublished doctoral dissertation). Vanderbilt University, Nashville, TN.
Brooks-Young, S. (2010). *Teaching with the tools kids really use: Learning with Web and mobile technologies.* Thousand Oaks, CA: Corwin.
Brown, T.M., & Rodriguez, L.F. (2009). School and the co-construction of dropout. *International Journal of Qualitative Studies in Education, 22*(2), 221–242.
Brozo, W.G. (2002). *To be a boy, to be a reader: Engaging teen and preteen boys in active literacy.* Newark, DE: International Reading Association.
Brozo, W.G. (2004). Gaining and keeping students' attention. *Thinking Classroom/Peremena, 5*, 38–39.
Brozo, W.G. (2005). Connecting with students who are disinterested and inexperienced. *Thinking Classroom/Peremena, 6*, 42–43.
Brozo, W. (2006). Bridges to literacy for boys. *Educational Leadership, 64*(1), 71–74.
Brozo, W.G. (2010). *To be a boy, to be a reader: Engaging teen and preteen boys in active literacy* (2nd ed.). Newark, DE: International Reading Association.
Brozo, W.G. (2013). Outside interest and literate practices as contexts for increasing engagement and critical reading for adolescent boys. In B. Guzzetti & T. Bean (Eds.), *Adolescent literacies and the gendered self: (Re)constructing gender through global literacy practices and policies* (pp. 3–12). New York: Routledge.
Brozo, W.G. (2017). *Disciplinary and content literacy for today's adolescents: Honoring diversity and building competence* (6th ed.). New York: Guilford.
Brozo, W.G. (2018). Literacy achievement and motivation reconsidered: Linking home and school literate practices for struggling adolescent males. In P. Orellana García & P. Baldwin Lind (Eds.), *Reading achievement and motivation in boys and girls* (pp. 185–200). New York: Springer.
Brozo, W.G., & Crain, S. (2015). Schooling in United States: What we know from international assessments of reading and math literacy. In H. Morgan & C.T. Barry (Eds.), *The world leaders in education: Lessons from the successes and drawbacks of their methods* (pp. 37–60). New York: Peter Lang.
Brozo, W.G., & Flynt, E.S. (2008). Motivating students to read in the content classroom: Six evidence-based principles. *The Reading Teacher, 62*(2), 172–174.

Brozo, W.G., & Gaskins, C. (2009). Engaging texts and literacy practices for adolescent boys. In K. Wood & W. Blanton (Eds.), *Literacy instruction for adolescents: Research-based practice* (pp. 170–186). New York: Guilford.

Brozo, W.G., & Hargis, C. (2003). Taking seriously the idea of reform: One high school's efforts to make reading more responsive to all students. *Journal of Adolescent & Adult Literacy, 47*(1), 14–23.

Brozo, W.G., & Schmelzer, R.V. (1997). Wildmen, warriors, and lovers: Reaching boys through archetypal literature. *Journal of Adolescent & Adult Literacy, 41*(1), 4–11.

Brozo, W.G., Moorman, G., & Meyer, K. (2014). *Wham! Teaching with graphic novels across the curriculum*. New York: Teachers College Press.

Brozo, W.G., Shiel, G., & Topping, K. (2007). Engagement in reading: Lessons learned from three PISA countries. *Journal of Adolescent & Adult Literacy, 51*(4), 304–315.

Brozo, W.G., Sulkunen, S., Shiel, G., Garbe, C., Pandian, A., & Valtin, R. (2014). Reading, gender, and engagement: Lessons from five PISA countries. *Journal of Adolescent & Adult Literacy, 57*(7), 584–593.

Brozo, W.G., Walter, P., & Placker, T. (2002). "I know the difference between a real man and a TV man": A critical exploration of violence and masculinity through literature and the media in a junior high school in the 'hood. *Journal of Adolescent & Adult Literacy, 45*(6), 530–538.

Brunn, R., & Kao, G. (2008). Where are all the boys? Examining the black-white gender gap in postsecondary attainment. *Du Bois Review, 5*(1), 137–60.

Buckingham, D. (2007). Digital media literacies: Rethinking media education in the age of the Internet. *Research in Comparative and International Education, 2*(1), 43–55.

Bull, G., Thompon, A., Searson, M., Garofalo, J., Park, J., Young, C., & Lee, J. (2008). Connecting informal and formal learning: Experiences in the age of participatory media. *Contemporary Issues in Technology and Teacher Education, 8*(2), 100–107.

Bunn V. (2012). Researching the Tin Tin effect: How can the active promotion of graphic novels support and enhance boys' enthusiasm for leisure reading? *The School Librarian, 60*(2), 74–76.

Burbules, N., & Callister, T. (2000). *Watch it: The risks and promises of information technologies for education*. Boulder, CO: Westview Press.

Burrus, J., & Roberts, R.D. (2012, February). *Dropping out of high school: Prevalence, risk factors, and remediation strategies*. Educational Testing Service. Retrieved from www.ets.org/Media/Research/pdf/RD_Connections18.pdf.

Bussiere, P., & Gluszynski, T. (2004). *The impact of computer use on reading achievement of 15-year-olds*. Learning Policy Directorate, Strategic Policy and Planning Branch Human Resources and Skills Development Canada. Retrieved from http://citeseerx.ist.psu.edu/viewdoc/download?doi=10.1.1.494.5476&rep=rep1&type=pdf.

Calderon, M., & Minaya-Rowe, L. (2011). *Preventing long-term ELs: Transforming schools to meet core standards*. Thousand Oaks, CA: Corwin.

Caldwell, J.E., Swan, S.C., & Woodbrown, V.D. (2012). Gender differences in intimate partner violence outcomes. *Psychology of Violence*, *2*(1), 42–57.

Callanan, V.J., & Davis, M.S. (2011). Gender differences in suicide methods. *Social Psychiatry and Psychiatric Epidemiology*. Retrieved from http://news.medlive.cn/uploadfile/2011/1118/20111118110957720.pdf.

Cambria, J., & Guthrie, J.T. (2011). Motivating and engaging students in reading. *The NERA Journal*, *46*(1), 16–29.

Canadian Council on Learning. (2008). *State of learning in Canada: Toward a learning future: Report on Learning in Canada 2008*. Ottawa, ON: Author.

Canadian Council on Learning. (2010). *More than just funny books: Comics and prose literacy for boys*. Retrieved from www.ccl-cca.ca/CCL/Reports/LessonsinLearning.

Carnoy, M., & Garcia, E. (2017, January). Five key trends in U.S. student performance: Progress by blacks and Hispanics, the takeoff of Asians, the stall of non-English speakers, the persistence of socioeconomic gaps, and the damaging effect of highly segregated schools. Washington, DC: Economic Policy Institute. Retrieved from www.epi.org/files/pdf/113217.pdf.

Carr, J., & Pauwels, A. (2006). *Boys and foreign language learning: Real boys don't do languages*. New York: Palgrave Macmillan.

Caughy, M.O., O'Campo, P.J., Randolph, S.M., & Nickerson, K. (2002). The influence of racial socialization practices on the cognitive and behavioral competence of African American preschoolers. *Child Development*, *73*, 1611–1625.

Chai, C.S., & Tan, S.C. (2010). Collaborative learning and ICT. In C.S. Chai & Q.Y. Wang (Eds.), *ICT for self-directed and collaborative learning* (pp. 52–69). Singapore: Pearson.

Chetty, R., & Hendren, N. (2015). *The impacts of neighborhoods on intergenerational mobility: Childhood exposure effects and county-level estimates*. Washington, DC: National Bureau of Economic Research. Retrieved from https://scholar.harvard.edu/files/hendren/files/nbhds_paper.pdf.

Chetty, R., Hendren, N., Lin, F., Majerovitz, J., & Scuderi, B. (2016). *Childhood environment and gender gaps in adulthood*. Working Paper No. 21936. Cambridge, MA: National Bureau of Economic Research. Retrieved from www.equality-of-opportunity.org/images/gender_paper.pdf.

Child Trends Data Bank. (2015). *High school dropout rates*. Retrieved from www.childtrends.org/wp-content/uploads/2015/11/01_Dropout_Rates.pdf.

Childress, A. (1973). *A hero ain't nothin' but a sandwich*. New York: Coward, McCann & Geoghegan.

Chiu, M.M., Chow, B.W.-Y., & Mcbride-Chang, C. (2007). Universals and specifics in learning strategies: Explaining adolescent mathematics, science, and reading achievement across 34 countries. *Learning and Individual Differences*, *17*, 344–365.

Cho, G., Choi, H., & Krashen, S. (2005). Hooked on comic book reading: How comic books make an impossible situation less difficult. *Knowledge Quest*, *33*(4), 32–34.

Cho, H. (2012). *The use of cartoons as a teaching tool in middle school mathematics* (Dissertation). Retrieved from ProQuest Dissertations and Theses. (Accession Order No. AAT3517272.)

Christianakis, M. (2011). Hybrid texts: Fifth graders, rap music, and writing. *Urban Education, 46*(5), 1131–1168.

Chu, J.Y. (2008). A relational perspective on adolescent boys' identity development. In D.L. Browning (Ed.), *Adolescent identities: A collection of readings* (pp. 183–206). New York: Taylor & Francis.

Chudowsky, N., & Chudowsky, V. (2010). *Are there differences in achievement between boys and girls?* Washington, DC: Center on Education Policy. Retrieved from www.cepdc.org/document/docWindow.cfm?fuseaction=document.viewDocument&documentid=304&documentFormatId=4643.

Chun, C.W. (2009). Critical literacies and graphic novels for English language learners: Teaching *Maus*. *Journal of Adolescent & Adult Literacy, 53*(2), 144–153.

Chuy, M., & Nitulescu, R. (2013). *PISA 2009: Explaining the gender gap in reading through reading engagement and approaches to learning*. Canada: Council of Ministers of Education. Retrieved from www.cmec.ca/Publications/Lists/Publications/Attachments/302/PISA2009_Research_CMEC_HRSDC_EN.pdf.

Chuy, M., Scardamalia, M., & Bereiter, C. (2012). Development of ideational writing through knowledge building: Theoretical and empirical bases. In E. L. Grigorenko, E. Mambrino, & D. D. Preiss (Eds.), *Writing: A mosaic of new perspectives* (pp. 175–190). New York: Psychology Press.

Clark, C. (2014). *Children's and young people's reading in 2013. Findings from the 2013 National Literacy Trust's annual survey*. London: National Literacy Trust.

Clarke, L.W., & Besnoy, K. (2010). Connecting the old to the new: What "technology-crazed" adolescents tell us about teaching content area literacy. *The Journal of Media Literacy Education, 2*(2), 47–56.

Cohen, S. (2010, December 25). A $5 children's book vs. a $47,000 jail cell— Choose one. *Forbes*. Retrieved from www.forbes.com/sites/stevecohen/2010/12/25/a-5-childrens-book-vs-a-47000-jail-cell-choose-one/#24a7b467615b.

Coiro, J. (2009). Promising practices for supporting adolescents' online literacy development. In K. Wood & W.E. Blanton (Eds.), *Literacy instruction for adolescents: Research-based practice* (pp. 442–471). New York: Guilford.

Coiro, J., Knobel, M., Lankshear, C. & Leu, D. (2008). Central issues in new literacies and new literacies research. In J. Coiro, M. Knobel, C. Lankshear, & D.J. Leu (Eds.), *Handbook of research on new literacies* (pp. 1–21). New York: Lawrence Erlbaum.

Coleman, W. (2011). "Fish out of water?" Targeted intervention for boys' writing at Padstow School. *Children Youth and Environments, 21*(1), 149–156.

Collier, D.R. (2015). "I'm just trying to be tough, okay": Masculine performances of everyday practices. *Journal of Early Childhood Literacy, 15*(2), 203–226.

Collie, R.J., Martin, A.J., & Curwood, J. S. (2016). Multidimensional motivation and engagement for writing: Construct validation with a sample of boys. *Educational Psychology, 36*(4), 771–791.

Colwell, J., Hunt-Barron, S., & Reinking, D. (2013). Obstacles developing digital literacy on the Internet in middle-school science instruction. *Journal of Literacy Research, 45*(3), 295–324.

Common Core State Standards Initiative. (2010). *Common core state standards for English language arts and literacy in history/social studies, science, and technical subjects.* Retrieved from www.corestandards.org/.

Common Sense Media. (2014). *Children, teens, and reading: A Common Sense Media research brief.* Retrieved from file:///C:/Users/wbrozo/AppData/Local/Temp/csm-childrenteensandreading-2014_0.pdf.

Common Sense Media. (2015). *The common sense census: Media use by tweens and teens.* Retrieved from http://static1.1.sqspcdn.com/static/f/1083077/26645197/1446492628567/CSM_TeenTween_MediaCensus_FinalWebVersion_1.pdf.

Common Sense Media. (2017). *Watching gender: How stereotypes in movies and on TV impact kids' development.* Retrieved from www.commonsensemedia.org/research/watching-gender.

Compton-Lilly, C., & Nayan, R. (2016). Literacy capital in two immigrant families: Longitudinal case studies. In P.R. Schmidt & A.M. Lazar (Eds.), *Reconceptualizing literacy in the new age of multiculturalism and pluralism* (2nd ed., pp. 191–213). Charlotte, NC: IAP Information Age Publishing.

Condie, R., & Munro, B. (2007). *The impact of ICT in schools: A landscape review.* UK: Department for Education and Skills. Retrieved from http://dera.ioe.ac.uk/1627/7/becta_2007_landscapeimpactreview_report_Redacted.pdf.

Conger, D., & Long, M.C. (2010). Why are men falling behind? Gender gaps in college performance and persistence. *The ANNALS of the American Academy of Political and Social Science, 627*(1), 184–214.

Cook-Sather, A. (2010). Students as learners and teachers: Taking responsibility, transforming education, and redefining accountability. *Curriculum Inquiry, 40*(4), 555–575.

Cooper-Mullin, A., & Coye, J.M. (1998). *Once upon a heroine: 450 books for girls to love.* Chicago: NTC/Contemporary Publishing Group.

Copley, R.E. (2000). *The tall Mexican: The life of Hank Aguirre all-star pitcher, businessman, humanitarian.* Houston, TX: Arte Publico.

Courtland, M.C., & Paddington, D. (2008). Digital literacy in a grade 8 classroom: An e-zine WebQuest. *Language and Literacy, 10*(1), 1–23.

Covert, B. (2014, May 19). In the real world, the so-called "boy crisis" disappears. *The Nation.* Retrieved from www.thenation.com/article/real-world-so-called-boy-crisis-disappears/.

Crawford, C., Macmillan, L., & Vignoles, A. (2016). When and why do initially high-achieving poor children fall behind? *Oxford Review of Education, 43*(1), 88–108.

Cromer, M., & Clark, P. (2007). Getting graphic with the past: Graphic novels and the teaching of history. *Theory and Research in Social Education, 35*(4), 574–591.

Crutcher, C. (1995). *Ironman.* New York: Greenwillow.

Dabell, J., Keogh, B., & Naylor, S. (2008). *Concept cartoons in mathematics education*. Millgate House.

Dalgarno, B., & Lee, M.J.W. (2009). What are the learning affordances of 3-D virtual environments? *British Journal of Educational Technology, 41*(1), 10–32.

Dalton, B., & Proctor, P. (2008). The changing landscape of text and comprehension in the age of new literacies. In J. Coiro, M. Knobel, C. Lankshear, & D.J. Leu (Eds.), *Handbook of research on new literacies* (pp. 297–324). Mahwah, NJ: Erlbaum.

Daly, C. (2002). *Literature search on improving boys' writing*. London, UK: Office for Standards in Education.

Damico, J.S., & Carpenter, M. (2005). Evoking hearts and heads: Exploring issues of social justice through poetry. *Language Arts, 83*(2), 137–146.

Dance, L.J. (2001). Shadows, mentors, and surrogate fathers: Effective schooling as critical pedagogy for inner-city boys. *Sociological Focus, 34*(4), 399–415.

Dastiger, A.E. (2017, October 10). "Guns don't kill people; men and boys kill people," experts say. *USA Today*. Retrieved from www.usatoday.com/story/news/2017/10/10/men-special-risk-guns-they-love/734961001/.

de Bellis, M.D., Keshavan, M.S., Beers, S.R. et al. (2001). Sex differences in brain maturation during childhood and adolescence. *Cerebral Cortex, 11*(6), 552–557.

Dede, C. (2010). Comparing frameworks for 21st century skills. In J.A. Bellanca & R. Brandt (Eds.), *21st century skills: Rethinking how students learn* (pp. 51–75). Bloomington, IN: Solution Tree Press.

DeFauw, D.L. (2016). Supporting boy writers. *Literacy Practice & Research, 41*(2), 52–53.

DeGennaro, D. (2008). Learning designs: An analysis of youth-initiated technology use. *Journal of Research on Technology in Education, 4*(1), 1–20.

Del Favero, L., Boscolo, P., Vidotto, G., & Vicentini, M. (2007). Classroom discussion and individual problem-solving in the teaching of history: Do different instructional approaches affect interest in different ways? *Learning and Instruction, 17*, 635–657.

Dennis, J., Basañez, T., & Farahmand, A. (2005). Intergenerational conflicts among Latinos in early adulthood: Separating values conflicts with parents from acculturation conflicts. *Hispanic Journal of Behavioral Science, 32*(1), 118–135.

Dewey, J. (1913). *Interest and effort in education*. Boston: Houghton Mifflin.

Diamond, J. E., & Gaier Knapik, M.C. (2014). *Literacy lessons for a digital world: Using blogs, wikis, podcasts, and more to meet the demands of the Common Core*. New York: Scholastic.

Diaz-Rico, L. (2017). *The crosscultural, language, and academic development handbook: A complete K-12 reference guide* (6th ed.). New York: Pearson.

Disenhaus, N. (2015). *Boys, writing, and the literacy gender gap: What we know, what we think we know*. Graduate College Dissertations and Theses. Paper 330.

Dredger, K., Woods, D., Beach, C., & Sagstetter, V. (2010). Engage me: Using new literacies to create third space classrooms that engage student writers. *Journal of Media Literacy, 2*(2), 85–101.

Dronkers, J., & Kornder, N. (2014). Do migrant girls perform better than migrant boys? Deviant gender differences between the reading scores of 15-year-old children of migrants compared to native pupils. *Educational Research and Evaluation, 20*(1), 44–66.

Dronkers, J., & Kornder, N. (2015). Can gender differences in educational performance of 15- year-old migrant pupils be explained by societal gender equality in origin and destination countries? *Compare: A Journal of Comparative and International Education, 45*(4), 610–634.

Dumka, LE, Gonzales, N.A., Bonds, D.D., & Millsap, R.E. (2009). Academic success of Mexican origin adolescent boys and girls: The role of mothers' and fathers' parenting and cultural orientation. *Sex Roles, 60,* 588–599.

Eberstadt, N. (2016). *Men without work: America's invisible crisis.* West Conshohocken, PA: John Templeton Foundation.

Edwards, J. (2012). *Multilingualism: Understanding linguistic diversity.* London: Continuum.

Education First. (2016). *EF English Proficiency Index.* Retrieved from http://media2.ef.com/__/~/media/centralefcom/epi/downloads/full-reports/v6/ef-epi-2016-english.pdf.

Ellis, N.C. (2012). Frequency-based accounts of SLA. In S.M. Gass & A. Mackey (Eds.), *Handbook of second language acquisition* (pp. 193–210). New York: Routledge.

Elmore, K.C., & Oyserman, D. (2012). If "we" can succeed, "I" can too: Identity-based motivation and gender in the classroom. *Contemporary Educational Psychology, 37*(3), 176–185.

Enriquez, G. (2017). "But they won't let you read!" A case study of an urban middle school male's response to school reading. *Journal of Education, 193*(1), 35–46.

Entwisle, D.R., Alexander, K.L., & Olson, L.S. (2007). Early schooling: The handicap of being poor and male. *Sociology of Education, 80*(2), 114–138.

Erikson, E. (1980). *Identity and the life cycle.* New York: W.W. Norton.

Ertmer, P.A., & Ottenbreit-Leftwich, A.T. (2010). Teacher technology change: How knowledge, confidence, beliefs, and culture intersect. *Journal of Research on Technology in Education, 42*(3), 255–284.

Ertmer, P.A., Ottenbreit-Leftwich, A.T., Sadik, O., Sendurur, E., & Sendurur, P. (2012). Teacher beliefs and technology integration practices: A critical relationship. *Computers in Education, 59,* 423–435.

ETS. (2016). *Test and score data summary for TOEFL iBT tests.* Educational Testing Service. Retrieved from www.ets.org/s/toefl/pdf/94227_unlweb.pdf.

European Commission. (2012). *ECEC for children from disadvantaged backgrounds: Findings from a European literature review and two case studies.* Brussels: European Commission. Retrieved from http://ec.europa.eu/dgs/education_culture/repository/education/policy/school/doc/ecec-report_en.pdf.

European Commission. (2016). *Upskilling pathways: New opportunities for adults*. Retrieved from http://eur-lex.europa.eu/legal-content/EN/TXT/PDF/?uri=CELEX:32016H1224(01)&from=EN.

EU High Level Group of Experts on Literacy. (2012). *Final report*. Retrieved from http://ec.europa.eu/dgs/education_culture/repository/education/policy/school/doc/literacy-report_en.pdf.

Eurydice. (2005). *How boys and girls in Europe are finding their way with information and communication technology?* Eurydice in brief. Retrieved from http://youth-partnership-eu.coe.int/youth partnership/documents/EKCYP/Youth_Policy/docs/Citizenship/Research/euridyce -study-on-IT.pdf.

Eurydice. (2010). *Gender differences in educational outcomes: Studies on the measures taken and current situation in Europe*. Brussels: Education, Audiovisual and Culture Executive Agency. Retrieved from http://eacea.ec.europa.eu/education/eurydice/documents/thematic_reports/120en.pdf.

Expert Panel on Literacy in Grades 4 to 6 in Ontario. (2004). *Literacy for learning: The report of the expert panel on literacy in Grades 4 to 6 in Ontario*. Toronto, ON: Ontario Ministry of Education.

Extra, G., & Yagmur, K. (2012). *Language rich Europe: Trends for policies and practices for multilingualism in Europe*. Cambridge, UK: Cambridge University Press.

Fantuzzo, J. (2009). *The educational well-being of African American boys: A Philadelphia story of challenges & possibilities*. Retrieved from www.documentcloud.org/documents/239463-the-educational-well-being-of-african-american.html.

Fantuzzo, J., LeBoeuf, W., Rouse, H., & Chen, C-C. (2012). Academic achievement of African American boys: A city-wide community-based investigation of risk and resilience. *Journal of School Psychology, 50*, 559–579.

Farrant, B., & Zubrick, S. (2012). Early vocabulary development: The importance of joint attention and parent-child book reading. *First Language, 32*(3), 343–364.

Farrell, A.D., & Meyer, A.L. (1997). The effectiveness of a school-based curriculum for reducing violence among urban sixth-grade students. *American Journal of Public Health, 87*(6), 979–984.

Farris, P.J., Werderich, D.E., Nelson, P.A., & Fuhler, C.J. (2009). Male call: Fifth-grade boys' reading preferences. *The Reading Teacher, 63*(3), 180–188.

Fecho, B. (2011). *Teaching for the students: Habits of heart, mind, and practice in the engaged classroom*. New York: Teachers College Press.

Feliciano, C. (2012). The female educational advantage among adolescent children of immigrants. *Youth and Society, 44*(3), 431–449.

Filmer, D., Hasan A., & Pritchett, L. (2006, August). *A millennium learning goal: Measuring real progress in education*, Working Paper, No. 97. Washington, DC: Center for Global Development.

Fingon, J. (2012). Nontraditional texts and the struggling/reluctant reader. *Voices From the Middle, 19*(4), 70–75.

Fisher, D., & Frey, N. (2012). Motivating boys to read: Inquiry, modeling, and choice matter. *Journal of Adolescent & Adult Literacy, 55*(7), 587–596.

Fisher, D., & Ivey, G. (2007). Farewell to *A Farewell to Arms*: Deemphasizing the whole-class novel. *Phi Delta Kappan, 88*(7), 494–497.

Fisher, M.T. (2007). *Writing in rhythm: Spoken word poetry in urban classrooms.* New York: Teachers College Press.

Fletcher, R. (2006). *Boy writers: Reclaiming their voices.* Markham, ON: Pembroke Publishers.

Flynt, S., & Brozo, W.G. (2009). It's all about the teacher. *The Reading Teacher, 62*(6), 536–538.

Freeman, J.G., McPhail, J.C., & Berndt, J.A. (2002). Sixth graders' views of activities that do and do not help them to learn. *Elementary School Journal, 102*, 335–347.

Freeman, Y., & Freeman, D. (2008). *Academic language for English language learners and struggling readers: How to help students succeed across content areas.* Portsmouth, NH: Heinemann.

Friere, P. (1987). *Literacy: Reading the word and the world.* South Hadley, MA: Bergin & Garvey.

Fruh, S.M., Fulkerson, J.A., Kendrick, L.A.J., & Clanton, C. (2011). The surprising benefits of the family meal. *The Journal for Nurse Practitioners, 7*(1), 18–22.

Fulkerson, J.A, Kubik, M.Y, Story, M., Lytle, L., & Arcan, C. (2009). Are there nutritional and other benefits associated with family meals among at-risk youth? *Journal of Adolescent Health, 45*(4), 389–395.

Fung, I.Y.Y., Wilkinson, I.A.G., & Moore, D.W. (2003). L1-assisted reciprocal teaching to improve ESL students' comprehension of English expository text. *Learning and Instruction, 13*, 1–13.

Gambrell, L. (2011). Seven rules of engagement: What's most important to know about motivation to read. *The Reading Teacher, 65*(3), 172–178.

Gandara, P., & Contreras, F. (2009). *The Latino education crisis: The consequences of failed social policies.* Boston: Harvard University Press.

García-Valcárcel, A., Basilotta, V., & López, C. (2014). ICT in collaborative learning in the classrooms of primary and secondary education. *Media Education Research Journal, 42*(21), 65–74.

Gates, A. (1961). Sex differences in reading ability. *The Elementary School Journal, 61*(8), 431–434.

Gavigan, K.W. (2010). *Examining struggling male adolescent readers' responses to graphic novels: A multiple case study of four, eighth-grade males in a graphic novel book club.* Retrieved from http://libres.uncg.edu/ir/uncg/f/gavigan_uncg_0154d_10480.pdf.

Gaylord-Harden, N.K., Burrow, A.L., & Cunningham, J.A. (2012). A cultural-asset framework for investigating successful adaptation to stress in African American youth. *Child Development Perspectives, 6*(3), 264–271.

Gee, J.P., & Hayes, E.R. (2011). *Language and learning in the digital age.* New York: Routledge.

Gershenson, S., Lindsay, C., Hart, C.M.D., & Papageorge, N.W. (2017). *The long-run impacts of same-race teachers.* IZA Institute of Labor Economics. Retrieved from www.iza.org/publications/dp/10630

Gibson, K.R., & Petersen, A.C. (2010). *Brain maturation and cognitive development*. Oxford, UK: Blackwell.

Gibson, M.A., & Carrasco, S. (2009). The education of immigrant youth: Some lessons from the U.S. and Spain. *Theory into Practice, 48*, 249–257.

Gilbert, J., & Graham, S. (2010). Teaching writing to elementary students in grades 4–6: A national survey. *The Elementary School Journal, 110*(4), 495–518.

Gilles, A. (2012). *The benefits of learning math vocabulary with context strategies alone versus with comics as a visual: A case study*. Dissertation. Fordham University.

Gillespie, A., Graham, S., Kiuhara, S., & Hebert, M. (2014). High school teachers' use of writing to support students' learning: A national survey. *Reading and Writing, 27*(6), 1043–1072.

Ging, D. (2005). A "manual on masculinity"? The consumption and use of mediated images of masculinity among teenage boys in Ireland. *Irish Journal of Sociology, 14*(2), 29–52.

Glowka, D. (2014). The impact of gender on attainment in learning English as a foreign language. *Studies in Second Language Learning and Teaching, 4*(4), 617–635.

Gluszynski, T., & Dhawan-Biswal, U. (2008). *Reading skills of young immigrants in Canada: The effects of duration of residency, home language exposure and schools*. Quebec, Canada: Human Resources and Social Development Canada.

Godley, A.J. (2003). Literacy learning as gendered identity work. *Communication Education, 52*(3–4), 273–285.

Gogan, B. (2013). Reading at the threshold. *Across the Disciplines, 10*(4). Retrieved from wac.colostate.edu/atd/reading/gogan.cfm.

Gonzales, N.A., German, M., Kim, S.Y., George, P., Fabrett, F.C., Millsap, R., & Dumka, L.E. (2008). Mexican American adolescents' cultural orientation, externalizing behavior and academic engagement: The role of traditional cultural values. *American Journal of Community Psychology, 41*(1–2), 151–164.

Goodman, J., & Rogers, R. (2010). Crossing borders in girls' secondary education. In J. Goodman, R. Rogers, & J. Albisetti (Eds.), *Girls' secondary education in the western world: From the 18th to the 20th century* (pp. 191–202). New York: Palgrave Macmillan.

Gorman-Smith, D., Henry, D.B., & Tolan, P. (2004). Exposure to community violence and violence penetration: The protective effects of family functioning. *Journal of Clinical Child and Adolescent Psychology, 33*(3), 439–449.

Graham, S., & Hebert, M. (2010). *Writing to read: Evidence for how writing can improve reading*: A report from Carnegie Corporation of New York.

Graham, S., & Perin, D. (2007). *Writing next: Effective strategies to improve writing of adolescents in middle and high schools: A report to Carnegie Corporation of New York*. Washington, DC: Alliance for Excellent Education.

Gray, K. (2014). Graphic novels: Providing a different perspective. *Connections, 91*(4),4–6.

Gray, L., Thomas, N., & Lewis, L. (2010). *Educational technology in U.S. public schools: Fall 2008*. Washington, DC: US Department of Education, National

Center for Education Statistics. Retrieved from https://nces.ed.gov/pubs2010/2010034.pdf.
Greenhow, C., & Robelia, B. (2009). Informal learning and identity formation in online social networks. *Learning, Media and Technology, 34*(2), 119–140.
Greenleaf, C.L., Jimenez, R.T., & Roller, C.M. (2002). Reclaiming secondary reading interventions: From limited to rich conceptions, from narrow to broad conversations. *Reading Research Quarterly, 37*, 484–496.
Greig, C., & Hughes, J. (2009). A boy who would rather write poetry then throw rocks at cats is also considered to be wanting in masculinity: Poetry, masculinity, and baiting boys. *Discourse: Studies in the Cultural Politics of Education, 30*(1), 91–105.
Griffith, P.E. (2010). Graphic novels in the secondary classroom and school libraries. *Journal of Adolescent & Adult Literacy, 54*(3), 181–189.
Grin, F., Sfreddo, C., & Vaillancourt, F. (2010). *The economics of the multilingual workplace*. London: Routledge.
Guevremont, A., Roos, N.P., & Brownell, M. (2007). Predictors and consequences of grade retention: Examining data from Manitoba, Canada. *Canadian Journal of School Psychology, 22*(1), 50–67.
Guthrie, J. (Ed.). (2008). *Engaging adolescents in reading*. Thousand Oaks, CA: Corwin.
Guthrie, J.T., & Klauda, S.L. (2014). Effects of classroom practices on reading comprehension, engagement, and motivations for adolescents. *Reading Research Quarterly, 49*(4), 387–416.
Guthrie, J.T., & McRae, A. (2011). Reading engagement among African American and European American students. In S.J. Samuels & A.E. Farstrup (Eds.), *What research has to say about reading instruction* (pp. 115–142). Newark, DE: IRA.
Guthrie, J.T., Wigfield, A., & You, W. (2012). Instructional contexts for engagement and achievement in reading. In S.L. Christenson, A.L. Reschly, & C. Wylie (Eds.), *Handbook of research on student engagement* (pp. 601–634). New York: Springer.
Guthrie, J.T., Hoa, L.W., Wigfield, A., Tonks, S.M., & Perencevich, K.C. (2006). From spark to fire: Can situational reading interest lead to long-term reading motivation? *Reading Research and Instruction, 45*(2), 91–117.
Gutnick, A., Robb, M., Takeuchi, L., & Kotler, J. (2011). *Always connected: The new digital media habits of young children*. New York: The Joan Ganz Cooney Center at Sesame Workshop. Retrieved from www.joanganzcooneycenter.org/wpcontent/uploads/2011/03/jgcc_alwaysconnected.pdf.
Guzzetti, B., Elliott, K., & Welsch, D. (2010). *DIY media in the classroom: New literacies across content areas*. New York: Teachers College Press.
Haddix, M. (2009). Black boys can write: Challenging dominant framings of African American males in literacy research. *Journal of Adolescent & Adult Literacy, 53*(4), 341–343.
Halat, E. (2008). A good teaching technique: WebQuests. *The Clearing House: A Journal of Educational Strategies, Issues and Ideas, 81*(3), 109–112.

Halimun, J.M. (2011). *A qualitative study of the use of content-related comics to promote student participation in mathematical discourse in a math I support class* (2011). Dissertations, Theses and Capstone Projects. Paper 471. http://digital commons.kennesaw.edu/etd/471

Hällgren, C., Dunkels, E., & Frånberg, G-M. (2015). *Invisible boy: The making of contemporary masculinities.* Umeå, Sweden: Print & Media, Umeå University.

Halpern, D.F. (2012). *Sex differences in cognitive abilities* (4th ed.). New York: Psychology Press.

Hamilton, S.K., & Wilson, J.H. (2009). Family mealtimes: Worth the effort? *ICAN: Infant, Child, & Adolescent Nutrition, 1*(6), 346–350.

Hammett, R., & Sanford, K. (2008). *Boys and girls and the myths of literacies and learning.* Toronto: Canadian Scholars' Press.

Hample, Z. (2011). *Baseball: Stunts, scandals and secrets beneath the stitches.* New York: Anchor Books.

Hanke, U. (2012). Generative learning. In N. Seel (Ed.), *Encyclopedia of the sciences of learning* (pp. 1356–1358). New York: Springer.

Hanushek, E.A., & Woessmann, L. (2008). The role of cognitive skills in economic development. *Journal of Economic Literature, 46*(3), 607–668.

Hanushek, E.A., & Woessmann, L. (2010). *The high cost of low educational performance: The long-run economic impact of improving PISA outcomes.* Paris: OECD. Retrieved from www.sourceoecd.org/education/9789264077485.

Hanushek, E.A., & Woessmann, L. (2015). *Universal basic skills: What countries stand to gain.* Paris: OECD. Retrieved from http://dx.doi.org/10.1787/978926 4234833-en.

Harders, P., & Macken-Horarik, M. (2008). Scaffolding literacy and the year 9 boys: Developing a language-centred literacy pedagogy. *TESOL in Context, 18*(2), 4–21.

Harper, S.R., & Williams, C.D. (2014). *Succeeding in the city: A report from the New York City Black and Latino male high achievement study.* Philadelphia: University of Pennsylvania, Center for the Study of Race and Equity in Education.

Harris, K.R., & Graham, S. (2013). Integrating reading and writing instruction. In B. Miller, P. McCardle, & R. Long (Eds.), *Teaching reading and writing: Improving instruction and student achievement* (pp. 35–44). Baltimore, MD: Paul H. Brookes Publishing.

Harris, T.S., & Graves Jr., S. L. (2010). The influence of cultural capital transmission on reading achievement in African American fifth grade boys. *The Journal of Negro Education, 79*(4), 447–457.

Harrison, B. (2010). Boys and literature: Challenging constructions of masculinity. *New Zealand Journal of Educational Studies, 45*(2), 47–60.

Harrison, C. (2016). Are computers, smartphones, and the Internet a boon or a barrier for the weaker reader? *Journal of Adolescent & Adult Literacy, 60*(2), 221–225.

Hartman, D.K., Morsink, P.M., & Zheng, J. (2010). From print to pixels: The evolution of cognitive conceptions of reading comprehension. In E.A.

Baker (Ed.), *The new literacies: Multiple perspectives on research and practice* (pp. 131–164). New York: Guilford Press.

Hattie, J. (2006). Cross-age tutoring and the Reading Together program. *Studies in Educational Evaluation, 32*(2), 100–124.

Hattie, J. (2011). *Visible learning for teachers: Maximizing impact on teachers.* New York: Routledge.

Hawisher, G.E., Selfe, C.L., Kisa, G., & Ahmed, S. (2009). Globalism and multimodality in a digitized world: Computers and composition studies. *Pedagogy, 10*(1), 55–68.

Hawke, J.L., Olson, R.K., Willcut, E.G., Wadsworth, S.J., & DeFries, J.C. (2009). Gender ratios for reading difficulties. *Dyslexia, 15,* 239–242.

Hawke, J.L., Wadsworth, S.J., Olson, R.K., & DeFries, J.C. (2007). Etiology of reading difficulties as a function of gender and severity. *Reading and Writing, 20,* 13–25.

Hawkins, L.K., & Certo, J.L. (2014). "It's something that I feel like writing, instead of writing because I'm being told to": Elementary boys' experiences writing and performing poetry. *Pedagogies: An International Journal, 9*(3), 196–215.

Heath, A., & Kilpi-Jakonen, E. (2012). *Immigrant children's age at arrival and assessment results.* OECD Education Working Papers, No. 75. Paris: OECD Publishing. http://dx.doi.org/10.1787/5k993zsz6g7h-en.

Hebert, M., Gillespie, A., & Graham, S. (2013). Comparing effects of different writing activities on reading comprehension: A meta-analysis. *Reading and Writing, 26*(1), 111–138.

Hebert, T.P., & Pagnani, A.R. (2010). Engaging gifted boys in new literacies. *Gifted Child Today, 33*(3), 36–45.

Heckman, J.J., & Kautz, T. (2012). *Hard evidence on soft skills.* Bonn, Germany: Institute for the Study of Labor.

Heckman, J.J., Stixrud, J., & Urzua, S. (2006). The effects of cognitive and noncognitive abilities on labor market outcomes and social behavior. *Journal of Labor Economics, 24*(3), 411–482.

Heinzmann, S. (2009). "Girls are better at language learning than boys": Do stereotypic beliefs about language learning contribute to girls' higher motivation to learn English in primary school? *Bulletin VALS-ASLA, 89,* 19–36.

Hernandez, D.J. (2012). *Double jeopardy: How third-grade reading skills and poverty influence high school graduation.* Baltimore, MD: The Annie E. Casey Foundation. Retrieved from www.aecf.org/m/resourcedoc/AECF-DoubleJeopardy-2012-Full.pdf.

Hicks, T., & Turner, K.H. (2013). No longer a luxury: Digital literacy can't wait. *English Journal, 102*(6), 58–65.

Hilburn, J. (2014). Challenges facing immigrant students beyond the linguistic domain in a new gateway state. *The Urban Review, 46*(4), 654–680.

Hildreth, P.M., & Kimble, C. (2004). *Knowledge networks: Innovation through communities of practice.* Hershey, PA: Idea Group Publications.

Hill, A.E. (2014). *Predictive effects of black fathers' class and status on their adolescent sons' reading proficiency.* Fairfax, VA: George Mason University. Retrieved from

http://digilib.gmu.edu/jspui/bitstream/handle/1920/8968/Hill_gmu_0883E_10686.pdf?sequence=1.
Hinchman, K.A., Alvermann, D.E., Boyd, F.B., Brozo, W.G., & Vacca, R.T. (2003/2004). Supporting older students' in- and out-of-school literacies. *Journal of Adolescent & Adult Literacy, 47*, 304–310.
Ho, A.N., & Guthrie, J.T. (2013). Patterns of association among multiple motivations and aspects of achievement in reading. *Reading Psychology, 34*(2), 101–147.
Hobbs, R. (2010). *Digital and media literacy: A plan of action.* Washington, DC: The Aspen Institute. Retrieved from https://files.eric.ed.gov/fulltext/ED523244.pdf.
Hoff, E. (2009). *Language development.* Boston, MA: Wadsworth/Cengage Learning.
Hofstetter, C.R., Sticht, T.G., & Hofstetter, C.H. (1999). Knowledge, literacy, and power. *Communication Research, 26*(1), 58–80.
Hogan-Brun, G. (2017). *Linguanomics: What is the market potential of multilingualism?* London: Bloomsbury.
Holstermann, N., Grube, D., & Bögeholz, S. (2010). Hands-on activities and their influence on students' interest. *Research in Science Education, 40*(5), 743–757.
Hong, G., & Yu, B. (2007). Early-grade retention and children's reading and math learning in elementary years. *Educational Evaluation and Policy Analysis, 29*(4), 239–261.
Houry, D., Rhodes, K., Demball, R.S., Click, L., Cerulli, C., McNutt, L.A., & Kaslow, N.J. (2008). Differences in female and male victims and perpetrators of partner violence with respect to WEB scores. *Journal of Interpersonal Violence, 23*(8), 1041–1055.
Hughes-Hassell, S., & Rodge, P. (2007). The leisure reading habits of urban adolescents. *Journal of Adolescent & Adult Literacy, 51*(1), 22–33.
Hulleman, C.S, Godes, O., Hendricks, B.L., & Harackiewicz, J.M. (2010). Enhancing interest and performance with a utility value intervention. *Journal of Educational Psychology, 102*(4), 880–895.
Husband, T. (2012). Addressing reading underachievement in African American boys through a multi-contextual approach. *Reading Horizons, 52*(1), 1–25.
Hutchison, A.C., & Colwell, J. (2014). The potential of digital technologies to support literacy Instruction relevant to the Common Core State Standards. *Journal of Adolescent & Adult Literacy, 58*(2), 147–156.
Hutchison, A.C., & Reinking, D. (2011). Teachers' perceptions of integrating information and communication technologies into literacy instruction: A national survey in the U.S. *Reading Research Quarterly, 46*(4), 312–333.
Illich, I. (1970). *Deschooling society.* New York: Harper & Row.
International Reading Association. (2009). *New literacies and 21st century technologies* (Position statement). Newark, DE: Author. Retrieved from: www.reading.org/General/AboutIRA/Position Statements/21stCenturyLiteracies.aspx.
International Reading Association. (2012). *Adolescent literacy: A position statement of the International Reading Association.* Retrieved from www.literacyworldwide.org/docs/default-source/where-we-stand/adolescent-literacy-position-statement.pdf.

Irving, J. (1997). *The imaginary girlfriend: A memoir*. New York: Acacia Press.
Ivey, G. (2011). What not to read: A book intervention. *Voices from the Middle, 19* (2), 22–26.
Ivey, G., & Broaddus, K. (2007). A formative experiment investigating literacy engagement among adolescent Latina/o students just beginning to read, write, and speak English. *Reading Research Quarterly, 42*, 512–545.
Jacob, B.A., & Lefgren, L. (2007). *The effect of grade retention on high school completion*. Cambridge, MA: National Bureau of Economic Research. NBER Working Paper 13514.
Janzen, J. (2008). Teaching English language learners in the content areas. *Review of Educational Research, 78*(4), 1010–1038.
Jendricks, N. (2006). *Dunks, doubles, doping: How steroids are killing American athletics*. Guilford, CT: Globe Pequot.
Jenkins, S. (2009). How to maintain school reading success: Five recommendations from a struggling male reader. *The Reading Teacher, 63*(2), 159–162.
Jensen, A. (2009). *Teaching with poverty in mind*. Alexandria, VA: ASCD.
Jensen, L.A. (2008). Coming of age in a multicultural world: Globalization and adolescent cultural identity formation. In D.L. Browning (Ed.), *Adolescent identities: A collection of readings* (pp. 3–18). New York: Taylor & Francis.
Jerrim, J. (2013). *The reading gap: The socio-economic gap in children's reading skills: A cross- national comparison using PISA 2009*. London: Sutton Trust. Retrieved from www.suttontrust.com/wp-content/uploads/2013/07/READINGGAP.pdf.
Jerrim, J., & Vignoles, A. (2013). Social mobility, regression to the mean and the cognitive development of high ability children from disadvantaged homes. *Journal of the Royal Statistical Society: Series A (Statistics in Society), 176*(3), 887–906.
Jeynes, W.H. (2005). *Parental involvement and student achievement: A meta-analysis*. Harvard Family Research Project. Retrieved from www.hfrp.org/family-involvement/publications-resources/.
Jiménez, R.M., & Ojeda, J. (2008). The English vocabulary of girls and boys: Evidence from a quantitative study. In L. Litosseliti, H. Sauton, K. Harrington, & J. Sunderland (Eds.), *Theoretical and methodological approaches to gender and language study* (pp. 103–115). London/New York: Palgrave Macmillan.
Jimerson, S.R., & Ferguson, P. (2007). A longitudinal study of grade retention: Academic and behavioral outcomes of retained students through adolescence. *School Psychology Quarterly, 22*(3), 314–339.
Johnson, C., & Gooliaff, S. (2013). Teaching to strengths: Engaging young boys in learning. *Reclaiming Children and Youth, 21*(4), 28–31.
Johnson, C.W., Richmond, L., & Kivel, B.D. (2008). "What a man ought to be, he is far from": Collective meanings of masculinity and race in media. *Leisure, 32* (2), 303–330.
Johnson, M., & Pleece, W. (2008). *Incognegro*. Milwaukie, OR: Dark Horse Books.
Jolliffe, L. (2011). Hard targets: Men as a disposable sex. In S.D. Ross & P.M. Lester (Eds.), *Images that injure: Pictorial stereotypes in the media* (3rd ed., pp. 173–182). Santa Barbara, CA: Praeger.

Juvonen, J., Espinoza, G., & Knifsend, C. (2009). The role of peer relationships in student academic and extracurricular engagement. In: K.R. Wenzel & A. Wigfield (Eds.), *Handbook of motivation at school* (pp. 387–403). New York: Routledge.

Jyotsna, J., & Pouezevara, S. (2016). *Boy's underachievement in education: A review of the literature with a focus on reading in the early years.* Washington, DC: USAID. Retrieved from www.ungei.org/Boys_Underachievement.pdf.

Kanaan, R.A., Allin, M. Picchioni, M. et al. (2012). Gender differences in white matter microstructure. *PloS ONE, 7*(6).e38272. https://doi.org/10.1371/journal.pone.0038272

Kajder, S.B. (2010). *Adolescents and digital literacies: Learning alongside our students.* Urbana, IL: National Council of Teachers of English.

Kamil, M. (2004). *Reading for the 21st century: Adolescent literacy and learning strategies.* Washington, DC: Alliance for Excellent Education.

Kanno, Y. & Kanagas, S. (2014). "I'm not going to be, like, for the AP": English language learners' limited access to advanced college-preparatory courses in high school. *American Educational Research Journal, 52*(3), 848–878.

Karcher, M. (2009). Increases in academic connectedness and self-esteem among high school students who serve as cross-age peer mentors. *Professional School Counseling, 12*(4), 292–299.

Kehler, M., & Martino, W. (2007). Questioning masculinities: Interrogating boys' capacities for self-problematization in schools. *Canadian Journal of Education, 30*(1), 90–112.

Kellogg, R.T., & Whiteford, A.P. (2009). Training advanced writing skills: The case for deliberate practice. *Educational Psychologist, 44*(4), 250–266.

Kennedy, M.D. (2015). *Globalizing knowledge: Intellectuals, universities, and publics in transformation.* Stanford, CA: Stanford University Press.

Kerpelman, J.L., Eryigit, S., & Stephens, C. J. (2008). African American adolescents' future education orientation: Associations with self-efficacy, ethnic identity, and perceived parental support. *Journal of Youth and Adolescence, 37*(8), 997–1008.

Kessels, U., Heyder, A., Latsch, M., & Hannover, B. (2014). How gender differences in academic engagement relate to students' gender identity. *Educational Research, 56*(2), 220–229.

Kessler, B. (2009). Comic books that teach mathematics. In C.S. Kaplan & R. Sarhangi (Eds.), *Proceedings of Bridges 2009: Mathematics, music, art, architecture, culture* (pp. 97–104). Banff, AB, Canada: Banff International Research Station, The Banff Centre.

Khamisi, H.A., Barwani, T.A., Mekhlafi, A.A., & Osman, M.E.T. (2016). EFL reading achievement: Impact of gender and self-efficacy beliefs. *International Journal of Learning, Teaching and Educational Research, 15*(3), 54–73.

Kieffer, M.J. (2012). Early oral language and later reading development in Spanish-speaking English language learners: Evidence from a nine-year longitudinal study. *Journal of Applied Developmental Psychology, 33*(3), 146–157.

King, M.L., Jr. (1963). Letter from Birmingham Jail. In *Why we can't wait* (pp. 23–33). New York: Harper & Row.

King, R. (2016). Gender differences in motivation, engagement and achievement are related to students' perceptions of peer – but not of parent or teacher – attitudes toward school. *Learning and Individual Differences, 52*, 60–71.

Kinzer, C.K., & Leander, K. (2003). Technology and the language arts: Implications of an expanded definition of literacy. In J. Flood, D. Lapp, J.R. Squires, & J.M. Jensen (Eds.), *Handbook of research and teaching the English language arts* (2nd ed., pp. 546–566). Mahwah, NJ: Erlbaum.

Kirkland, D.E. (2011a). Books like clothes: Engaging young black men with reading. *Journal of Adolescent & Adult Literacy, 55*(3), 199–208.

Kirkland, D.E. (2011b). Listening to echoes: Teaching young black men literacy and the problem of ELA standards. *Language Arts, 88*(5), 373–380.

Kishiyama, M.M., Boyce, W.T., Jimenez, A.M., Perry, L.M., & Knight, R.T. (2009). Socioeconomic disparities affect prefrontal function in children. *Journal of Cognitive Neuroscience, 21*(6), 1106–1115.

Kissau, S., & Turnbull, M. (2008). Boys and French as a second language: A research agenda for greater understanding. *Canadian Journal of Applied Linguistics, 11*(3), 151–170.

Klein, P.D., Arcon, N., & Baker, S. (2016). Writing to learn. In C. MacArthur, S. Graham, & J. Fitzgerald (Eds.), *Handbook of writing research* (2nd ed., pp. 243–256). New York: Guilford Press.

Knight, J. (2013). *High-impact instruction: A framework for great teaching*. Thousand Oaks, CA: Corwin.

Kohnen, A.M. (2013). Informational writing in high school science: The importance of genre, apprenticeship, and publication. *Journal of Adolescent & Adult Literacy, 57*(3), 233–242.

Koltay, T. (2011). The media and the literacies: Media literacy, information literacy, digital literacy. *Media, Culture & Society, 33*(2), 211–221.

Kong, A., & Fitch, E. (2002). Using book club to engage culturally and linguistically diverse learners in reading, writing, and talking about books. *The Reading Teacher, 56*(4), 352.

Kreidler, M. (2007). *Four days to glory: Wrestling with the soul of the American heartland*. New York: HarperCollins.

Kuhl, D. & Martino, W. (2017) "Sissy" boys and the pathologization of gender non-conformity. In S. Talburt (Ed.), *Youth sexualities: Public feelings and contemporary cultural politics* (pp. 31–60). Santa Barbara: Praeger.

Ladbrook, J., & Probert, E. (2011). Information skills and critical literacy: Where are our digikids at with online searching and are their teachers helping? *Australasian Journal of Educational Technology, 27*(1), 105–121.

Ladd, H. F. (2012). Education and poverty: Confronting the evidence. *Journal of Policy Analysis and Management, 31*(2), 203–227.

Land, M. (2013). Full STEAM ahead: The benefits of integrating the arts into STEM. *Procedia Computer Science, 20*, 547–552.

Langker, S. (1995). Boys' team also does well. In R. Browne & R. Fletcher (Eds.), *Boys in schools: Addressing the real issues – behaviour, values and relationships* (pp. 190–200). Sydney, NSW, Australia: Finch Publishing.

Lankshear, C., & Knobel, M. (2013). *A new literacies reader: Educational perspectives*. New York: Peter Lang.

Lapp, D., & Fisher, D. (2009). It's all about the book: Motivating teens to read. *Journal of Adolescent & Adult Literacy, 52*(7), 556–561.

Lapp, D., & Fisher, D. (2011). *Handbook of research on teaching the English language arts* (3rd ed.). New York: Routledge.

Larson, R.W., Wiley, A.R., & Branscomb, K.R. (2006). *Family mealtime as a context of development and socialization: New directions for child and adolescent development*. San Francisco: Jossey-Bass.

Lattanzi, J.A. (2014). *"Just don't call it a book club": Boys' reading experiences and motivaton in school and in an after school book club*. Retrieved from https://rucore.libraries.rutgers.edu/rutgers-lib/42347/PDF/1/play/.

Leander, K.M., & Sheehy, M. (2004). *Spatializing literacy research and practice*. New York: Peter Lang.

Lee, J.-S. (2014). The relationship between student engagement and academic performance: Is it a myth or reality? *The Journal of Educational Research, 107*(3), 177–185.

Leino, K. (2014). *The relationship between ICT use and reading literacy: Focus on 15-year-old Finnish students in PISA studies*. Jyvaskyla, Finland: University of Jyvaskyla. Retrieved from https://jyx.jyu.fi/dspace/bitstream/handle/123456789/44930/978-951-39-5828-2.pdf?sequence=1.

Lietz, P. (2006). A meta-analysis of gender differences in reading achievement at the secondary school level. *Studies in Educational Evaluation, 32*(4), 317–344.

Lenhart, A., Arafeh, S., Smith, A., & Macgill, A.R. (2008). *Writing, technology and teens*. Pew Internet & American Life Project. Retrieved from www.pewinternet.org/files/oldmedia/Files/Reports/2008/PIP_Writing_Report_FINAL3.pdf.pdf.

Lenters, K. (2007). From storybooks to games, comics, bands, and chapter books: A young boy's appropriation of literacy practices. *Canadian Journal of Education, 30*, 113–136.

Lesaux, N.K., Kieffer, M.J., Faller, S.E., & Kelley, J.G. (2010). The effectiveness and ease of implementation of an academic vocabulary intervention for linguistically diverse students in urban middle schools. *Reading Research Quarterly, 45*(2), 196–228.

Leu, D.J., Forzani, E., Rhoads, C., Maykel, C., Kennedy, C., & Timbrell, N. (2015). The new literacies of online reading and comprehension: Rethinking the reading achievement gap. *Reading Research Quarterly, 50*(1), 37–59.

Leu, D.J., Kinzer, C.K., Coiro, J.L., & Cammack, D.W. (2004). Toward a theory of new literacies emerging from the Internet and other information and communication technologies. In R. Ruddell & N. Unrau (Eds.), *Theoretical Models and Processes of Reading* (5th ed., pp. 1568–1611). Newark, DE: International Reading Association.

Leu D.J., Kinzer, C.K., Coiro, J., Castek, J., & Henry, L.A. (2013). New literacies: A dual-level theory of the changing nature of literacy, instruction, and assessment. In D. Alvermann, N. Unrau, & R. Ruddell (Eds.), *Theoretical models and processes of reading* (6th ed., pp. 1150–1181). Newark, DE: International Reading Association.

Leventhal, T., Xue, Y., & Brooks-Gunn, J. (2006). Immigrant differences in school-age children's verbal trajectories: A look at four racial/ethnic groups. *Child Development, 77*(5), 1359–1374.

Li, X., Feigelman, S., & Stanton, B. (2000). Perceived parental monitoring and health risk behaviors among urban low-income African-American children and adolescents. *Journal of Adolescent Health, 27*(1), 43–48.

Liederman, J., Kantrowitz, L., & Flannery, K. (2005). Male vulnerability to reading disability is not likely to be a myth: A call for new data. *Journal of Learning Disabilities, 38*, 109–129.

Lietaert, S., Roorda, D., Laevers, F., Verschueren, K., & De Fraine, B. (2015). The gender gap in student engagement: The role of teachers' autonomy support, structure, and involvement. *British Journal of Educational Psychology, 85*(4), 498–518.

Lingard, B., Martino, W., & Mills, M. (2009). *Boys and schooling: Beyond structural reform*. London: Palgrave Macmillan.

Livingstone, S. (2008). Internet literacy: Young people's negotiation of new online opportunities. In T. McPherson (Ed.), *Digital youth, innovation, and the unexpected* (pp. 101–122). Cambridge, MA: The MIT Press.

Livingstone, S. (2012). Critical reflections on the benefits of ICT in education. *Oxford Review of Education, 38*(1), 9–24.

Llach, M.P.A., & Gallego, M.T. (2012). Vocabulary knowledge development and gender differences in a second language. *ELIA, 12*, 45–75.

Lloyd, T. (2011). *Boys underachievement in schools literature review*. Belfast, Ireland: Centre for Young Men's Studies, Ulster University. Retrieved from www.boysdevelopmentproject.org.uk/wp-content/uploads/2013/06/Boys-and-underachievement-literature-review-edited-in-pdf.pdf.

Lockhart, T., & Soliday, M. (2016). The critical place of reading in writing transfer (and beyond): A report of student experiences. *Pedagogy, 16*(1), 23–37.

Loera, G., Rueda, R., & Nakamoto, J. (2011). The association between parental involvement in reading and schooling and children's reading engagement in Latino families. *Literacy Research and Instruction, 50*, 133–155.

Logan, S., & Johnston, R. (2009). Gender differences in reading ability and attitudes: Examining where these differences lie. *Journal of Research in Reading, 32*(2), 199–214.

Logan, S., & Medford, E. (2011). Gender differences in the strength of association between motivation, competency beliefs and reading skill. *Educational Research, 53*(1), 85–94.

Long, J.F, Monoi, S., Harper, B., Knoblauch, D., & Murphy, P.K. (2007). Academic motivation and achievement among urban adolescents. *Urban Education, 42*(3), 196–222.

Love, K., & Hamston, J. (2003). Teenage boys' leisure reading dispositions: Juggling male youth culture and family cultural capital. *Educational Review*, *55*, 161–177.
Loveless, T. (2015). *The 2015 Brown Center Report on American Education: How well are American students learning?* Retrieved from www.brookings.edu/~/media/research/files/reports/2015/03/bcr/2015-brown-center-report_final.pdf.
Low, B.E. (2010). The tale of the talent night rap: Hip-hop culture in schools and the challenge of interpretation. *Urban Education*, *45*(2), 194–220.
Luppicini, R. (2007). Review of computer mediated communication research for education. *Instructional Science*, *35*(2), 141–185.
Ma, X. (2003). Measuring up: Academic performance of Canadian immigrant children in reading, mathematics, and science. *Journal of International Migration and Integration*, *4*(4), 541–576.
MacArthur, C., Graham, S., & Fitzgerald, J. (2008). *Best practices in writing instruction*. New York: Guilford Press.
MacDonald, J. (2004). *Great battles of World War II*. Edison, NJ: Chartwell.
Mady, C., & Seiling, A. (2017). The coupling of second language learning motivation and achievement according to gender. *Theory and Practice in Language Studies*, *7*(12), 1149–1159.
Malloy, J., Marinak, B., & Gambrell, L.B. (Eds.). (2010). *Essential readings on motivation*. Newark, DE: International Reading Association.
Manninen, S., Huuki, T., & Sunnari, V. (2011). Earn yo' respect! Respect in the status struggle of Finnish school boys. *Men and Masculinities*, *14*(3), 335–357.
Manzo, U., & Manzo, A.V. (2013). The Informal Reading-Thinking Inventory: Twenty-first-century assessment formats for discovering reading and writing needs – and strengths. *Reading & Writing Quarterly: Overcoming Learning Difficulties*, *29*(3), 231–251.
Marinak, B.A., & Gambrell, L.B. (2010). Reading motivation: Exploring the elementary gender gap. *Literacy Research and Instruction*, *49*(2), 129–141.
Marks, G.N. (2008). Accounting for the gender gaps in student performance in reading and mathematics: Evidence from 31 countries. *Oxford Review of Education*, *34*(1), 89–109.
Marmot, M. (2004). *The status syndrome: How social standing affects our health and longevity*. New York: Owl Books.
Martin, A.C. (2008). Television media as a potential negative factor in the racial identity development of African American youth. *Academic Psychiatry*, *32*, 338–342.
Martin, A.J. (2009). Motivation and engagement across the academic life span: A developmental construct validity study of elementary school, high school, and university/college students. *Educational and Psychological Measurement*, *69*, 794–824.
Martin, D., Martin, M., Gibson, S.S., & Wilkins, J. (2007). Increasing prosocial behavior and academic achievement among adolescent African American males. *Adolescence*, *42*, 689–698.

Martinez, R.M., Slate, J.R., & Martinez-Garcia, C. (2014). English language learner boys and girls reading and math achievement as a function of early-exit and late-exit bilingual programs: A multiyear, statewide analysis. *Education Research International*. Retrieved from www.hindawi.com/journals/edri/2014/508459/.

Martino, W., & Kehler, M. (2007). Gender-based literacy reform: A question of challenging or recuperating gender binaries. *Canadian Journal of Education, 30* (2), 406–431.

Massinger, P. (1910). A new way to pay old debts. In C. Eliot (Ed.), *Elizabethan drama in two volumes* (pp. 859–943). New York: P.F. Collier & Son.

Massoud, S., & Sudic, E. (2014). *Since reading is a girly thing: A study on boys' underachievement in reading literacy in relation to PISA*. Malmo, Sweden. Retrieved from https://dspace.mah.se/bitstream/handle/2043/17896/FINAL E&S.pdf?sequence=2.

Matthews, J.S., Kizzie, K.T., Rowley, S.J., & Cortina, K. (2010). African Americans and boys: Understanding the literacy gap, tracing academic achievement, and evaluating the role of learning-related skills. *Journal of Educational Psychology, 102*, 757–771.

Mazer, H. (2007). *Heroes don't run: A novel of the Pacific War*. New York: Simon & Schuster.

McCartney, R. (2014, January 29). Teen pregnancies stay stubbornly high in poor D.C. wards; low expectations are cited. *The Washington Post*. Retrieved from www.washingtonpost.com/local/teen-pregnancies-stay-stubbornly-high-in-poor-dc-wards-low-expectations-are-cited/2014/01/29/0e65b1a4-8927-11e3-a5bd-844629433ba3_story.html?utm_term=.cdf2a0f0f04f.

McCormack, M. (2011). Hierarchy without hegemony: Locating boys in an inclusive school setting. *Sociological Perspectives, 54*(1), 83–101.

McDaniel, M.A., Waddill, P.J., Finstad, K., & Bourg, T. (2000). The effects of text-based interest on attention and recall. *Journal of Educational Psychology, 92* (3), 492–502.

McGeown, S., Goodwin, H., Henderson, N., & Wright, P. (2012). Gender differences in reading motivation: Does sex or gender identity provide a better account? *Journal of Research in Reading, 35*(3), 328–336.

McKenna, M., Conradi, K., Lawrence, C., Jang, B.G., & Meyer, J.P. (2012). Reading attitudes of middle school students: Results of a U.S. survey. *Reading Research Quarterly, 47*(3), 283–306.

McKool, S.S., & Gespass, S. (2009). Does Johnny's reading teacher love to read? How teachers' personal reading habits affect instructional practices. *Literacy Research and Instruction, 48*(3), 264–276.

McNally, J.W. (2016). *Creating a lifeline back to books for adolescent boys through multimedia enhanced read-alouds*. National Louis University. Retrieved from http://digitalcommons.nl.edu/cgi/viewcontent.cgi?article=1166&context=diss.

McNaught, K. (2010). Reflective writing in mathematics education programmes. *Reflective Practice, 11*(3), 369–379.

Mead, S. (2006, June). *The evidence suggests otherwise: The truth about boys and girls*. Washington, DC: Education Sector.

Meade, B., Gaytan, F., Fergus, E., & Noguera, P. (2009). *A close look at the dropout crisis: Examining Black and Latino Males in New York City*. New York: Metropolitan Center for Urban Education, New York University.

Meier, T. (2015). "The Brown Face of Hope": Reading engagement and African American boys. *The Reading Teacher, 68*(5), 335–343.

Meltzer, J., & Hamann, E.T. (2005). *Meeting the literacy development needs of adolescent English language learners through content-area learning – part two: Focus on classroom teaching and learning strategies*. Faculty Publications: Department of Teaching, Learning and Teacher Education. 53. Retrieved from http://digitalcommons.unl.edu/teachlearnfacpub/53.

Menken, K. (2009, April). The difficult road for long-term English learners. *Educational Leadership, 66* (7). Retrieved from www.ascd.org/publications/educational_leadership/apr09/vol66/num07/The_Difficult_Road_for_Long-Term_English_Learners.aspx.

Merchant, G. (2009). Literacy in virtual worlds. *Journal of Research in Reading, 32* (1), 38–56.

Merisuo-Storm, T. (2006). Girls and boys like to read and write different texts. *Scandinavian Journal of Educational Research, 50*(2), 111–125.

Meyer, W.D. (2004). *Monster*. New York: HarperTempest.

Miller, J.G. (2011). *Search and destroy: African-American males in the criminal justice system*. New York: Cambridge University Press.

Miniño A.M. (2013). *Death in the United States*, 2011 (NCHS data brief, No 115). Hyattsville, MD: National Center for Health Statistics. Retrieved from www.cdc.gov/nchs/data/databriefs/db115.htm.

Mirel, J. (1999). *The rise and fall of an urban school system: Detroit, 1907–81* (2nd ed.). Ann Arbor: University of Michigan Press.

Mistler-Jackson, M., & Songer, N.B. (2000). Student motivation and Internet technology: Are students empowered to learn science? *Journal of Research in Science Teaching, 37*(5), 459–479.

Mochizuki, K. (1993). *Baseball saved us*. New York: Lee & Low Books.

Moje, E. (2007). Youth cultures, literacies and identities in and out of school. In J. Flood, S.B. Heath, & D. Lapp (Eds.), *Handbook of research on teaching literacy through the communicative and visual arts* (vol. 2, pp. 207–219). Mahway, NJ: Erlbaum.

Moje, E.B. (2010). *Disciplinary literacy: Why it matters and what we should do about it*. Orlando, FL: National Writing Project Annual Meeting.

Moje, E.B., & Tysvaer, N. (2010). *Adolescent literacy development in out-of-school time: A practitioner's guide*. New York: Carnegie Corporation of New York.

Mol, S., & Jolles, J. (2014). Reading enjoyment amongst non-leisure readers can affect achievement in secondary school. *Frontiers in Psychology, 5*(1214), 1–10.

Moley, P.F., Bandre, P.E., & George, J.E. (2011). Moving beyond readability: Considering choice, motivation, and learner engagement. *Theory into Practice, 50*(3), 247–253.

Monte-Sano, C., & De La Paz, S. (2012). Using writing tasks to elicit adolescents' historical reasoning. *Journal of Literacy Research, 44*(3), 273–299.

Moore, J.L., Henfield, M.S., & Owens, D. (2008). African American males in special education: Their attitudes and perceptions toward high school counselors and school counseling services. *American Behavioral Scientist, 51*(7), 907–927.
Morey, W. (1993). *Death walk*. Portland, OR: Blue Heron Publishing.
Morgan, P.L., Farkas, G, Hillemeier, M.M., & Maczuga S. (2009). Risk factors for learning- related behavior problems at 24 months of age: Population-based estimates. *Journal of Abnormal Child Psychology, 37*(3), 401–413.
Morrell, E. (2008). *Critical literacy and urban youth: Pedagogies of access, dissent, and liberation*. New York: Routledge.
Morrell, E., & Duncan-Andrade, J.M.R. (2002). Promoting academic literacy with urban youth through engaging hip-hop culture. *English Journal, 91*(6), 88–92.
Morris, E.W. (2011). Bridging the gap: "Doing gender," "hegemonic masculinity," and the educational troubles of boys. *Sociology Compass, 5*(1), 92–103.
Mou, Y., & Peng, W. (2008). Gender and racial stereotypes in popular video games. In R. Ferdig (Ed.), *Handbook of research on effective electronic gaming in education* (pp. 922–937). Hershey, PA: IGI Global.
Mullis, I.V.S., Martin, M.O., Foy, P., & Drucker, K.T. (2012). *PIRLS 2011 international results in reading*. Chestnut Hill, MA: TIMSS & PIRLS International Study Center, Boston College.
Mullis, I.V.S., Martin, M.O., & Sainsbury, M. (2016). *Chapter 1: PIRLS 2016 reading framework*. Retrieved from https://timssandpirls.bc.edu/pirls2016/downloads/P16_FW_Chap1.pdf
Murray, D. (2007). *D-Day: The liberation of Europe begins*. New York: Rosen Central.
Murray, D. (2004). *Write to learn* (8th ed.). Boston: Cengage Learning.
Murry, V.M., Berkel, C., Brody, G.H., Miller, S.J., & Chen, Y.F. (2009). Linking parental socialization to interpersonal protective processes, academic self-presentation, and expectations among rural African American youth. *Cultural Diversity and Ethnic Minority Psychology, 15*(1), 1–10.
Murry, V.M., Block, E.P., & Liu, N. (2016). Adjustment and developmental patterns of African American males: The roles of families, communities, and other contexts. In L.M. Burton, D. Burton, S.M. McHale, V. King, & J. Van Hook (Eds.), *National symposium on family issues: Vol. 7. Boys and men in African American families* (pp. 7–32). http://dx.doi.org.mutex.gmu.edu/10.1007/978-3-319-43847-4_2.
Mussman, D.C. (2013). *Gender and English language learners*. Annapolis, MD: TESOL Publications.
Myers, W.D. (1990). *Scorpions*. New York: HarperTrophy.
Myers, W.D. (1999). *Hoops*. Minneapolis, MN: Econo-Clad.
Myers, W.D. (2000). *Monster*. New York: HarperCollins.
Najman, J.M., Aird, R., Bor, W., O'Callaghan, M., Williams, G.M., & Shuttlewood, G.J. (2004). The generational transmission of socioeconomic inequalities in child cognitive development and emotional health. *Social Science and Medicine, 58*(6), 1147–1158.

National Alliance to End Homelessness. (2016). *The state of homelessness in America*. Washington, DC: NAEH. Retrieved from http://endhomelessness.org/wp-content/uploads/2016/10/2016-soh.pdf.

National Center for Education Statistics. (2011). *The Nation's Report Card: Writing 2011: National Assessment of Educational Progress at Grades 8 and 12*. Retrieved from https://nces.ed.gov/nationsreportcard/pdf/main2011/2012470.pdf.

National Center for Education Statistics. (2012). *The nation's report card: Trends in academic progress 2012*. Washington, DC: NCES.

National Center for Educational Statistics. EdDataExpress. (2014). *Report on regulatory adjusted cohort graduation rates limited English proficient 2010*. US Department of Education. Retrieved from http://eddataexpress.ed.gov/data-element-explorer.cfm.

National Center for Education Statistics. (2016). *The condition of education 2016*. Washington, DC: Institute of Education Sciences, US Department of Education. https://nces.ed.gov/pubs2016/2016144.pdf.

National Center for Education Statistics. (2017, April). *Status dropout rates*. Retrieved from https://nces.ed.gov/programs/coe/indicator_coj.asp.

National Commission on Writing for America's Families, Schools, and Colleges. (2003). *The neglected "R": Need for a writing revolution*. New York: College Board.

National Council of Teachers of Mathematics. (2000). *Executive summary: Principles and standards for school mathematics*. Retrieved from www.nctm.org/uploadedFiles/Standards_and_Positions/PSSM_ExecutiveSummary.pdf.

National Institutes of Health. (n.d.). *Sex and gender differences in substance use*. Washington, DC: National Institute on Drug Abuse.

Nelson, K.J. (2008). *Teaching in the digital age: Using the Internet to increase student engagement and understanding*. Thousand Oaks, CA: Corwin.

Newkirk, T. (2006). Media and literacy: What's good? *Educational Leadership*, 64(1), 62–66.

Nijkamp, M. (2016). *This is where it ends*. Naperville, IL: Sourcebooks.

Noguera, P.A. (2008). *The trouble with Black boys: And other reflections on race, equity, and the future of public education*. New York: Jossey-Bass.

Oakhill, J.V., & Petrides, A. (2007). Sex differences in the effects of interest on boys' and girls' reading comprehension. *British Journal of Psychology*, 98, 223–235.

O'Brien, D. (2001, June). "At-risk" adolescents: Redefining competence through the multiliteracies of intermediality, visual arts, and representation. *Reading Online*, 4(11). Retrieved from www.readingonline.org/newliteracies/lit_index.asp?HREF=/newliteracies/obrien/index.html.

O'Brien, D., & Scharber, C. (2008). Digital literacies go to school: Potholes and possibilities. *Journal of Adolescent & Adult Literacy*, 52(1), 66–68.

Oddny, J.S., & Lundetræ, K. (2016). Can test construction account for varying gender differences in international reading achievement tests of children, adolescents and young adults? – A study based on Nordic results in PIRLS, PISA and PIAAC. *Assessment in Education: Principles, Policy & Practice*. Retrieved from www.tandfonline.com/doi/full/10.1080/0969594X.2016.1239612.

OECD. (2012). *Literacy, numeracy and problem solving in technology-rich environments: Framework for the OECD Survey of Adult Skills*. Paris: OECD Publishing.
OECD. (2013a). *PISA 2012 results: Excellence through equity: Giving every student the chance to succeed* (vol. II). Paris: Author.
OECD. (2013b). *PISA 2012 results: What students know and can do – Student performance in mathematics, reading and science* (vol. I). Paris: OECD Publishing.
OECD. (2013c). *PISA 2012 results: Ready to learn – Students' engagement, drive and self-beliefs* (vol. III). Paris: Author.
OECD. (2013d). *PISA 2012 results: Excellence through equity – Giving every student the chance to succeed* (vol. II). Paris: Author.
OECD. (2015a). *The ABC of gender equality in education: Aptitude, behavior, confidence*. Paris: PISA, OECD Publishing.
OECD. (2015b). *Education at a glance 2015: OECD indicators*. Paris: OECD Publishing. Retrieved from http://download.ei-ie.org/Docs/WebDepot/Ea G2015_EN.pdf
OECD. (2015c). *Students, computers and learning: Making the connection*. Paris: OECD Publishing.
OECD. (2016a). A global competency for an inclusive world. Paris: OECD Publishing. Retrieved from www.oecd.org/education/Global-competency-for-an-inclusive-world.pdf.
OECD. (2016b). *PISA 2015 results: Excellence and equity in education* (vol. I). Paris: OECD Publishing.
OECD. (2016c). *PISA 2018 draft analytical frameworks*. Retrieved from www.oecd.org/pisa/data/PISA-2018-draft-frameworks.pdf.
Oei, A.C., & Patterson, M.D. (2013). Enhancing cognition with video games: A multiple game training study. *PLoS One, 8*(3). Retrieved from www.ncbi.nlm.nih.gov/pmc/articles/PMC3596277/.
Office of English Language Acquisition, National Clearinghouse for English Language Acquisition. (February 2017). *Profiles of English Learners (ELs)*. Retrieved June 9, 2017, from www.ncela.us/files/fast_facts/05-19-2017/Profiles OfELs_FastFacts.pdf.
OISE Research Team. (2009). *The road ahead: Boys' literacy teacher inquiry project 2005 to 2008: Final report*. Retrieved from www.edu.gov.on.ca/eng/curriculum/RoadAhead2009.pdf.
Olsen, L. (2012). *Secondary school courses designed to address the language needs and academic gaps of long term English learners*. Long Beach: Californians Together.
Opitz, M.F., & Guccione, L.M. (2009). *Comprehension and English language learners: 25 oral reading strategies that cross proficiency levels*. Portsmouth, NH: Heinemann.
The Opportunity Agenda. (2011). *Media representations and impact on the lives of black men and boys*. New York: Author. Retrieved from www.racialequitytools.org/resourcefiles/Media-Impact-onLives-of-Black-Men-and-Boys-OppAgenda.pdf.

Osman, M. (2012). *Gender gaps in student academic performance: Patterns of disparities in the global context.* A Paper presented at the ICET 56th World Assembly, Capa Coast University. Ghana.

Pajares, F., & Urdan, T. (Eds.). (2006). *Self-efficacy beliefs of adolescence.* Greenwich, CT: Information Age.

Pajares, F., & Valiante, G. (2001). Gender differences in writing motivation and achievement of middle school students: A function of gender orientation. *Contemporary Educational Psychology, 26,* 366–381.

Palancılar, N.A. (2017). Mars or Venus? gender differences in language learning: A sociolinguistic study on language and gender. *PEOPLE: International Journal of Social Sciences, 3*(2), 563–574.

Pape, K., Bjorngaard, J., Westin, S., Holmen, T., & Krokstad, S. (2011). Reading and writing difficulties in adolescence and later risk of welfare dependence: A ten year follow-up, the HUNT Study, Norway. *BMC Public Health, 11,* 1–8.

Palmer, D.H. (2009). Student interest generated during an inquiry skills lesson. *Journal of Research in Science Teaching, 46*(2), 147–165.

Parker, J.R. (2010). *Teaching tech-savvy kids: Bringing digital media into the classroom, grades 5–12.* Thousand Oaks, CA: Corwin.

Pascoe, C.J. (2011). *Dude you're a fag: Masculinity and sexuality in high school* (2nd ed.). Berkley: University of California Press.

Patall, E.A., Cooper H., & Wynn, S.R. (2010). The effectiveness and relative importance of providing choices in the classroom. *Journal of Educational Psychology, 102*(4), 896–915.

Paterson, P.O., & Elliott, L.N. (2006). Struggling reader to struggling reader: High school students' responses to a cross-age tutoring program. *Journal of Adolescent & Adult Literacy, 49,* 378–389.

Patterson, R.E. (2012). *The role of culturally relevant texts and comprehension strategy instruction in the literacy engagement of African American adolescent males.* Pittsburg, PA: University of Pittsburg.

Pavy, S. (2006). Boys learning languages: The myth busted. *Babel, 41*(1), 2–9.

Payne, R.K., & Slocumb, P.D. (2011). *Boys in poverty: A framework for understanding dropout.* Bloomington, IN: Solution Tree Press.

Pearson, H. (2016). *The life project: The extraordinary story of 70,000 ordinary lives.* Berkeley, CA: Soft Skull Press.

Pelton, L.F., & Pelton, T. (2009). The learner as teacher: Using student authored comics to "teach" mathematics concepts. In G. Siemens & C. Fulford (Eds.), *Proceedings of world conference on educational multimedia, hypermedia and telecommunications 2009* (pp. 1591–1599). Chesapeake, VA: AACE. Retrieved from www.editlib.org/p/31690.

Perriera, K.M., Kiang, L., & Potochnick, S. (2013). Ethnic discrimination: Identifying and intervening in its effects on the education of immigrant children. In E.L. Grigorenko (Ed.), *U.S. immigration and education: Cultural and policy issues across the lifespan* (pp. 137–162). New York: Springer.

Perrin, A. (2016). *Book reading 2016.* Retrieved from www.pewinternet.org/2016/09/01/book-reading-2016/.

Perry, T. (2018). Using texts to nurture reading, writing, and intellectual development: A conversation with Alfred Tatum. *Voices from the Middle*, 25(3), 13–15.
Peterson, S.S., & McClay, J. (2014). A national study of teaching and assessing writing in Canadian middle grades classrooms. *McGill Journal of Education*, 49(1), 17–40.
Peterson, S.S., & Parr, J.M. (2012). Gender and literacy issues and research: Placing the spotlight on writing. *Journal of Writing Research*, 3(3), 151–161.
Pettit, B. (2012). *Invisible men: Mass incarceration and the myth of black progress.* New York: Russell Sage Foundation.
The Pew Charitable Trusts. (2010). *Collateral costs: Incarceration's effect on economic mobility.* Retrieved from www.pewtrusts.org/-/media/legacy/uploadedfiles/pcs_assets/2010/collateralcosts1pdf.pdf.
Piasecka, L. (2010). Gender differences in L1 and L2 reading. In J. Arabski & A. Wojtaszek (Eds.), *Neurolinguistic and psycholinguistic perspectives on SLA* (pp. 145–158). Toronto: Multilingual Matters.
Piki, A. (2008). The visions and challenges of ICT for collaborative learning: A review of the literature. *Themes in Science and Technology Education*, 1(2), 113–134.
Pitre, E., Lewis, C.L., & Hillton-Pitre, T. (2007). The overrepresentation of African American males in special education: A qualitative analysis of the students perspective. *Journal of the Alliance of Black School Educators*, 6(2), 61–75.
Powell-Brown, A. (2003/2004). Can you be a teacher of literacy if you don't love to read? *Journal of Adolescent & Adult Literacy*, 47, 284–288.
Prensky, M. (2009). H. Sapiens digital: From digital immigrants and digital natives to digital wisdom. *Innovate: Journal of Online Education*, 5(3). Retrieved from http://nsuworks.nova.edu/cgi/viewcontent.cgi?article=1020&context=innovate.
Prieur, A. (2002). Gender remix: On gender constructions among children of immigrants in Norway. *Ethnicities*, 2(1), 53–77.
Proctor, C.P., Dalton, B., & Grisham, D. (2007). Scaffolding English language learners and struggling readers in a universal literacy environment with embedded strategy instruction and vocabulary support. *Journal of Literacy Research*, 39(1), 71–93.
Qin, D.B. (2006). The role of gender in immigrant children's educational adaptation. *Current Issues in Comparative Education*, 91(1), 8–19.
Qin, D.B. (2009). Being "good" or being "popular": Gender and ethnic identity negotiations of Chinese immigrant adolescents. *Journal of Adolescent Research*, 24(1), 37–66.
Quane, J.M., Wilson, W.J., & Hwang, J. (2015). Black men and the struggle for work. *Education Next*, 15(2). Retrieved from http://educationnext.org/black-men-struggle-work/.
Rampey, B.D., Finnegan, R., Goodman, M., Mohadjer, L., Krenzke, T., Hogan, J., & Provasnik, S. (2016). *Skills of U.S. unemployed, young, and older adults in sharper focus: Results from the Program for the International Assessment of*

Adult Competencies (PIAAC) 2012/2014: First look (NCES 2016–039). US Department of Education. Washington, DC: National Center for Education Statistics. Retrieved from http://nces.ed.gov/pubsearch.

Rampey, B.D., Keiper, S., Mohadjer, L., Krenzke, T., Li, J., Thornton, N., & Hogan, J. (2016). *Highlights from the U.S. PIAAC survey of incarcerated adults: Their skills, work experience, education, and training*: Program for the International Assessment of Adult Competencies: 2014 (NCES 2016–040). US Department of Education. Washington, DC: National Center for Education Statistics. Retrieved from http://nces.ed.gov/pubsearch.

Rauch, D.P., & Hartig, J. (2010). Multiple-choice versus open-ended response formats of reading test items: A two-dimensional IRT analysis. *Psychological Test and Assessment Modeling, 52*(4), 354–379.

Reardon, S., Robinson-Cimpian, J., & Weathers, E. (2015). Patterns and trends in racial/ethnic and socio-economic achievement gaps. In H. Ladd & M. Goertz (Eds.), *Handbook of research in education finance and policy* (pp. 491–509). New York: Routledge.

Redfield, S.E., & Nance, J.P. (2016). *School-to-prison pipeline*. American Bar Association. Retrieved from www.americanbar.org/content/dam/aba/adminis trative/diversity_pipeline/stp_preliminary_report_final.authcheckdam.pdf.

Retelsdorf, J., Schwartz, K., & Asbrock, F. (2015). "Michael can't read!": Teachers' gender stereotypes and boys' reading self-concept. *Journal of Educational Psychology, 107*(1), 186–194.

Reynolds, J. (2016). *Ghost*. New York: Atheneum.

Riegle-Crumb, C. (2010). More girls go to college: Exploring the social and academic factors behind the female postsecondary advantage among Hispanic and White students. *Research in Higher Education, 51*(6), 573–593.

Riegle-Crumb, C., & Humphries, M. (2012). Exploring bias in math teachers' perceptions of students' ability by gender and race/ethnicity. *Gender & Society, 26*(2), 290–322.

Richmond, M., Robinson, C., & Sachs-Israel, M. (2008). *The global literacy challenge: A profile of youth and adult literacy at the mid-point of the United Nations Literacy Decade 2003–2012*. Paris: UNESCO. Retrieved from http://unesdoc.unesco.org/images/0016/001631/163170e.pdf.

Rideout, V.J., Foehr, U.G., & Roberts, D.F. (2010). *Generation M2: Media in the lives of 8- to 18-year-olds*. Menlo Park, CA: Kaiser Family Foundation.

Riley, R., & Reedy, D. (2000). *Developing writing for different purposes*. London: Paul Chapman.

Ritchie, S.J., & Bates, T.C. (2013). Enduring links from childhood mathematics and reading achievement to adult socioeconomic status. *Psychological Science, 20*(10), 1–8.

Roberts, J. (2009). *Rey Mysterio: Behind the mask*. New York: Pocket Books.

Robinson, J., & Lubienski, S. (2011). The development of gender achievement gaps in mathematics and reading in elementary and middle school: Examining direct cognitive assessments and teacher ratings. *American Educational Research Journal, 48*(2), 268–302.

Robinson, M., & Mackey, M. (2006). Assets in the classroom: Comfort and competence with media among teachers present and future. In J. Marsh & E. Millard (Eds.), *Popular literacies, childhood and schooling* (pp. 200–220). New York: Routledge.

Roche, K.M., Ensminger, M.E., & Cherlin, A.J. (2007). Variations in parenting and adolescent outcomes among African American and Latino families living in low-income, urban areas. *Journal of Family Issues, 28*, 882–909.

Roosa, M.W., Weaver, S.R., White, R.M., Tein, J.Y., Knight, G.P., Gonzales, N., & Saenz, D. (2009). Family and neighborhood fit or misfit and the adaptation of Mexican Americans. *American Journal of Community Psychology, 44*(1–2), 15–27.

Rosen, M. (2002). *ChaseR: A novel in emails*. Cambridge, MA: Candlewick.

Rosselli, M., Ardila, A., Matute, E., & Velez-Uribe, I. (2014). Language development across the life span: A neuropsychological/neuroimaging perspective. *Neuroscience Journal, 2014*, 1–21. Retrieved from www.hindawi.com/journals/neuroscience/2014/585237/.

Rotgans, J.I., & Schmidt, H.G. (2011). The role of teachers in facilitating situational interest in an active-learning classroom. *Teaching and Teacher Education, 27*(1), 37–42.

Rotgans, J.I., & Schmidt, H.G. (2014). Situational interest and learning: Thirst for knowledge. *Learning and Instruction, 32*, 37–50.

Rouland, K.K., Rowley, S.J., & Kurtz-Costes, B. (2013). Self-views of African-American youth are related to the gender stereotypes and ability attributions of their parents. *Self and Identity, 12*(4), 382–399.

Rousseau, J.J. (1979). *Emile, or on education*. New York: Basic.

Rowsell, J., & Kendrick, M. (2013). Boys' hidden literacies: The critical need for the visual. *Journal of Adolescent & Adult Literacy, 56*(7), 587–599.

Rua, P.L. (2006). The sex variable in foreign language learning: An integrative approach. *Porta Linguarium, 6*, 99–114.

Ryan, C. (2013, August). *Language use in the United States: 2011*. Retrieved from www.census.gov/prod/2013pubs/acs-22.pdf.

Saiz, A., & Zoido, E. (2005). Listening to what the world says: Bilingualism and earnings in the US. *The Review of Economics and Statistics, 87*(3), 523–538.

Salsovic, A.R. (2009). Designing a WebQuest. *Mathematics Teacher, 102*(9), 666–671.

Sanderson, G. (1995). Being "cool" and a reader. In R. Browne & R. Fletcher (Eds.), *Boys in schools: Addressing the real issues – behaviour, values and relationships* (pp. 152–167). Sydney, NSW, Australia: Finch Publishing.

Sanford, K. (2006). Gendered literacy experiences: The effects of expectation and opportunity for boys' and girls' learning. *Journal of Adolescent & Adult Literacy, 49*(4), 302–325.

Sanford, K., & Madill, L. (2007). Understanding the power of new literacies through video game play and design. *Canadian Journal of Education, 30*(2), 432–455.

Santiago, C.D., Gudino, O.G., Baweja, S., & Nadeem, E. (2014). Academic achievement among immigrant and U.S.-born Latino adolescents:

Associations with cultural, family, and acculturation factors. *Journal of Community Psychology, 42*(6), 735–747.

Sarroub, L.K., & Pernicek, T. (2016). Boys, books, and boredom: A case of three high school boys and their encounters with literacy. *Reading & Writing Quarterly: Overcoming Learning Difficulties, 32*(1), 27–55.

Saunders, W., & O'Brien, G. (2006). Oral language. In F. Genesee, K. Lindholm-Leary, W.M. Saunders, & D. Christian (Eds.), *Educating English language learners: A synthesis of research evidence* (pp. 14–63). New York: Cambridge University Press.

Scanlan, M. (2012). "Cos um it like put a picture in my mind of what I should write": An exploration of how home–school partnership might support the writing of lower-achieving boys. *Support for Learning, 27*(1), 4–10.

Scharber, C. (2009). Online book clubs: Bridges between old and new literacies. *Journal of Adolescent & Adult Literacy, 52*(5), 433–437.

Schiff, R., & Lotem, E. (2011). Effects of phonological and morphological awareness on children's word reading development from two socioeconomic backgrounds. *First Language, 31*(2), 139–163.

Schoon, I. (2008). A transgenerational model of status attainment: The potential mediating role of school motivation and education. *National Institute Economic Review, 205*, 72–82.

Schott Foundation for Public Education. (2012). *The urgency of now: The Schott 50 state report on public education and Black males*. Cambridge, MA: Schott Foundation for Public Education.

Schott Foundation. (2015). *Black lives matter: The Schott 50 state report on public education and Black males*. New York: Schott Foundation for Public Education. Retrieved from www.blackboysreport.org/2015-black-boys-report.pdf.

Schraff, A.E. (2008). *Jackie Robinson*. Costa Mesa, CA: Saddleback Educational.

Schunk, D.H., Meece, J.L., & Pintrich, P.R. (2013). *Motivation in education: Theory, research, and applications* (4th ed.). Englewood Cliffs, NJ: Prentice Hall.

Schwartz, L.H. (2015). A funds of knowledge approach to the appropriation of new media in a high school writing classroom. *Interactive Learning Environments, 23*(5), 595–612.

Schwarzschild, M. (2000). Alienated youth: Help from families and schools. *Professional Psychology, Research and Practice, 31*(1), 95–96.

Scieszka, J. (2003). Guys and reading. *Teacher Librarian, 30*(3), 17–18.

Scutts, J. (2000). *World War II dioramas*. New York: Compendium.

Scwabe, F., McElvany, N., & Trentel, M. (2015). The school age gender gap in reading achievement: Examining the influences of item format and intrinsic reading motivation. *Reading Research Quarterly, 50*(2), 219–232.

Sengul, S., & Dereli, M. (2010). Does instruction of "integers" subject with cartoons effect students' mathematics anxiety? *Procedia Social and Behavioral Sciences, 2*(2), 2176–2180.

Senn, N. (2012). Effective approaches to motivate and engage reluctant boys in literacy. *The Reading Teacher, 66*(3), 211–220.

Shaffer, S. (2015). *Bilingual Latino high school boys' reading motivation: Seven case studies examining factors that influence motivation to read*. Retrieved from https://repository.asu.edu/attachments/157977/content/Shaffer_asu_0010E_15191.pdf.

Shakespeare, W., Appignanesi, R., & Leong, S. (2007). *Romeo and Juliet*. New York: Abrams Books for Young Readers.

Shanahan, T. (1997). Reading-writing relationships, thematic units, inquiry learning: In pursuit of effective integrated literacy instruction. *The Reading Teacher*, *51*, 12–20.

Shanahan, T. (2006). Relations among oral language, reading and writing development. In C.A. MacArthur, S. Graham, & J. Fitzgerald (Eds.), *Handbook of writing research* (pp. 171–183). New York: Guilford Press.

Shanks, T.R., & Robinson, C. (2012). *Assets, economic opportunity, and toxic stress: A framework for understanding child educational outcomes*. St. Louis, MO: Washington University in St. Louis. Retrieved from https://csd.wustl.edu/Publications/Documents/WP12-22.pdf.

Shaywitz, S.E., Shaywitz, B.A., Fletcher, J.M., & Escobar, M.D. (1990). Prevalence of reading disability in boys and girls: Results of the Connecticut Longitudinal Study. *JAMA*, *264*(8), 998–1002.

Shields, B., & Sullivan, K. (2009). *WWE encyclopedia*. New York: BradyGames.

Shulman, E.P., Stienberg, L.D., & Piquero, A.R. (2013). The age-crime curve in adolescence and early adulthood is not due to age differences in economic status. *Journal of Youth and Adolescence*, *42*(6), 848–860.

Silberglitt, B., Appleton, J.J., Burns, M.K., & Jimerson, S.R. (2006). Examining the effects of grade retention on student reading performance: A longitudinal study. *Journal of School Psychology*, *44*(4), 255–270.

Silverstein, O., & Rashbaum, B. (1995). *The courage to raise good men*. New York: Penguin.

Simon, R. (2012). "Without comic books, there would be no me": Teachers as connoisseurs of adolescents' literate lives. *Journal of Adolescent & Adult Literacy*, *55*(6), 516–526.

Simon, R.I. (1987). Empowerment as a pedagogy of possibility. *Language Arts*, *64*(4), 370–382.

Sing, C.C., Wei-Ying, L., Hyo-Jeong, S., & Mun, C.H. (2011). *Advancing collaborative learning with ICT: Conception, cases and design*. Singapore: Ministry of Education. Retrieved from https://ictconnection.moe.edu.sg/ictconnection/slot/u200/mp3/monographs/advancing%20collaborative%20learning%20with%20ict.pdf.

Skerrett, A., & Bomer, R. (2011). Borderzones in adolescents' literacy practices: Connecting out-of-school literacies to the reading curriculum. *Urban Education*, *46*(6), 1256–1279.

Smiley, T. (2011). *Too important to fail: Saving America's boys*. New York: Smiley

Smith, G.A. (2002). Place-based education: Learning to be where we are. *Phi Delta Kappan*, *83*(8), 584–594.

Snyder, H.N. (2012). *Arrest in the United States, 1990–2010*. Washington, DC: Bureau of Justice Statistics. Retrieved from www.bjs.gov/content/pub/pdf/aus9010.pdf.

So, H.J., Seah, L.H., & Toh-Heng, H.L. (2010). Designing collaborative knowledge building environments accessible to all learners: Impacts and design challenges. *Computers & Education, 54*(2), 479-490.

Soto-Hinman, I. (2011). Increasing academic oral language development: Using English language learner shadowing in classrooms. *Multicultural Education, 18*(2), 21–23.

Souto-Manning, M., Dernikos, B., & Yu, H.M. (2016). Rethinking normative literacy practices, behaviors, and interactions: Learning from young immigrant boys. *Journal of Early Childhood Research, 14*(2), 163–180.

Soza, R.A., Yzaguirre, R., & Perilla, A. (2007). *Pathways to Prevention: The Latino male dropout crisis.* Center for Community Development and Civil Rights, Arizona State University, Tempe, AZ.

Sparrow, B., Liu, J., & Wegner, D.M. (2011). Google effects on memory: Cognitive consequences of having information at our fingertips. *Science, 333*(6043), 776-778.

Spiegel, A.N., McQuillan, J., Halpin, P., Matuk, C., & Diamond, J. (2013). Engaging teenagers with science through comics. *Research in Science Education, 43*(6), 2309–2326.

Spiegelman, A. (1986). *Maus I: A survivor's tale.* New York: Pantheon.

Squire, K. (2011). *Video games and learning: Teaching and participatory culture in the digital age.* New York: Teachers College Press.

Staples, J.M. (2012). "Niggaz dyin' don't make no news": Exploring the intellectual work of an African American urban adolescent boy in an after-school program. *Educational Action Research, 20*(1), 55–73.

Steinberg, L. (2008). *Adolescence.* New York: McGraw-Hill.

Steinkuehler, C., & King, E. (2009). Digital literacies for the disengaged: Creating after school contexts to support boys' game-based literacy skills. *On the Horizon, 17*(1), 47–59.

Steinmayr, R., & Spinath, B. (2009). The importance of motivation as a predictor of school achievement. *Learning and Individual Differences, 19*(1), 80–90.

Stetser, M., & Stillwell, R. (2014). Public high school four-year on-time graduation rates and event dropout rates: School years 2010–11 and 2011–12. *First look* (NCES 2014–391). Washington, DC: US Department of Education. National Center for Education Statistics. Retrieved from http://nces.ed.gov/pubsearch.

Stevenson, H.C. (2004). Boys in men's clothing: Racial socialization and neighborhood safety as buffers to hypervulnerability in African American adolescent males. In N. Way & J.Y. Chu (Eds.), *Adolescent boys: Exploring diverse cultures of boyhood* (pp. 59–77). New York: New York University Press.

Strasser, T. (2002). *Give a boy a gun.* New York: Simon Pulse.

Straus, L.P. (2011). *Adolescent reading engagement: Predictors of eighth grade reading achievement on the 2007 NAEP with an examination of gender and ethnicity differences.* Claremont, CA: Claremont University.

Stroud, J.B., & Lindquist, E.F. (1942). Sex differences in achievement in the elementary and secondary schools. *Journal of Educational Psychology, 33*(9), 657–667.

Sturtevant, E., Boyd, F., Brozo, W.G., Hinchman, K., Alvermann, D., & Moore, D. (2006). *Principled practices for adolescent literacy: A framework for instruction and policy*. Mahwah, NJ: Erlbaum.

Styslinger, M.E., Gavigan, K., & Albright, K. (2017). *Literacy behind bars*. Lanham, MD: Rowman & Littlefield.

Suarez-Orozco, C., & Qin, D.B. (2005). Immigrant boys' experiences in U.S. schools. In M.M. Suarez-Orozco, C. Suarez-Orozco, & D.B. Qin (Eds.), *The new immigration: An interdisciplinary reader* (pp. 345–360). New York: Routledge.

Sum, A., Khatiwada, I., & McLaughlin, J. (2011). *The "jobless and wageless" recovery from the great recession of 2007–2009*. Northeastern University: Sheila Palma Center for Labor Market Studies. Retrieved from www.employmentpolicy.org/sites/www.employmentpolicy.org/files/field-content-file/pdf/Mike%20Lillich/Revised%20Corporate%20Report%20May%2027th.pdf.

Sum, A., Khatiwada, I., McLaughlin, J., & Palma, S. (2009). *The consequences of dropping out of high school: Joblessness and jailing for high school dropouts and the high cost for taxpayers*. Boston, MA: Center for Labor Market Studies, Northeastern University. Retrieved from https://repository.library.northeastern.edu/downloads/neu:376324?datastream_id=content.

Sunderland, J. (2010). Theorizing gender perspectives in foreign and second language learning. In R.M. Jiménez Catalán (Ed.), *Gender perspectives on vocabulary in foreign and second languages* (pp. 1–22). Basingstoke: Palgrave Macmillan.

Sunderland, J., Dempster, S., & Thistlethwaite, J. (2016). *Children's literacy practices and preferences: Harry Potter and beyond*. New York: Routledge.

Taboada, A., & Rutherford, V. (2011). Developing reading comprehension and academic vocabulary for English Language Learners through science content: A formative experiment. *Reading Psychology*, 32(2), 113–157.

Takahashi, S. (2009). *The manga guide to statistics*. Tokyo: Ohmsha Ltd.

Tapscot, D. (1999). Educating the Net Generation. *Educational Leadership*, 56, 7–11.

Tatum, A. (2006) Adolescents' multiple identities and teacher professional development. In D. Alvermann, K. Hinchman, D. Moore, S. Phelps, & D. Waff (Eds.), *Reconceptualizing the literacies in adolescents' lives* (2nd ed., pp. 65–70). Mahwah, NJ: Lawrence Erlbaum Associates, Inc.

Tatum, A. (2008). Toward a more anatomically complete model of literacy instruction: A Focus on African American male adolescents and texts. *Harvard Educational Review*, 78(1), 155–180.

Tatum, A.W. (2009). *Reading for their life: (Re)Building the textual lineages of African American adolescent males*. Portsmouth, NH: Heinemann.

Tatum, A.W., & Muhammad, G. (2012). African American males and literacy development in contexts that are characteristically urban. *Urban Education*, 47(2), 434–463.

Thiessen, V., & Looker, E. D. (2007). Digital divides and capital conversion: The optimal use of information and communication technology for youth reading achievement. *Information, Communication & Society*, 10(2), 159–180.

Thomas Fordham Institute. (2004). *The mad, mad world of textbook adoption*. Washington, DC: Thomas Fordham Institute.
Thomas, P.L. (2011) Adventures in genre!: Rethinking genre through comics/graphic novels. *Journal of Graphic Novels and Comics*, 2(2), 187–201.
Thompson, P., & Hall, C. (2008). Opportunities missed and/or thwarted?: "Funds of knowledge" meet the English national curriculum. *Curriculum Journal*, 19(2), 87–103.
Thompson, S., Provasnik, S., Kastberg, D., Ferraro, D., Lemanski, N., Roey, S., & Jenkins, F. (2013). *Highlights from PIRLS 2011: Reading achievement of U.S. fourth-grade Students in international context*. (NCES 2013–010). National Center for Education Statistics, Institute of Education Sciences, US Department of Education, Washington, DC. Retrieved from http://nces.ed.gov/pubs2013/2013101.pdf.
Thompson, T. (2008). *Adventures in graphica: Using comics and graphic novels to teach comprehension, 2–6*. Portland, ME: Stenhouse.
Thompson, T. (2011). *Fact sheet: Outcomes for young, black men*. Retrieved from www.pbs.org/wnet/tavissmiley/tsr/too-important-to-fail/fact-sheet-outcomes-for-young-black-men/.
Tierney, R.J., & Shanahan, T. (1991). Research on the reading-writing relationship: Interactions, transactions, and outcomes. In R. Barr, M.L. Kamil, P. Mosenthal, & P.D. Pearson (Eds.), *Handbook of reading research* (vol. II, pp. 246–280). New York: Longman.
Tømte, C. (2008). *Return to gender: Gender, ICT and education*. Oslo, Norway: OECD Expert Meeting. Retrieved from https://pdfs.semanticscholar.org/e1ff/3e4f510cbd8a7e12facc55b0a5e396e5c26f.pdf.
Tong, F., Lara-Alecio, R., Irby, B., Mathes, P., & Kwok, O-M. (2008). Accelerating early academic oral English development in transitional bilingual and structured English immersion programs. *American Educational Research Journal*, 45(4), 1011–1044.
Tonne, I., & Pihl, J. (2012). Literacy education, reading engagement, and library use in multilingual classes. *Journal of Intercultural Education*, 23(3), 183–194.
Topping, K.J., Samuels, J., & Paul, T. (2008). Independent reading: The relationship of challenge, non-fiction and achievement. *British Educational Research Journal*, 34, 505–524.
Tramonte, T., & Willms, J.D. (2010). Cultural capital and its effects on education outcomes. *Economics of Education Review*, 29(2), 200–213.
UNESCO. (2014). *Reading in the mobile era: A study of mobile reading in developing countries*. Paris: UNESCO.
United States Census Bureau. (2014). *Census Bureau's American Survey provides new state and Local income, poverty, health insurance statistics*. Retrieved from www.census.gov/newsroom/press-releases/2014/cb14-170.html
United States Census Bureau. (n.d.). *Current Population Survey data on school enrollment*. Retrieved from www.census.gov/topics/education/school-enrollment.html.

US Department of Justice, Bureau of Justice Statistics. (2015). *Prisoners in 2014*. Retrieved from www.bjs.gov/content/pub/pdf/p14.pdf.
United Nations Office on Drugs and Crime. (2015). *Homicide and gender*. Retrieved from www.heuni.fi/material/attachments/heuni/projects/wd2vDSKcZ/Homicide_and_Gender.pdf.
van De Gaer, E., Pustjens, H., Van Damme, J., & De Munter, A. (2007). Impact of attitudes of peers on language achievement: Gender differences. *Journal of Educational Research, 101*(2), 78–90.
van de Gaer, E., Pustjens, H., Van Damme, J., & De Munter, A. (2009). School engagement and language achievement: A longitudinal study of gender differences across secondary school. *Merrill-Palmer Quarterly, 55*(4), 373–405.
van de Werfhorst, H.G., & Mijs, J.J.B. (2010). Achievement inequality and the institutional structure of educational systems: A comparative perspective. *Annual Review of Sociology, 36*(1), 407–428.
van der Slik, F., van Hout, R., & Schepens, J. (2015). The gender gap in second language acquisition: Differences in the acquisition of Dutch among immigrants from 88 countries with 49 mother tongues. *PLoS One, 10*(11). Retrieved from www.ncbi.nlm.nih.gov/pmc/articles/PMC4634989/.
Van Duinen, D., & Vriend Malu, K.F. (2015). Craigslist, LEGO, and wakeboarding: Examining the out-of-school sponsorship of early adolescent boys' literacy practices. In M.B. Schaefer (Ed.), *Research on teaching and learning with the literacies of young adolescents* (pp. 151–172). Charlotte, NC: Information Age Publishing.
Van Keer, H., & Vanderlinde, R. (2010). The impact of cross-age peer tutoring on third and sixth graders' reading strategy awareness, reading strategy use, and reading comprehension. *Middle Grades Research Journal, 5*(1), 33–46.
Van Langen, A., Bosker, R., & Dekkers, H. (2006). Exploring cross-national differences in gender gaps in education. *Educational Research and Evaluation, 12*(2), 155–177.
Vantieghem, W., Vermeersch, H., & Van Houtte, M. (2014). Transcending the gender dichotomy in educational gender gap research: The association between gender identity and academic self-efficacy. *Contemporary Educational Psychology, 39*(4), 369–378.
Vekiri, I., & Chronaki, A. (2008). Gender issues in technology use: Perceived social support, computer self-efficacy and value beliefs, and computer use beyond school. *Computers & Education, 51*(3), 1392–1404.
Verlinden, F. (2003). *Building military dioramas* (vol. VII). Chicago: Verlinden Productions.
Vieira Jr., E. T., & Grantham, S. (2011). Perceptions of control facilitate reading engagement. *Reading Psychology, 32*(4), 322–348.
Villalón, R., Mateos, M., & Cuevas, I. (2015). High school boys' and girls' writing conceptions and writing self-efficacy beliefs: What is their role in writing performance? *Educational Psychology, 35*(6), 653–674.
Villiger, C., Wandeler, C., & Niggli, A. (2014). Explaining differences in reading motivation between immigrant and native students: The role of parental involvement. *International Journal of Educational Research, 64*, 12–25.

Retrieved from https://doc.rero.ch/record/235813/files/01Villiger_et_al_2014_immigrants.pdf.
Voyer, D., & Voyer, S.D. (2014). Gender differences in scholastic achievement: A meta- analysis. *Psychological Bulletin, 140*(4), 1174–1204.
Vygotsky, L.S. (1978). *Mind in society*. Cambridge, MA: Harvard University Press.
Waddell, E.N., Orr, M.G., Sackoff, J., & Santelli, J.S. (2010). Pregnancy risk among black, white, and Hispanic teen girls in New York City Public Schools. *Journal of Urban Health, 87*(3), 426–439.
Walczak, A., & Geranpayeh, A. (n.d.). *The gender gap in English language proficiency: Insights from a test of academic English*. Retrieved from www.cambridgeassessment.org.uk/Images/gender-differences-cambridge-english.pdf.
Walsh, M. (2010). Multimodal literacy: What does it mean for classroom practice? *The Australian Journal of Language and Literacy, 33*(3), 211–239.
Wang, T.J. (2008). Using ICT to enhance academic learning: pedagogy & practice. *Educational Research and Review, 3*(4), 101–106.
Wang, Q. (2015). A study of the influence of gender differences on English learning of senior high school students. *Higher Education of Social Science, 8*(6), 66–69.
Watson, A., Kehler, M., & Martino, W. (2010). The problem of boys' literacy underachievement: Raising some questions. *Journal of Adolescent & Adult Literacy, 53*(5), 356–361.
Weaver-Hightower, M.B., & Skelton, C. (2013). *Leaders in gender and education: Intellectual self-portraits*. Rotterdam: Sense.
Weber, D., Skirbekk, V., Freund, I., & Herlitz, A. (2014). The changing face of cognitive gender differences in Europe. *PNAS, 111*(32), 11673–11678.
Weih, T.G. (2007, September). A book club sheds light on boys and reading. *Middle School Journal*, 19–25.
Western, B., & Rosenfeld, J. (2011). Unions, norms, and the rise in U.S. wage inequality. *American Sociological Review, 76*(4), 513–537.
Wheldall, K., & Limbrick, L. (2010). Do more boys than girls have reading problems? *Journal of Learning Disabilities, 43*(5), 418–429.
Whitman, W. (1993). *Leaves of grass*. New York: Modern Library.
Whitmire, R. (2010). *Why boys fail: Saving our sons from an educational system that's leaving them behind*. New York: AMACOM.
Whittingham, J.L., & Huffman, S. (2009). The effects of book clubs on the reading attitudes of middle school students. *Reading Improvement, 46*(3), 130–136.
Wigfield, A. (1997). Children's motivations for reading and reading engagement. In J.T. Guthrie & A. Wigfield (Eds.), *Reading engagement: Motivating readers through integrated instruction* (pp. 14–33). Newark, DE: International Reading Association.
Wigfield, A., Guthrie, J.T., Perencevich, K.C., Taboada, A., Klauda, S.L., McRae, A., & Barbosa, P. (2008). The role of reading engagement in mediating effects of reading comprehension instruction on reading outcomes. *Psychology in the Schools, 45*(5), 432–445.
Wilfong, L.G. (2008). Building fluency, word-recognition ability, and confidence in struggling readers: The poetry academy. *The Reading Teacher, 62*(1), 4–13.

Wilhelm, J.D. (2016). Recognising the power of pleasure: What engaged adolescent readers get from their free-choice reading, and how teachers can leverage this for all. *Australian Journal of Language and Literacy, 39*(1), 30–41.
Williams, A., & Merten, M. (2008). A review of online social networking profiles by adolescents: Implications for future research and intervention. *Adolescence, 43*, 253–74.
Williams, B.T. (2004). Boys may be boys, but do they have to read and write that way? *Journal of Adolescent & Adult Literacy, 47*(6), 510–515.
Williams, J.A. (2010). Taking on the role of questioner: Revisiting reciprocal teaching. *The Reading Teacher, 64*(4), 278–281.
Winton, T. (1991). *Lockie Leonard, human torpedo*. Boston: Little, Brown.
Winton, T. (1999). *Lockie Leonard, scumbuster*. New York: Margaret K. McElderry.
Wissinger, D.R., & De La Paz, S. (2015). Effects of critical discussions on middle school students' written historical arguments. *Journal of Educational Psychology, 108*(1), 43–59.
Wright, J., & Cleary, K.S. (2006). Kids in the tutor seat: Building schools' capacity to help struggling readers through cross-age peer tutoring program. *Psychology in the Schools, 43*(1), 99–107.
Wu, J.-Y. (2014). Gender differences in online reading engagement, metacognitive strategies, navigation skills and reading literacy. *Journal of Computer Assisted Learning, 30*(3), 252–271.
Wu, X., Anderson, R.C., Nguyen-Jahiel, K., & Miller, B. (2013). Enhancing motivation and engagement through collaborative discussion. *Journal of Educational Psychology, 105*(3), 622–632.
Wyatt-Smith, C., & Elkins, J. (2008). Multimodal reading and comprehension in online environments. In J. Coiro, M. Knobel, C. Lankshear, & D.J. Leu (Eds.), *Handbook of research on new literacies* (pp. 899–942). Mahwah, NJ: Erlbaum.
Wyllie, C. et al. (2012). *Men, suicide and society.* Samaritans. Retrieved from www.samaritans.org/sites/default/files/kcfinder/files/Men%20and%20Suicide%20Research%20Report%20210912.pdf.
Xia, N., & Kirby, S.N. (2009). *Retaining students in grade: A literature review of the effects of retention on students' academic and nonacademic outcomes.* Rand Corporation. www.rand.org/content/dam/rand/pubs/technical_reports/2009/RAND_TR678.pdf.
Yancey, K.B. (2009). *Writing in the 21st century*. Urbana, IL: National Council of Teachers of English.
Yang, G. (2008). Graphic novels in the classroom. *Language Arts, 85*, 185–192.
Yonezawa, S., Jones, M., & Joselowsky, F. (2009). Youth engagement in high schools: Developing a multidimensional, critical approach to improving engagement for all students. *Journal of Educational Change, 10*, 191–209.
Yoon, B. (2012). Junsuk and Junhyuck: Adolescent immigrants' educational journey to success and identity negotiation. *American Educational Research Journal, 49*(5), 971–1002.
Young, J.P., & Brozo, W.G. (2001). Boys will be boys, or will they? Literacy and masculinities. *Reading Research Quarterly, 36*(3), 316–325. doi:10.1598/RRQ.36.3.4.

Younge, G. (2016). *Another day in the death of America: A chronicle of ten short lives.* New York: Nation Books.

Younger, M., & Cobbett, M. (2014). Gendered perceptions of schooling: Classroom dynamics and inequalities within four Caribbean secondary schools. *Educational Review, 66*(1), 1–21.

Zambo, D., & Brozo, W.G. (2009). *Bright beginnings for boys: Engaging young boys in active literacy.* Newark, DE: International Reading Association.

Zickafoose, R. (2009). *"Oye mi voz!" (hear my voice!): The perceptions of Hispanic boys regarding their literacy experiences.* Graduate Theses and Dissertations. http://scholarcommons.usf.edu/etd/104.

Zirkel, S. (2002). Is there a place for me? Role models and academic identity among white students and students of color. *Teachers College Record, 104*(2), 357–376.

Zoghi, M., Kazemi, S., & Kalani, A. (2013). The effect of gender on language learning. *Journal of Novel Applied Sciences, 2*(S4), 1124–1128.

Zong, J., & Batalova, J. (2015). *The limited English proficient population in the United States.* Washington, DC: Migration Policy Institute. www.migrationpolicy.org/article/limited-english-proficient-population-united-states#Age,%20Race,%20and%20Ethnicity.

Zwiers, J., & Crawford, M. (2011). *Academic conversations: Classroom talk that fosters critical thinking and content understandings.* Portland, ME: Stenhouse.

Index

Adams, A., 182–183
Additional language learners. *See* New language learners
African-Americans
  dropout rates among, 12
  gender disparity in literacy among, 11–12
  graduation rates among, 10–11
  growth in population of, 28
  homicide rates among, 13
  incarceration rates among, 12–13, 95
  masculinities and identities and
    correlation with literacy development, 35–36
    development of, 46
  in remedial reading and learning disabilities classes, 9–10
  socio-economic status and
    community buffers against negative effects of, 97–98
    correlation with literacy development, 27
    family buffers against negative effects of, 97–98
    "poverty penalty," 93–94, 96
    school buffers against negative effects of, 98–99
  writing, correlation with literacy development, 181
Allusion, digital media as teaching tool for, 174–176
Alternative texts, 169–170
Andon, A., 111–112
Annie E. Casey Foundation, 96
Applebee, A., 183–184
Arellano, M.D.C., 117
Asbrock, F., 34–35
Austria, correlation between immigrants and literacy development in, 113
Author perspective, 2–3

Barkley, Charles, 78
Baseball, combining reading with, 150–151

Baseball: Stunts, Scandals and Secrets Beneath the Stitches (Hample), 42
Baseball Saved Us (Mochizuki), 42
Basketball as reading topic, 146
Bates, T.C., 94–95
Batista, Dave, 128
Batista Unleashed (Batista), 128
Beard, R., 183
Belgium
  immigrants, correlation with literacy development in, 113
  literacy engagement, correlation with literacy development in, 38–39
Berliner, David, 90
Bilger, R., 34
Birkerts, Sven, 1
Blair, H., 42–43
Bodybuilding as reading topic, 50, 128
Book clubs as reading tool
  family book clubs, 106–109
  immigrants and new language learners, 130–134
    fun as priority, 131–132
    linking book selection to interests, 131–132
    multiple modes of expression, 131–132
Bourke, L., 182–183
Boyd, D., 161
Boys & Books (website), 152–153
Boys Life, 141
Boy with a Pack (Meader), 141–142
Bozack, A., 43
Brandt, D., 181
Bridge-building texts, 170–171
Bright Beginnings for Boys (Brozo), 17
Brown Center Report on American Education, 8
Brozo, William G., 17
Buddha Boy (Koja), 14
Building Military Dioramas (Verlinden), 154
Burbules, N.C., 166–167
Burrell, A., 183
Bussiere, P., 159

Callister, T.A., 166–167
Cambria, J., 150
Canada
  gender disparity in literacy in, 8
  immigrants, correlation with literacy development in, 110, 112–113
  information and communication technologies, correlation with literacy development in, 159, 160
  new language learners, gender disparity among, 115–116
  writing, gender disparity in, 182
Carnoy, M., 11–12
Carr, J., 115, 116
Carson, Harry, 101
ChaseR: A Novel in E-Mails (Rosen), 131–132
Chavez, Cesar, 119, 120
Chetty, R., 27
Children of Immigrants Longitudinal Study (CILS), 28–29
Childress, Alice, 1
China, correlation between socio-economic status and literacy development in, 26
Chow, B.W.-Y., 112
Chui, M.M., 112
Chuy, M., 38
Cohen, S., 12
Collier, D.R., 87
Comic books as literacy tool, 169–170
Common Core Standards, 164, 191
Conger, D., 10–11
Counternarrative to crisis paradigm. *See* Nuanced perspective on crisis paradigm
Crisis, literacy in boys as, 7–8, 21–23
Cross-age reading buddies, 99–106
The Crossover (Alexander), 14
Crutcher, Chris, 50

Daly, C., 182
D-Day: The Liberation of Europe Begins (Murray), 154
Death Walk (Morey), 132–133
de Bellis, M.D., 41
Definition of literacy, 18–19
Denmark
  immigrants, correlation with literacy development in, 113
  socio-economic status, correlation with literacy development in, 26
Dernikos, B., 29
Development. *See* Literacy development
Dewey, John, 145
Digital technology. *See* Information and communication technologies (ICT)
Dioramas, combining reading with, 153–155

Domestic violence
  gender disparity in, 13
  as reading topic, 48–49
Drake, 107
Dronkers, J., 28, 115
Dropout rates
  gender disparity in, 12
  socio-economic status and, 96–97
Drug addiction, gender disparity in, 13
Dunks, Doubles, Doping: How Steroids are Killing American Athletics (Jendricks), 101–102
Durant, Kevin, 107

Eastwood, Clint, 78
Education First, 30
Electronic reading. *See* Information and communication technologies (ICT)
Elmore, K.C., 35
Emile, or on Education (Rousseau), 126
Engagement. *See* Literacy engagement
English Learners (ELs), 31–32
Equal Rights Amendment, 17
Ertmer, P.A., 164–165
Esquire, 77
European Commission, 21, 90
European Union. *See also specific country*
  High Level Group of Experts on Literacy, 8, 110, 158
  immigrants, correlation with literacy development in, 28, 113
  literacy engagement, correlation with literacy development in, 38–39
  literacy skills in, 21
  new language learners, correlation with literacy development in, 30
  writing, gender disparity in, 182–183

Family book clubs, 106–109
"Family Guy" (television program), 176
Farrell, A.D., 85
Feliciano, C., 28–29
Finland
  adulthood, males "catching up" by, 17
  immigrants, correlation with literacy development in, 113
  information and communication technologies, correlation with literacy development in, 159–160
  masculinities and identities in, 46–47
  writing, gender disparity in, 183
Football as reading topic, 100–102
"Fortnite" (video game), 163
Four Days to Glory: Wrestling with the Soul of the American Heartland (Kreidler), 50

France, correlation between immigrants and literacy development in, 113
Freire, Pablo, 166
Frost, Robert, 135–137
Future (rap artist), 107

Garcia, E., 11–12
Gates Foundation, 148
"Gears of War" (video game), 102
Gender disparity
  domestic violence, 13
  dropout rates, 12
  drug addiction, 13
  graduation rates, 10–11
  HIV/AIDS, 13
  homelessness, 13
  homicide, 13
  immigrants, gender disparity in literacy among, 11, 113–115
  incarceration, 12–13
  learning disabilities classes, 9–10
  literacy engagement, 9
  NAEP and, 11
  new language learners, gender disparity in literacy among, 115–118
    cognitive tools and, 117
    instructional methods and, 116
  postsecondary education, 10–11
  remedial reading classes, 9–10
  retained students, 10
  socio-economic status and, 12
  suicide, 13
  underperformance, 8–9
  weak readers, 9
  in writing, 181, 182–183
Germany
  adulthood, males "catching up" by, 17
  Boys & Books, 152–153
  Kicking and Reading Program, 151–152
  literacy engagement in
    correlation with literacy development, 38
    programs, 151–153
  socio-economic status, correlation with literacy development in, 26
  underperformance of boys in, 9
Gershenson, S., 98–99
The Ghost (Reynolds), 163
Gibbs, Stuart, 92–93
Gifford, Frank, 101
Ging, D., 77–78
Give a Boy a Gun (Strasser), 73
The Global Literacy Challenge (UNESCO), 21
Global literacy context, 18–21
Glowka, D., 116
Gluszynski, T., 159

Godley, A.J., 46
Goodman, J., 30
Goodson, B.J., 101
Google, 161
GQ, 77
Graduation rates, gender disparity in, 10–11
Graham, S., 192
Graphic novels
  as literacy tool, 169–170
  mathematics, as teaching tool for, 202–204
Graves, S.L., Jr., 96–97
Great Battles of World War II (MacDonald), 154
Gurian, David, 7–8
Guthrie, J.T., 150

Hample, Zack, 42
Hanushek, E.A., 20, 25–26, 89–90
Harper, S.R., 35–36
Harris, T.S., 96–97
Harrison, C., 162
Head Start, 97
Heckman, James, 36, 143
Hegemonic masculinity, 4–5, 18, 34, 47, 85
Hernandez, D.J., 12
A Hero Ain't Nothin' But a Sandwich (Childress), 1
Heroes Don't Run: A Novel of the Pacific War (Mazer), 155
Hill, A.E., 12
Hispanics
  dropout rates among, 12
  gender disparity in literacy among, 11–12
  growth in population of, 28
  as immigrants, 111, 114 (*See also* Immigrants)
  incarceration rates among, 95
  masculinities and identities, correlation with literacy development, 35–36
  in remedial reading and learning disabilities classes, 9–10
  writing, correlation with literacy development, 181
HIV/AIDS, 13
Hobbies, combining reading with, 153–155
Hogan-Brun, G., 115
Homelessness, gender disparity in, 13
Homicide, gender disparity in, 13
Hong Kong, correlation between socio-economic status and literacy development in, 26
Hoops (Myers), 108
Hughes-Hassell, S., 43, 169
Huuki, T, 46–47
Hwang, J., 96

"I Celebrate Myself" (Whitman), 83
ICT. *See* Information and communication technologies (ICT)
Illich, I., 155
"I Love to Give You Light" (Snoop Dogg), 173–174
The Imaginary Girlfriend: A Memoir (Irving), 51
Immigrants
  overview, 5, 110–111, 138–139
  additional needs of, 111
  book clubs as reading tool, 130–134
    fun as priority, 133–134
    linking book selection to interests, 131–132
    multiple modes of expression, 132–133
  developing language through discussion, 118–121
  gender disparity in literacy among, 11, 113–115
  Hispanics as, 111, 114
  holistic treatment of, 111
  independent word learning prompts and strategies, 137–138
  literacy development, correlation with, 28–29
  in-school versus outside-of-school literacies, 29
  morphological analysis and, 134–137, 138
  My Bag, 123–129
    generally, 140
    bodybuilding as reading topic, 128
    digital My Bags, 128
    windsurfing as reading topic, 123–127
    wrestling as reading topic, 127–129
  native-born students versus, 111–113
  outside-of-school interests, texts related to, 122–129
  PIRLS and, 111–112
  PISA and
    correlation with literacy development, 111, 112–113
    gender disparity in literacy, 115
  popular music as reading tool, 129–130
  value line discussion and, 119–121
Incarceration rates
  gender disparity in, 12–13
  socio-economic status and, 95
Inconegro (Johnson and Pleece), 32–33
Information and communication technologies (ICT)
  overview, 5, 157–158, 178
  allusion, digital media as teaching tool for, 174–176
  alternative texts, 169–170
  bridge-building texts, 170–171
  comic books as literacy tool, 169–170
  graphic novels as literacy tool, 169–170
  guidelines for use of
    overview, 164–165
    authentic communication, promoting, 167–168
    collaboration, promoting, 168–169
    collective learning, promoting, 168–169
    creative use, providing opportunities for, 165–166
    critical thinking, promoting, 166–167
    motivation, increasing, 168
  literacy development, correlation with, 39–40, 158–160
  manga as literacy tool, 171–172
  memory processes, changes resulting from, 161
  multiple literacies perspective for boys, 160–162
  negative effects of, 161–162
  new forms of discourse, necessity of, 162
  PIRLS and, 160
  PISA and, 158
    correlation with literacy development, 40
    gender disparity, 159
    home computers, effect of presence of, 159
    negative effects of, 161
    prevalence of, 161
  rap music as literacy tool, 172–174
  shift in reading resulting from, 162
  video games as teaching tool, 176–178
Interests
  immigrants and new language learners
    book clubs, linking book selection to interests, 131–132
    outside-of-school interests, texts related to, 131–132
  literacy development, effect of changes in interests on, 42–43
  literacy engagement, factors influencing, 145–146
  local interests, 147
  masculinities and identities, importance of interesting reading material to, 48–52
Ironman (Crutcher), 50
Irving, John, 51

James, LeBron, 100, 107, 108, 146
Jet, 99
"Jimmy Neutron–Boy Genius" (television program), 176
Jordan, Michael, 83

Kennedy, Michael, 44
Kessels, U., 38
Kiang, L., 114
Kicking and Reading Program, 151–152
King, Martin Luther, Jr., 84

Index

Kissau, S., 116
Kornder, N., 28, 115
Kreidler, Mark, 50
Kurtz-Costes, B., 46

Langer, J.A., 77, 183–184
Learning disabilities classes, gender disparity in, 9–10
Leaves of Grass (Whitman), 83
Lee, J.-S., 38
Leino, K., 159–160
"Letter from Birmingham Jail" (King), 84
Leventhal, T., 113–114
Lietaert, S., 39
Literacy. *See specific topic*
Literacy development
  overview, 4, 24–25, 44
  brain growth and, 40–41
  cognitive development and, 40–41
  immigrants, correlation with, 28–29
    in-school versus outside-of-school literacies, 29
  information and communication technologies, correlation with, 39–40, 158–160
  interests, effect of changes in, 42–43
  level of reading difficulty, effect of changes in, 41–42
  literacy engagement, correlation with, 36–39
    overview, 142–143
    gender disparity and, 37–38
  masculinities and identities, correlation with, 33–36
    African-Americans and Hispanics, 35–36
    gender disparity and, 33–35
    hegemonic masculinity and, 34
  new language learners, correlation with, 30–32
    English Learners (ELs), 31–32
    Long-Term English Learners (LTELs), 31
  reading identity and, 43
  socio-economic status, correlation with, 25–27
    African-Americans, 27
    data analysis, 26
  in transition from childhood to adolescence, 40–43
Literacy engagement
  overview, 5, 140–144, 155–156
  in adults, 141
  baseball, combining reading with, 150–151
  basketball as reading topic, 146
  benefits of, 37, 143–144
  Boys & Books, 152–153
  controlling test data for, 16
  factors influencing
    overview, 144

    accessibility, 148–149
    choice, 149–150
    collaboration, 150
    interests, 145–146
      local interests, 147
      outside-of-school literacies, 147
    self-efficacy, 145
  gender disparity in, 9
  hobbies, combining reading with, 153–155
  Kicking and Reading Program, 151–152
  libraries and, 141–142
  literacy development, correlation with, 36–39
    overview, 142–143
    gender disparity and, 37–38
  military dioramas, combining reading with, 153–155
  motivational strategies, 143
  NAEP and, 37, 38, 143–144, 148
  PISA and
    controlling test data for, 16
    correlation with literacy development, 37–38, 94, 144
    gender disparity, 9
    socio-economic status and, 144
  soccer, combining reading with, 151–152
  social context of, 143
  socio-economic status and, 144
  as "soft skill," 36–37, 143, 155–156
Little League, 150–151
Lockie Leonard, Human Torpedo (Winton), 124–127
Long, M.C., 10–11
Long-Term English Learners (LTELs), 31
Looker, E.D., 160
The Lord of the Rings (Tolkein), 196
Lubienski, S., 25
"Lucky Star" (anime), 176

Ma, X., 112–113
Mackey, M., 164
Manga
  as literacy tool, 171–172
  mathematics, as teaching tool for, 202–204
The Manga Guide to Statistics (Takahashi), 202–204
"Manhunt" (video game), 102
Manninen, S., 46–47
Martinez, R.M., 117–118
Martinez-Garcia, C., 117–118
Masculinities and identities
  overview, 4–5, 45, 88
  African-Americans and, 46
  correlation with literacy development, 35–36
  development of, 46

Masculinities and identities (cont.)
  bodybuilding as reading topic, 50
  domestic violence as reading topic, 48–49
  hegemonic masculinity, 4–5, 18, 34, 47, 85
  Hispanics, correlation with literacy development, 35–36
  interesting reading material, importance of, 48–52
  literacy development, correlation with, 33–36
    African-Americans and Hispanics, 35–36
    gender disparity and, 33–35
    hegemonic masculinity and, 34
    outside-of-school images as source of, 46
    parents as source of, 46
  "Real Men" Unit (*See* "Real Men" Unit)
  relational formation of, 47
  sources of, 46
  stereotypes, overcoming, 46–47
  wrestling as reading topic, 50–51
Mathematics
  graphic novels as teaching tool, 202–204
  manga as teaching tool, 202–204
  writing and, 201–204
Maus I: A Survivor's Tale (Spiegelman), 170
Mcbride-Change, C., 112
McCormack, M., 47
Mead, S., 11
Meader, Stephen, 141–142
"The Melancholy of Haruhi Suzumiya" (anime), 176
Men's Health, 77
Merisou-Storm, T., 183
Mexico, correlation between socio-economic status and literacy development in, 26
Meyer, A.L., 85
Middle School (Patterson), 163
Military dioramas, combining reading with, 153–155
Mr. Bungle (band), 175–176
Mochizuki, Ken, 42
Monster (Myers), 108, 199–201
Morphological analysis, 134–137, 138
Morrell, E., 28
Morris, E.W., 8
"Mortal Kombat" (video game), 102
Motivation. *See* Literacy engagement
MS Word, 204
My Bag, 123–129
  generally, 140
  bodybuilding as reading topic, 128
  digital My Bags, 128
  windsurfing as reading topic, 123–127
  wrestling as reading topic, 127–129
"My Boy Lollypop" (song), 175
My Brother's a Superhero, 121

Myers, Walter Dean, 53, 57, 80–81, 108, 199–200
My Gym Teacher is a Superhero, 122

National Assessment of Educational Progress (NAEP)
  gender disparity in literacy and, 11
  literacy engagement and, 37, 38, 143–144, 148
  underperformance of boys and, 8
  writing and, 181–182
National Center for Education Statistics, 28
National Commission on Writing, 183
National Council of Teachers of Mathematics (NCTM), 201–202
National Weather Service Climate Prediction Center, 203
National Writing Project, 179–180
Netherlands
  literacy engagement, correlation with literacy development in, 39
  new language learners, correlation with literacy development in, 30
New language learners
  overview, 5, 110–111, 138–139
  book clubs as reading tool, 130–134
    fun as priority, 133–134
    linking book selection to interests, 131–132
    multiple modes of expression, 132–133
  developing language through discussion, 118–121
  gender disparity among, 115–118
    cognitive tools and, 117
    instructional methods and, 116
  independent word learning prompts and strategies, 137–138
  literacy development, correlation with, 30–32
    English Learners (ELs), 31–32
    Long-Term English Learners (LTELs), 31
  morphological analysis and, 134–137, 138
  My Bag, 123–129
    generally, 140
    bodybuilding as reading topic, 128
    digital My Bags, 128
    windsurfing as reading topic, 123–127
    wrestling as reading topic, 127–129
  outside-of-school interests, texts related to, 122–129
  popular music as reading tool, 129–130
  value line discussion and, 119–121
New technology. *See* Information and communication technologies (ICT)
A New Way to Pay Old Debts (play), 84
Niggli, A., 28
Nijkamp, Marieke, 73
Nitulescu, R., 38

Norway
  literacy engagement, correlation with literacy development in, 39
  writing, gender disparity in, 183
Nuanced perspective on crisis paradigm
  overview, 4, 45–46
  adulthood, males "catching up" by, 16–17
  formatting of tests and, 15–16
  hegemonic masculinity and, 18
  literacy engagement, controlling test data for, 16
  sexism and, 17–18
  unidimensional conception of boys and, 18

Oakhill, J.V., 39
Obama, Barack, 99
O'Brien, D., 160–161
Oyserman, D., 35

Pape, K., 183
Patterson, James, 163
Pauwels, A., 115, 116
Pavy, S., 116
Performance-enhancing drugs, 101–102
Perin, D., 192
Perriera, K.M., 114
Petrides, A., 39
Physics4kids.com, 203
PIAAC. *See* Program for International Assessment of Adult Competencies (PIAAC)
Pihl, J., 39
PIRLS. *See* Progress in International Reading Literacy Study (PIRLS)
PISA. *See* Programme for International Student Assessment (PISA)
Pixton (software), 204
Poetry writing
  overview, 196–197
  outside of school, 198–199
  rap lyrics as poetry, 198–199
  in school, 197–198
Poland, gender disparity among new language learners in, 116
Popular music as literacy tool
  among immigrants and new language learners, 129–130
  poetry, rap lyrics as, 198–199
  word families, rap music as teaching tool for, 172–174
Postsecondary education, gender disparity in, 10–11
Potochnick, S., 114
"Poverty penalty" for boys, 93–97
PowToon (software), 128

Prieur, A., 36
Prince Ea (rap artist), 205
Program for International Assessment of Adult Competencies (PIAAC)
  adulthood, males "catching up" by, 16–17
  definition of literacy, 19
Programme for International Student Assessment (PISA)
  definition of literacy, 19
  effect of higher scores, 30–31
  formatting of tests, 15–16
  immigrants and
    correlation with literacy development, 111, 112–113
    gender disparity in literacy, 115
  information and communication technologies and, 158
    correlation with literacy development, 40
    gender disparity, 159
    home computers, effect of presence of, 159
    negative effects of, 161
  literacy engagement and
    controlling test data for, 16
    correlation with literacy development, 37–38, 94, 144
    gender disparity, 9
    socio-economic status and, 144
  socio-economic status, correlation with literacy development, 12, 25, 26, 89–90, 91
  underperformance of boys and, 8–9, 33
  weak readers and, 9
Progress in International Reading Literacy Study (PIRLS)
  definition of literacy, 19
  immigrants, correlation with literacy development, 111–112
  information and communication technologies, gender disparity in, 160
  underperformance of boys and, 8–9
Purpose of book, 3–4

Qin, D.B., 29, 36, 114–115
Quane, J.M., 96

Rap music
  poetry, rap lyrics as, 198–199
  word families, as literacy tool for, 172–174
Reading. *See specific topic*
Reading identity, 43, 87
"Real Men" Unit
  overview, 53–55
  anticipation guide and compare-contrast activity (Week 3), 67–69
  compare-contrast essay, 58

"Real Men" Unit (cont.)
  end-of-book journal entry (Week 7), 80–81
  finale (Week 8), 81–85
  gun violence debate (Week 5), 72–76
  introductions and predictions (Week 1), 58–65
  masculine identity and, 85–87
  origins of, 55–56
  planning of, 56–57
  preparation for projects (Week 6), 76–79
  reading identity and, 87
  story impression and writing skills (Week 2), 65–67
  student projects, 58
  survey results, 57–58, 59, 85–86
  teacher anecdotal logs, 58
  university field trip (Week 4), 69–72
Remedial reading classes, gender disparity in, 9–10
Retained students, gender disparity in, 10
Retelsdorf, J., 34–35
Rey Mysterio (wrestler), 128–129
Reynolds, Jason, 163
Rihanna, 107
"The Ring" (film), 176
Ritchie, S.J., 94–95
"The Road Not Taken" (Frost), 135–137
Robinson, J., 25
Robinson, Jackie, 120
Robinson, M., 164
Rodge, P., 43, 169
Rogers, R., 30
Romeo and Juliet (Shakespeare), 171–172
Roosevelt, Franklin, 187, 188
Rouland, K.K., 35, 46
Rousseau, Jean-Jacques, 126, 145
Rowley, S.J., 46
Rua, P.L., 117

Sanford, K., 42–43
Santiago, C.D., 29, 114
Schepens, J., 30
Schoon, I., 94–95
Schwartz, K., 34–35
Schwarzchild, M., 108
Science
  vocabulary, video games as teaching tool for, 176–178
  writing and, 204–206
Scieszka, Jon, 133
Scorpions (Myers), 53, 57–59, 62, 64–65, 72–73, 76, 77, 78–79, 80–81, 82, 87
Scutts, Jerry, 154
SES. *See* Socio-economic status (SES)
Shakespeare, William, 171–172
Shields, Brian, 50

"Shrek 2" (film), 175
Simon, R.I., 49, 50, 196–197
"The Simpsons" (television program), 176
Singapore, correlation between socio-economic status and literacy development in, 26
Skateboard Science (website), 171
Slate, J.R., 117–118
Snoop Dogg, 173–174
Soccer, combining reading with, 151–152
Socio-economic status (SES)
  overview, 5, 89–92, 109
  African-Americans and
    community buffers against negative effects of, 97–98
    correlation with literacy development, 27
    family buffers against negative effects of, 97–98
    "poverty penalty," 93–94, 96
    school buffers against negative effects of, 98–99
  community buffers against negative effects of, 97–98
  cross-age reading buddies and, 99–106
  dropout rates and, 96–97
  effect of literacy on, 89–90, 94–95
  employment, and decline in, 95–96
  family book clubs and, 106–109
  family buffers against negative effects of, 97–98
  gender disparity in literacy and, 11–12
  incarceration rates and, 95
  literacy development, correlation with, 25–27
    African-Americans, 27
    data analysis, 26
  literacy engagement and, 144
  manufacturing, and decline in, 91, 95–96
  PISA and, 12, 25, 26, 89–90, 91
  "poverty penalty" for boys, 93–97
  school buffers against negative effects of, 98–99
  transgenerational nature of, 94, 96
"Soft skills," 36–37, 143, 155–156
Souto-Manning, M., 29
Spain, gender disparity among new language learners in, 117
Special attention to boys, need for, 7–8, 21–23
Spiegelman, A., 170
"Spongebob Squarepants" (television program), 176
Sports
  baseball, combining reading with, 150–151
  basketball as reading topic, 146
  bodybuilding as reading topic, 50, 128
  football as reading topic, 100–102
  performance-enhancing drugs and, 101–102
  soccer, combining reading with, 151–152

Index

windsurfing as reading topic, 123–127
wrestling as reading topic, 50–51, 127–129
Spy Camp (Gibbs), 92–93
Spy School (Gibbs), 92–93
Staples, J.M., 85–87
"Star Wars" (film series), 177
Stone Rabbit, 122
Strasser, Todd, 73
Straus, L.P., 38
Suarez-Orozco, C., 29
Suicide, gender disparity in, 13
Sullivan, Kevin, 50
Sum, A., 12–13
Sunnari, V., 46–47
Sweden
  immigrants, correlation with literacy development in, 113
  information and communication technologies, correlation with literacy development in, 160
Switzerland, correlation between immigrants and literacy development in, 28

The Tall Mexican: The Life of Hank Aguirre All-Star Pitcher, Businessman, Humanitarian (Copley), 120–121
Taylor, Lawrence, 101
Technology. *See* Information and communication technologies (ICT)
Test of English as a Foreign Language (TOEFL), 30
Thiessen, V., 160
This is Where it Ends (Nijkamp), 73
Thompson, Tamika, 97
"Thrill Kill" (video game), 102
The Time Warp Trio (Scieszka), 133
To Be a Boy, To Be a Reader (Brozo), 130
Tonne, I., 39
Tramonte, T., 96
Trino's Choice (Gonzalez-Bertrand), 105–106
Turnbull, M., 116

Underperformance, gender disparity and, 8–9, 33
UNESCO, 21, 162
United Kingdom
  Boys' Reading Commission, 8
  information and communication technologies in
    correlation with literacy development, 39
    shift in reading resulting from, 162
  literacy engagement, correlation with literacy development in, 39
  masculinities and identities in, 47
  National Literacy Trust, 8
  Office of Standards in Education, 182
  socio-economic status, correlation with literacy development in, 26, 94–95
  writing, gender disparity in, 182–183

Value line discussion, 119–121
van der Slik, F., 30
van Hout, R., 30
Verlinden, Francois, 154
Video games
  cross-age reading buddies and, 102
  science vocabulary, as teaching tool for, 176–178
Villiger, C., 28
Vygotsky, L.S., 150

Wandeler, C., 28
Warner Brothers, 175–176
Weak readers, gender disparity and, 9
Where the Wild Things Are (Sendak), 103
Whitman, Walt, 83
Why We Can't Wait (King), 84
Williams, C.D., 35–36
Willms, J.D., 96
Wilson, W.J., 96
Windsurfing as reading topic, 123–127
Woessmann, L., 20, 25–26, 89–90
Word families, rap music as teaching tool for, 172–174
"World War II" (video game), 163
World War II Dioramas (Scutts), 154
World Wrestling Entertainment (WWE), 51, 128
Wrestling as reading topic, 50–51, 127–129
Writing
  overview, 6, 179–180, 206
  African-Americans, correlation with literacy development, 181
  enhancing reading through writing, 186–189
  experience, boys writing from, 192–195
  gender disparity in, 181, 182–183
  guidelines for instruction
    evidence-based principles, using, 192
    low-stakes writing, integrating into daily lessons, 189–190
    real writing with real audiences, promoting, 191–192
    writing to learn, fostering, 190–191
  Hispanics, correlation with literacy development, 181
  mathematics and, 201–204
    graphic novels as teaching tool, 202–204
    manga as teaching tool, 202–204
  NAEP and, 181–182

Writing (cont.)
  poetry
    overview, 196–197
    outside of school, 198–199
    rap lyrics as, 198–199
    in school, 197–198
  reading compared
    cognitive processes and, 184
    drafting, 185
    editing and polishing, 185
    instructional methods and, 186
    motivation and, 186
    planning, 184–185
    post-writing and sharing, 185
    revising, 185
    science and, 204–206
    technology, impact of, 180–181
    young adult literature, in response to, 199–201
Writing Next (Graham and Perin), 192
Wu, J.-Y., 40, 158–159
WWE Encyclopedia (Shields and Sullivan), 50

Yancey, K.B., 192
Young adult literature, writing in response to, 199–201
Yu, H.M., 29